UNDER A VENICE MOON

MARGARET CAMERON

UNDER A VENICE MOON

hachette
AUSTRALIA

Published in Australia and New Zealand in 2022
by Hachette Australia
(an imprint of Hachette Australia Pty Limited)
Gadigal Country, Level 17, 207 Kent Street, Sydney, NSW 2000
www.hachette.com.au

Hachette Australia acknowledges and pays our respects to the past, present and future Traditional Owners and Custodians of Country throughout Australia and recognises the continuation of cultural, spiritual and educational practices of Aboriginal and Torres Strait Islander peoples. Our head office is located on the lands of the Gadigal people of the Eora Nation.

A catalogue record for this
book is available from the
National Library of Australia

ISBN: 978 0 7336 4831 1 (paperback)

Cover design by Christabella Designs
Cover photograph courtesy of Dmitry Rukhlenko / Alamy
Author photograph by David Broadway
Internal photographs courtesy author's collection and David Hannaford
Typeset in Sabon LT Std by Kirby Jones
Printed and bound in Australia by McPherson's Printing Group

The paper this book is printed on is certified against the Forest Stewardship Council® Standards. McPherson's Printing Group holds FSC® chain of custody certification SA-COC-005379. FSC® promotes environmentally responsible, socially beneficial and economically viable management of the world's forests.

CONTENTS

CHAPTER 1

BEGINNINGS ...

In short, he who doesn't go to Venice is a fool.

Anton Chekhov, Russian playwright and short story writer,
in *Letters of Anton Chekhov to His Family and Friends*

George Clooney and Amal Alamuddin are getting married today.

At three o'clock, Hollywood's most eligible single will be single no more. He's had some near misses over the years since his divorce in the early nineties, close brushes with the altar that have left a trail of disappointed contenders for the title of Mrs Clooney. But that's all in the past and now The Wedding is just hours away. At the Hotel Cipriani, on Giudecca Island, where the ceremony will take place, activity has reached fever pitch. Glasses are buffed to sparkling perfection; brooms are passed across already immaculate garden paths; Hollywood royalty graces the guest list and the world's media has assembled to record the event. I'll be there too – a kilometre away in my apartment on the other side of Venice.

On a scale of one to ten in the pay-attention stakes, I rated the Clooney nuptials at six: impossible to ignore, but without much bearing on my day. I wouldn't be sipping champagne and toasting the happy couple. The only toast I cared about was spread with marmalade and sat alongside my teacup. Sunday morning, nine o'clock. I was in Venice with Jenny, a friend from Perth, on day five of an Italian holiday.

Bellagio, an oh-so-cute village on the shores of Lake Como, had been the launching pad for our adventure. We'd opted for a DIY approach to travel arrangements this time around – totally hands-on and involved – an enterprise of online bookings, the successful and timely location of correct Trenitalia platforms, and a you-own-it-you-carry-it baggage-handling philosophy.

It could not have been more different from our holiday the previous year.

That holiday – a tour-company safari through East Africa – had delivered three weeks of carefully planned itineraries, seamless organisation and diligent staff ready to meet every travel need: luggage delivered with a smile, fresh towels folded and waiting by the swimming pool, hearty breakfasts before a day of savannah cruising. Candlelit dinners brought the curtain down on each well-ordered day. Even the animals seemed to understand their role in the affair, presenting themselves preened and perfect for photo opportunities at just the right moment. From the time we left the departure lounge of Perth Airport, someone else did the thinking for us.

And that suited me. A take-no-risks-and-blaze-no-trails sort of person, I was content to stand back and let someone else run the show. My golden rule ran along the lines of a decision avoided being the best decision. Over the years it had paid off, with numerous life choices – sound, rewarding choices – being made by other people on my behalf, requiring nothing of me but to follow the path of least resistance and simply go along with the plan.

My mother got the ball rolling. In my late teenage years she steered me towards a career in nursing, hoping to (let me guess here) clip the wings of a high-spirited and trouble-prone daughter. She'd expected the discipline of her own student nurse days, back in a time when hospital matrons came second only to God in the authority stakes. I sometimes caught a drift of nostalgia in her voice when she spoke of 'her' Matron Johnson, invoking all the reverence of a missionary wife describing her husband's evangelical work in Borneo.

Ideas can be perfect, but circumstances rarely are. Discipline wasn't what it used to be, and I fell way short in the good behaviour stakes. For the three years of my nurse training I kicked up my heels and made merry. So many parties, so little time. Fellow nurses always knew of some event that could benefit from our attendance and I simply tagged along with the rest of the crew, night after week after year, having a high old time. It was like Woody Allen said: ninety per cent of life is about just showing up.

But in other ways, Mum was right on the money. The day-to-day work – the actual business of being a nurse – gave me huge satisfaction. At the age of thirty-one, expecting a lifetime of nursing ahead, I married.

And it happened again.

My husband showed the same astute judgement as my mother when he suggested I trade my nursing career for a university degree program. His academic achievements included two degrees, in commerce and economics. My younger sister had notched up two teaching degrees. So, then. Was I letting the team down? University had never been on my radar, one way or another, but now it seemed like a reasonable idea. And my husband was a reasonable man. I felt I should at least give it a go.

What can I say? I fell on my feet and loved it all: the lectures, the friends I made, our endless discussions. My views were challenged and my perspectives broadened as I moved from learning the answers to asking the questions. For me, university took over where nursing left off.

I'd met Jenny soon after graduation. Along with my degree came a career rethink, and I started work in a state government department. Jenny managed the section I was assigned to.

'What a great boss,' I'd thought when she invited me to her home for dinner. 'I've done it again. Hit the jackpot without even trying.'

In our late thirties, Jenny and I were the same age and lived in neighbouring suburbs, making connection in both mindset and logistics an easy business. Friendship followed, seeing us through my romantic ups and downs – I'd separated and divorced by then – and Jenny's widowhood and remarriage.

Twenty-five years after first walking into my new boss' office, I sat opposite her on a train making its way from Bellagio to Milan and linking to Venice. I watched as Jenny raised her head for a last glimpse of Lake Como, then settled back to reading *Wines of Tuscany*, flicking over pages before stopping at one particular article. Food and wine were Jenny's passion. My knowledge of such things was stuck at Year One level and I had no interest in moving up through the grades. But on big-picture issues, the ones that mattered in life, we shared the same broad outlook.

'There's no point asking for your opinion,' Jenny once said to me. 'I know it will be the same as mine.'

I could understand, then, why we'd remained friends. What I struggled to explain was the recent shift from my usual follow-the-leader approach. Something had lit my inner Hillary Clinton and induced me to pursue my own first-time-in-history venture. I'd be the one in charge, I decided, I'd organise this holiday. Things snowballed. I sifted through one travel guide after another, writing memos and listing not-to-be-missed sights. With the resolve of a bargain hunter planning maximum coverage of the Boxing Day sales, I sketched out the most time-efficient paths to take us from this church to that museum and on to another gallery. Google Maps and I became best mates.

Only in occasional, reflective moments did I face the disquieting possibility that this all-out effort was no more than showing off to my former boss.

I turned from Jenny to gaze out the train window, feeling a twinge of anxiety settle near the pizza I'd eaten for lunch. Things had proved harder in off-screen, on-the-ground reality. Images I'd held of brisk efficiency, of knowing what to do and where to go, had become less clear in Bellagio's winding pathways. It was as though I'd bet everything on a horse named Miss Know-It-All and now she was running last. My thoughts moved ahead to our Venetian home. The address itself was a challenge: Campiello Riccardo Selvatico. I couldn't even say it, now I'd have to find it.

The things I did to myself.

I was still lost in rueful contemplation when the train jolted onto the lagoon causeway and crossed to Venice. Thirty-five years had passed since my last visit to the city. I'd forgotten the way Venice announces itself: suddenly there, just beyond the glass walls of the *ferrovia* (station). Ancient buildings rise from still water. The Grand Canal begins its serpentine course through the city, wrinkling beneath a tapestry of water craft. On the opposite bank, the green-domed church of San Simeon Piccolo lifts above the pavements, as if to oversee proceedings.

We planned to catch a vaporetto four stops along the Grand Canal, and from there walk to the apartment we'd rented. The ticket office stood across the station forecourt, abutting the Grand Canal, with a queue stretching back from it in a curving tail.

'I'm thinking a weekly ticket,' I said, guiding my suitcase over a bump in the forecourt paving. 'It's going to be our cheapest option. And it will mean we don't have to line up every time we need a ticket.'

Jenny nodded as she put on her sunglasses, displacing a tuft of curls above each ear. We joined the queue and shuffled forwards. I leaned out from my position and assessed the crowd ahead.

'This shouldn't take too long.' I unfolded seventy euro from my purse in readiness. Jenny looked around, smiled at me, at the crowds and at the golden Venetian afternoon.

Fifteen minutes later we stood on the deck of a vaporetto, wedged against our suitcases. Passengers crammed on all sides. I peered between bodies and over heads, struggling for balance against the boat's sway. Elbows poked my back as cameras were lifted and angled into position for holiday snaps. The fug of packed bodies, sweat and warring perfumes settled in thick folds. I thought of bundled clothes, ready for the washing machine.

And I thought of the day, thirty-five years ago, when I made this same trip with my then husband, John. We'd settled on the deck of a motor cruiser, lulled by the sun's warmth and the rush of water against the boat's hull.

Caught up in documentary wonder, I'd watched as one palazzo after another slipped by – a bizarre architectural fusion of Byzantine East and Gothic West. Nowhere else on earth looked like this. It had been easy, so easy, to succumb to the charms of Venice that July morning.

No doubt about it, I decided now, locked within my cocoon of humanity, there were better ways to arrive in Venice.

Yet magic still existed. Light fell in yellow sheets, washing Venice in a harmony of pale tones. Jumbled buildings enfolded labyrinthine walkways, like the Chinese puzzle of boxes within boxes. Faded terracotta tiles formed patches of larger squares, abutting or overlapping one another, shaping the outlines of a cubist painting.

At the Ca' d'Oro stop we hefted our suitcases onto the landing platform, all set to walk the remaining distance to our apartment. I looked up to the adjoining palazzo. Ca' d'Oro, or Palace of Gold: an in-your-face status symbol that had been decorated with gold leaf to advertise the wealth of its fifteenth-century owners, the aristocratic Contarini dynasty. A narrow pathway ran alongside it.

'It must be up this alleyway,' I said. 'Then we walk along an easy, straight section and that's it. We're there.'

Jenny looked at the alley with a questioning hitch of her eyebrows. It huddled in the shadow of Ca' d'Oro, as unpromising as the palazzo was impressive. But there was no other exit from the platform. She gripped her luggage and followed me, motivated less by trust than the lack of any alternative.

At the end of the pathway (referred to as a *calle* in Venice) we reached a wider thoroughfare linking the *ferrovia* to central Venice. Crowds thronged, pressing against us from every side. We were surrounded, part of a shoal of fish all moving upstream together. *Why so many people?* I wondered. I didn't remember Venice as being a noisy, crowded city of hustle and bustle; far from it. My memories were of gentle, dreamy *calli* opening to squares populated by no more than a solitary dog walker. Rising anxiety levels accompanied each shuffling step as we trudged onwards, hauling our suitcases. At a tiny square, hardly worth noting, we stopped to get our bearings.

'Where did this come from?' I said. 'It shouldn't be here. Google didn't mention it.'

Three storeys of ochre walls encased us, speckled with red geraniums falling in swoops from window flower boxes. We pulled out of the traffic to assess our new circumstances. On the opposite wall, just visible beneath the cascading horticulture, Jenny spotted something. She looked down to the address on our reservation slip, then back up again.

'Well,' she said, pointing. 'This is it. We're here.'

My eyes tracked the line of her finger. Campiello Riccardo Selvatico, a street sign announced: a grand name for such a tiny place. I forgave Google the oversight. But where to now? No apartment doorway broke the ring of shops and restaurants encircling the *campiello*. Our suitcases lay at anchor by our feet, and the human tide surged on past.

I looked from one window to another. Several levels up, two women rested their elbows on a window sill, scanning the *campiello* as though expecting someone. I tapped Jenny's shoulder and nodded in their direction.

'I think they could be looking for us.' I waved in a testing sort of way, not quite certain it was us they wanted. The signore smiled and waved back. One leaned from the window and beckoned, then pointed to the apartment's street entrance, tucked between a shoe shop and a cafe. The door, nondescript and unnumbered, seemed to be hiding between its neighbours.

Suitcases trailing in our wake, we crossed the *campiello* traffic. We'd found our Venetian home.

❁

So now, on this gently beautiful morning in late September, the start of our first full day in Venice, we sat in our kitchen, dawdling over breakfast and a second cup of tea.

'It's worked out well, don't you think?' I said. 'I loved the apartment in Bellagio, and now this is perfect. Definitely worth the effort. Remember the hours we spent on your computer?'

Jenny smiled. 'How could I forget?'

The memory was burnt into my brain. Jenny's computer screen had held us hostage for entire afternoons as we searched for our perfect Venetian apartment. Room sizes, photo checks, visitor reviews – we delved into every detail like terriers on the scent of a week-old bone. Complicating matters was my determination to live somewhere that mirrored the opulence of Venice itself. If only for a week, I wanted a little piece of Rococo excess or Gothic flight of fancy. I wasn't about to wake up thinking I was staying at a Holiday Inn.

'Yes, it's just what I had in mind,' I said, returning Jenny's smile. 'Baroque on a budget, you might say.'

Jenny was cutting fruit into wedges. She passed the plate to me and I picked up a melon slice, my gaze moving beyond her to the sitting room. I could picture myself there, over the coming week. Perhaps I'd come home after a day's sightseeing and kick off my shoes, walking barefoot across the cool, marble floor. Or perhaps I'd sit on the chaise longue to unwrap the latest shopping treasure, scattering tissue paper over the frayed mat and adding to the room's shabby-chic charm. If I glanced up at the mirror, the face looking back at me would smile. I'd sip tea and listen to sounds from the *campiello* as they drifted in through the open windows.

The windows were open now, inviting inside the crisp air of an autumn morning. Curtains stirred in a faint breeze.

'I feel so connected,' Jenny said. 'It's what I like most, I think.' She chose some grapes, then rested her elbows on the table and nodded towards the windows. 'I can be up here and still feel part of everything that's happening outside.'

Floating up to our kitchen came a whirlpool of noise. Footsteps shuffled and suitcases rumbled on paving. Laughter overlaid mingled conversations in different languages, a soundtrack to our breakfast. The *campiello* surrounded us, vivid and tangible.

'Another cup of tea?' I suggested. 'More toast?' The cosy fragrance of warm bread filled the kitchen.

'I'm fine, thanks, I should really start getting ready.' Jenny sorted through a stack of papers, removing a newspaper article on Verona. She had friends who'd spent three months living there, and she wanted to see something of the city they remembered with such fondness. I was keen to visit, too. An hour's train trip from Venice, Verona offered the ideal day excursion for later in the week. *And* it was the hometown of Romeo and Juliet. Who could pass that up? Verona rated five shiny, gold stars on my must-see list.

I cleared away the breakfast plates. Above the sink, another window opened over a canal. I leaned out, watching a gondola move along the canal and listening as the gondolier explained to his passengers a point of Venetian history.

'Serenissima? Ah, Serenissima was Venice. The Republic. Was beautiful. Is gone, after Napoleon.'

Splash. Plunk, plunk. Gondola oars pushed through still water. The history lesson continued, fading in volume as the gondolier steered his tourist cargo towards the busier waters of the Grand Canal. Splash. Plunk, plunk.

The canal below was a favourite route for gondoliers. Chocolate-box pretty, it was narrow and canyoned between buildings which shaded it from the brutal summer sun. No one warned passengers it was hot out there in the middle of a wide, shadeless canal. Hand on heart, I could honestly say I'd never seen a gondola passenger smile, unless a photo was being taken at the time.

'What do you think, then?' Jenny's voice cut into my thoughts. 'What time should we leave?' She re-homed the papers under the fruit bowl and stood, the chair creaking as she moved it backwards.

'It's just gone ten now. Say around eleven? That should give us plenty of time to come back here for lunch and then get ready.'

The Clooney nuptials didn't figure in our program for that glittering Sunday. We were going to the opera that afternoon, and a morning practice run to Teatro La Fenice, the opera house, was part of the plan. Just to be on the safe side. How many stories had I heard about people getting lost – hopelessly lost – in Venice? I just didn't get it. Attention to detail was the key; hadn't it worked so well in choosing our apartment? A little forethought and a small outlay of time now would guarantee an easy stroll to our matinee performance later on.

Besides, who wouldn't want to walk around Venice on such a glorious day?

✺

'Hmm. I think it's warmed up since this morning.' Jenny looked at the cloudless afternoon sky with just the faintest hint of an accusation. She closed the street door and we crossed the *campiello*. 'I'm glad it's only a twenty-five-minute walk to La Fenice.'

'Still very pleasant, though,' I said. 'Totally my sort of day.'

I adored hot weather. My teenage summer weekends, spent on the white sands of City Beach, still lingered in my mind as idyllic. A too-brief bikini, sand clinging to my sweaty, sunburnt body, then the knee-deep wade into swirling foam before losing balance and churning underwater like a load of laundry. Life in 1970s Perth could offer nothing finer.

'And at last I get to wear some decent shoes,' I continued, pleased with both weather and footwear.

Jenny looked down – distrustingly, or did I imagine it? – at my high heels. I'd packed four pairs for the month travelling around Italy. The mountain-goat streets of Bellagio hadn't encouraged high heels but Venice, with its cardboard-flat landscape, was ideal. It was high time they moved from my suitcase to my feet. Besides, I wanted to glam up a bit. How often in one lifetime do you go to the opera in Venice?

I glanced at my watch. 2.15 pm. The Wedding was forty-five minutes away, I remembered, the same time as the opening curtain at La Fenice. What a coincidence. I imagined the Cipriani at that moment: staff aflutter, with not a moment to lose before the curtain rose on their own performance. But Jenny and I had time to spare. Perhaps we could enjoy a pre-cultural prosecco in the super-posh bar, rubbing shoulders with Venetian A-listers. Who knew what might follow? Possibilities whirled like snowflakes in a blizzard.

We'd had no problems finding La Fenice that morning. Our trial run took us to the Ponte di Rialto (Rialto Bridge) in fifteen minutes and from there, in another ten, to Piazza di San Marco and the opera house. Forty-five minutes was more than enough time to see us safely from *campiello* to cushioned seat at La Fenice. Really, what was all the fuss about? Get lost in Venice? Not us.

'And there's the Clarks shoe store.' Jenny pointed to what had become our navigational landmark, easily recognised in the sea of unfamiliar Italian names. 'So from here it's straight ahead.'

'It's nice not to have so many people around,' I said, click-clacking along in my fancy footwear. 'I can actually see things this time.'

Our morning run had corresponded with tourist peak hour, and we'd stepped from our front door into a human tidal wave, carried along by the surge, funnelled into one *calle* after another until we washed up at San Marco. From the tourist sea which engulfed me, I'd seen little more than bobbing heads. But now it was siesta time, and only small clusters of slow-moving tourists took in the sights. Jenny and I ambled along with them.

'I love the ramshackle elegance of Venice,' I said. 'So much more interesting than clinical order. It must be an acquired taste. Like a spritz with Campari instead of Aperol.'

Time was on our side, as the song goes, and we wandered on, soaking up the peeling-paint ambience. Flourishes of mildew spread across ochre walls. Glimpses of foliage hinted at a lush courtyard oasis kept secret from the passer-by. Beneath a green and white awning a cake shop nestled, an Aladdin's cave of delights. Marzipan birds sang in a chocolate tree, and peanut brittle lay in nests of ruffled paper. Beauty and style were hard-wired into the Venetian consciousness, I thought, inescapable even on bakery shelves. I veered sideways for a closer inspection and bumped into another cake-loving window-shopper.

Then I bumped into a thought.

I hadn't seen the shop before. Never mind the crowds, it was the sort of thing I'd notice anywhere.

'Jenny.' I spoke in the subdued, contrite manner of a child summoned to the headmaster's office. 'I don't remember this shop.' Then, as an afterthought, 'And we seem to be going up and down a lot more steps. I'm sure it's not just because my feet are getting a bit sore.'

We stopped and looked at our surroundings. Nothing was familiar. Jenny pulled a map from her handbag and studied it, a frown appearing above her sunglasses. She pushed the glasses further up her nose and turned the map sideways, then upright again. The frown deepened. Not a good sign.

She faced me over the map. A pause opened and lengthened. Then: 'I can't even find where we started from.'

We looked at each other, then at the map. From a nearby rooftop, a complacent stone lion watched on.

'Let's go back to the Clarks shoe shop,' I said, attempting authority. 'That's what you're supposed to do. Go back to your starting point. We've still got plenty of time. We'll just turn around and start again.'

Which was about as easy as putting the pin back in the grenade. We recognised nothing. Had we passed this *ristorante* before or hadn't we? What about that mask shop? And the gelateria, its metal cannisters offering a choice of fifty flavours? I'd remember that, surely. I looked at

Jenny, hoping she remembered it. Her shrug came as the punctuation mark to end my hopes.

New, never-before-seen vistas appeared at every turn. Here was a *campo* (square), a pretty sight with its trattoria and umbrella-shaded tables, its water fountain and wisteria-draped archways. We stood in the *calle* leading into it and looked at the other three which led away from it.

'I think,' Jenny said, nodding to our right, 'if we just head in that direction we'll come to something that *is* on the map.'

A knot of anxiety lodged in my stomach. What little remained of the confidence that had blossomed pre-holiday now withered and fell. A brief flowering. I glanced at my watch, eyes widening. That late already? We picked one *calle* from the range of three and pushed ahead, like a couple of new recruits on their first orienteering course.

The balmy morning had ripened into a hot afternoon, breeze-less and sticky. An unwelcome dampness spread beneath the folds of my dress, making it cling to bosom and bottom in ways the designer could never have imagined. Glad rags became sad rags. Wonderful turned to wilted. How was Amal doing, I wondered, over on her side of Venice.

Heat spread across my face in a rich flush. 'I could murder a drink. Something cold and fizzy, to remind me I've still got a throat.' I glared at the sun as it continued its path across a cloudless sky. The sun glared back.

At the other end of my anatomy there were more issues. My feet had become a headache, so to speak. Those shoes, never intended for a walking tour of Venice, pinched my toes in a vice-like grip and with each uncharted step my ankles swelled to mock two half-inflated birthday balloons. Blistered skin morphed to the same shade of purple as my dress.

I checked my watch again. Twenty minutes to opening curtain. The knot of anxiety unravelled, spreading tendrils of alarm. We paced the northern reaches of Venice; to and fro, this way and that. The map passed between sweaty palms, occasionally moving to a handbag during moments of baseless confidence. It was becoming damp and creased, crumpled around the edges. Rather like us.

A church appeared on our left.

'Gothic, isn't it?' Jenny stopped, shading her eyes to admire Byzantine reliefs and white steeples. 'Quite magnificent.'

Magnificent, yes. And puzzling. The map promised a bridge should be expected at this spot. But no, there sat the church. There was no bridge in sight, no canal even, just a sun-drenched *campo* and its large church-tenant.

'I wonder which church it is?' Red patches glowed on Jenny's cheeks but, undaunted by heat and late or not, she remained the diligent tourist. 'I'd like to come back when we've got more time.'

More time. Now there's a thought.

Heat flowed through the *campo* like melting butter. Into its shadeless spaces we plunged, then out the other side, heading … neither of us had a clue. Secretly I suspected we were closer to the island of Murano than the opera house. In twenty-five minutes we'd covered more of Venice than most tourists managed in a week. We picked another of those two-peas-in-a-pod *calli* and pressed on. A zig to the right. A zag to the left.

The next landmark sighting was mine. 'I know this bridge,' I said, relieved. 'I've seen it before. We're on the right track. It's less than five minutes to San Marco.'

Jenny also recognised the bridge. As you would: we'd crossed it fifteen minutes earlier, going in the opposite direction. We trundled to a stop, forced to admit the unthinkable. We were lost. Completely. Hopelessly. All that googling – our morning practice run, even – had proved about as useful as a beach house in winter. Venice had tricked us.

I leaned against the bridge railings to rub my burning feet. That's when I remembered my mother's solution: a simple strategy, as effective in finding items at the back of supermarket shelves as for locating tricky destinations. It generally delivered the right result, Mum maintained, and saved a lot of time. And time was no longer on our side.

'Let's just ask the way to San Marco. If we can get there, we can find La Fenice.'

And so the oldest of all tourist questions asked in Venice – asked by so many visitors, in so many languages, over so many centuries – was put to whoever appeared in our path: Which way to San Marco?

It worked. *Calle* by *calle* and bridge by bridge we worked our way to the Piazza and trudged past those famous golden mosaics. With hand laid firmly across my heart, I swear no traveller ever found the sight of them more glorious.

Ten minutes until the opening curtain.

'At last,' I panted, as we turned into a *calle* behind the Piazza. Inside those punishing shoes my feet no longer throbbed. Worse. They were numb. The only sensation was a quivering about the ankles, like a twig ready to snap. I dreaded slipping and ending up in the emergency department of some hospital. There was bound to be a queue, like everywhere else in Italy.

For now I remained upright, propped against a stone column while I scanned our surroundings. My eyes landed on a wall plaque...

'Jenny, look!' I said. 'It's the Frezzeria. That's the name of the street we should be on. We go to the next corner and turn to the right. We're as good as there.'

I led the way to the next corner and we turned to the right. Then we turned to the left. To the right again. No La Fenice.

'I was sure it was right there.'

Jenny rummaged in her bag and out came the map. Such unfiltered trust in Venetian cartography.

I pointed to the ragged concertina expanding in her hands. 'It might be too late for that. We're going to have to ask directions again.'

The opening curtain was just minutes away. And time was not the only thing that had moved on. From being lost in the shadeless *calli* of northern Venice we'd moved closer to our target and were now lost in a 21st-century jungle. A dense growth of consumerism sprang up around us, and retail outlets hemmed us on every side. They all looked the same. We chose one at random and traipsed into the world of upscale retail.

Behind the counter, a woman rearranged her merchandise, moving each item a fraction of a millimetre to better display its charms. Groomed and perfumed, red lipped and dark haired, she epitomised Venetian chic. Her demeanour reflected the obvious and exceptional pleasure she took in merely being herself in this showy store in this showy city. With a whisking movement of her eyelids she completed a top-to-toe assessment of what now stood before her. It was clear we didn't measure up to the standard she expected of her clientele.

'Hello.' Jenny smiled and spoke in her pleasant voice. Good manners never failed her, even in the most testing circumstances. 'Could you tell us the way to La Fenice? We seem to be lost.'

Directing lost tourists fell outside the signora's remit. She sniffed, a sniff as delicate as a cat's sneeze, then tilted that sleekly groomed head to send hair spilling like ink over her shoulders. A long, flat stare directed at a point on the far wall completed the pantomime of disdain.

'Turn down the next *calle*,' she said to the air beside Jenny's right ear. 'There is La Fenice.'

I tottered to the door in a shuffling, dance-step motion. Jenny said a gracious thank you and followed. La Bella wiped the spot on the counter where we'd rested our elbows.

We turned down the next *calle* as instructed, then stopped. We looked at the *calle*. We looked at each other.

'We've already walked down here.'

It was four minutes until the performance started. It didn't matter if we had misunderstood the instructions. It didn't matter if we had been cunningly – *wilfully* – misled by a lady who didn't want sweaty tourists messing up her pretty, shiny store. It was game over. We weren't going to make it.

There we stood, stopped in our weary tracks. I remembered the anticipation I'd felt when we booked our tickets. I remembered the images I'd seen of La Fenice's interior, a confection of gilt and stucco rising over six levels of individual boxes. One was meant to contain me. I remembered how I'd fancied myself sitting there, tricked up in my flash rags as though I lived my life within the borders of wealth and ease.

Most of all, I remembered how we weren't going to get lost. Not us. A tissue, please, to wipe the egg from my scarlet, suffering face.

Then, from out of nowhere, a miracle. I recognised the opera house, familiar from our morning enterprise. Relief surged all the way to my pinched toes as I balanced against Jenny's shoulder and pointed. 'It's there! Just there! We've found it!'

It was. And we had. La Fenice, ten metres away. I can't be certain we hadn't walked past it before. Possibly several times. A final dash, then up the stairs *e presto*. We'd nailed it.

Jenny and I slid moistly into our seats.

On stage Ferrando launched into his aria as the Count di Luna pondered his love for Leonora.

Across town, Mr and Mrs Clooney said 'I do'.

❋

Later that evening, over pizza and several glasses of red, Jenny and I put together our Venice program. We sat and schemed in Oke, a pizzeria across the canal from the Hotel Cipriani, scene of the afternoon's nuptials.

'I fancy a day on the lagoon tomorrow,' I said. 'Especially if the weather is like today. We could start ...'

The sentence trailed to a halt as my eyes ricocheted to and fro like a ball in a ping-pong game. Oke was a fusion of New York loft, 1950s retro and Venetian Gothic. Chandelier met shabby chic. Pop art met punk. A battery of style statements came together with pulsing energy, demanding my attention.

A waiter approached and indicated my empty glass. 'Another, signora?'

'*Si, si. Grazie mille.*' A follow-up struck me as a wonderful idea.

He refilled my glass and I pointed outside to the crowded *fondamenta*. 'All those people. Are they here because of the wedding?'

'Wedding?' A frown appeared before understanding scudded across his face. 'Pfft. No one cares about wedding. Everyone comes for *la passeggiata*.'

La passeggiata, the evening stroll, was still a popular tradition in contemporary Venice. Couples, families and dog walkers took to the streets, aiming to see and be seen, to meet and greet, to chat and gossip. Others watched on from behind a cappuccino or an aperitif at a pavement cafe.

My gaze bounced from the waiter to a table against the far wall. A motorbike was parked beside it, as though James Dean had just stepped out and would be back shortly. Above a pinball machine dripped the crystal prisms of a chandelier. I wanted to package up Oke and take it home with me, so I could go there every Sunday night.

Our pizzas arrived, two bubbling discs covering most of the table's surface. I moved my wineglass to safety and redirected my attention to Jenny.

'The first time I saw someone eat a whole pizza, I was appalled. It was that lady in Lake Como, remember? We ordered poached sea bass and salad. So totally virtuous. Now I realise she was on the right track.'

I bit into the first slice. Elastic-like threads of mozzarella stretched from the plate to my mouth. 'Oh, yes. Definitely on the right track.'

The level in my wineglass was falling again. Three hours of La Fenice's opulence and the buzz of a dining-in-technicolour pizzeria had lifted my spirits. Ready for anything, I was, and fizzing with anticipation. Venice, here I come. Although I'd be revising my choice of footwear.

Jenny traced a finger around her wineglass. 'And how about we go to Verona on Tuesday?' She took a sip of wine. It was low tide in her glass, too.

'Sounds good to me.' Wall-poster advertisements for Coca-Cola, maple syrup and canned tomatoes, circa 1950, framed Jenny's head but her thoughts lay several centuries earlier, back with Romeo and Juliet. I smiled – at Jenny, at the parked motorbike, at my good fortune.

Pizzas eaten. Wine finished. Plan Venice sorted. We caught a vaporetto, then walked through the now chilly streets to our apartment, passing the Clarks shoe store, sitting right where it was meant to be. Jenny unlocked our *campiello* door.

'It's one of my small pleasures,' she said, as we started up the stairs. 'Walking through that door and away from the crowds. It's like saying, "Yes, I'm a local. This is my home."'

We ended the day much as we'd started, sitting at the kitchen table with a cup of tea. Fatigue wrapped around me. With a yawn and the promise of an early start the next day, I said goodnight.

In the apartment's study, I pulled on pyjamas before tackling the swarm of Designer Lifestyle cushions nesting on the sofa. The glam infusion, I guessed, was compensation for the fact that the sofa didn't unfold into the promised double bed. Its stubborn resistance had defied logical thought, brute force and invective in three languages. But despite the recalcitrant sofa, I loved my study–bedroom. Its atmosphere was cluttered and cosy, a welcoming retreat.

The curtains hung still beside open windows. Paintings glinted in light from the *campiello* – silent now, but for an occasional muffled voice. The tables and chairs of its restaurants were inside until tomorrow, tucked away like children under curfew. It wasn't noise that prevented sleep. My thoughts kept me awake until dawn outlined the *campiello*'s rooftops.

In a week's time I'd walk along the *ferrovia*'s platform and catch the train to Florence. I'd carry with me memories of Venice, like something packed into my luggage along with my toothbrush. I wanted more than that. Already I felt a sense of connection to the city, as if I somehow belonged among those *calli* that had so baffled me during the afternoon. Venice had cast its spell. I knew I'd be back.

CHAPTER 2

HENRI'S PARTY

*Whether for good or ill, those Venetians are always up
to something together ...*

Johann Wolfgang von Goethe, German philosopher,
in *Italian Journey 1761–88*

Silence enfolded the apartment. Two o'clock ticked by, then
three o'clock. My thoughts drifted, roaming back over the
day's events. The Wedding of the Year had come and gone
and, like me, Venice had been pretty much indifferent to the
whole affair. A perfect day was all it gave the couple.

Hardly surprising when you think about it. Venetians
were used to famous visitors. For longer than a millennium
they had played host to world notables, so a wedding was
nothing out of the ordinary. But there had been a time,
once, when Venice pulled out all stops to impress a visitor.
When it really mattered to the city, new heights of expense
and creative genius had been willingly scaled. Nothing was
too much trouble. If it could be done, then it was done. The
story is stitched into the tapestry of Venetian history.

✸

The French were up to mischief. They'd signed – *instigated*, if you please – a treaty with the Ottoman Turks, Venice's long-standing enemy. France needed a powerful ally like the Turks to deflect the military ambitions of its old enemy, Spain. The Franco–Turkish Alliance was intended to give France security rather than demonstrate any fondness for the Turks.

But just the same. The treaty was a matter of concern for Venice, who'd hoped to enlist France's support – or at least France's non-intervention – in its endless wars with the Turks. That now seemed less likely. So when an opportunity arose to advance their cause, the wily Venetians weren't about to pass it up.

The year was 1574. Henri, Duke de Valois and King of Poland, was returning to Paris from Poland following the death of his older brother, King Charles IX. In Paris he was to be crowned King Henri III of France. Before taking up the royal reins, Henri planned a little time in Venice.

Henri was mischief in a package. The favourite child of Catherine de' Medici – one of history's supreme trouble-makers – he shared her fascination with witchcraft and wizardry; a small eccentricity that could be overlooked in a younger son not expected to be king.

An obsession with the occult matched other unorthodox traits, and nowhere did Henri embrace the unconventional more than in his personal life. He lived surrounded by a coterie of young men, his *mignons*. The word means darlings or sweet ones, and the relationship of these men to their monarch was the subject of constant speculation. Was Henri homosexual? A transvestite? Or was the whole business nothing more than malicious gossip, put about by his political opponents? Voicing an opinion too freely could prove unwise: one detractor, the Parisian lawyer Le Breton, was publicly hanged for his comments regarding Henri's homosexual dalliances. So reviled had Henri become by then that crowds of Parisians gathered to kiss the feet of Le Breton's swinging corpse.

Along with his *mignons*, Henri enjoyed the company of beautiful women. At one time he'd been considered a possible husband for Elizabeth I of England, a union smiled upon by his scheming mother, Queen Catherine. But marriage plans stalled when Henri, then in his late teens, scathingly dismissed Elizabeth as 'an old woman with bad legs'. He'd heard about her varicose veins. Anglo–French relations of the royal and romantic kind had to wait a further ten years when Elizabeth, then aged forty-six, entertained the notion of a liaison with Henri's *younger* brother François, Duke of Alençon. He presumably was not concerned about her legs.[1]

So now Henri, the unexpected soon-to-be-King, was coming to Venice. Whispers circulated that Catherine had poisoned her own son, Henri's brother Charles, in order to have favoured-child Henri back in France as monarch. Perhaps it was just a wicked rumour. We'll never know.

But we do know that Henri liked to be the centre of attention, and that he adored luxury. So Venice delivered. Every mover and shaker from the ruling aristocracy attended his official arrival, jostling beneath the triumphal arch built in his honour, hoping to say *bonjour* before fleets of gilded,

---

1 The 1998 film *Elizabeth* depicts Elizabeth pacing the palace corridors, awaiting her imminent meeting with Henri. Henri, meanwhile, romps and plays dress-up with his *mignons*. Whatever the entertainment value of the scene, it flies in the face of history. The two never met. She did, however, meet François, Duke of Alençon.

silk-lined gondolas whisked him, *avec les mignons*, off to their lodgings.

Henri's retinue hunkered down in the grandly Gothic Ca' Foscari, located centrestage on the Grand Canal. Its already sumptuous rooms had received a right royal makeover in anticipation of the visit. Enough gold-threaded damask to form an awning over the Piazza di San Marco draped the walls, and priceless artworks were sprinkled about like so much confetti.

Along with luxury, Henry was also partial to a good time: lavish entertainments, no expense spared, that sort of thing. Venice was then at the peak of its maritime and trading power, the richest city on earth. So the world's richest city mounted an extravaganza for Henri's enjoyment.

Three thousand people attended the reception banquet. The women dazzled, bedecked with gold, diamonds and pearls. Every precious jewel to be found in Venice encircled a wrist, a finger, a throat. Henri was in awe. And the *mignons* ... although in mourning for Henri's brother, the besotted courtiers asked permission to remove their black coats and dance with the ladies. (Henri said *oui*.)

Then came the food. Guests chose from over one thousand dishes, prepared and presented by a small army of chefs and assistants. The entire meal was served on tableware made from a confection of hard-baked sugar. Ditto the table decorations, fashioned to a design by sculptor Jacopo Sansovino. Thousands of sugar plates and thousands of sets of sugar cutlery – those sixteenth-century Venetians knew how to throw a party.

And they knew *why* they were throwing a party. They wanted something. The basis of Venetian prosperity – the very lifeblood of the Republic – was trade. And for uninterrupted trade, alliances were a necessary survival tool. Henri, as King of France, would make a powerful Venetian ally. Everything in Venice had its price and its purpose. No such thing as a free lunch, not even for a monarch.

The ever-resourceful Venetians had more tricks, more rabbits to pull from the hat. They planned to demonstrate their war-readiness, the willingness of their citizens to fight.

Ritual battles between the city's two sparring factions, the Castellani and the Nicolotti, traditionally took place at the Ponte dei Pugni (Bridge of Punches) between September and Christmas. A special, one-off performance was arranged for Henri's benefit. Mindful of their distinguished spectator, the combatants rose to the occasion with heightened vigour and slugged it out using steel-tipped lances rather than the customary bare knuckles.

Everyone did their bit for Venice Inc.

More was to come. Prior to one banquet, Henri was escorted on a tour of the shipbuilding yards at the Arsenale, at that time the largest commercial operation in the world. Henri was mightily impressed by the display of naval prowess as he moved on with his hosts to a few hours of serious feasting.

The pièce de résistance came at the end of the banquet. Henri was taken back to the Arsenale where, since his earlier visit, a warship had been built and now awaited his inspection. A work force of thousands had constructed the vessel from absolute start to ocean-ready finish in the five or so hours of the banquet. Henry was astounded.

Oh, yes. The Arsenale did that sort of thing. It employed tens of thousands of workers in shipbuilding and allied trades. Carpenters alone numbered sixteen thousand. Its assembly-line techniques predated Henry Ford by more than three centuries. Four years earlier, when the Ottomans attacked the Venetian territory of Cyprus, the Arsenale furnished one hundred battle-ready galleys in under two months – a rate of two per day. The not-so-subtle message from Venetian rulers to Henri was that France would fare better as friend than as foe.

Ploys to further military and trade ambitions were set to one side when the Venetians pulled their final rabbit from the hat. Politics turned personal and romance found a place on the agenda.

The Great Council put together a list of the crème de la crème of Venetian courtesans and offered it to Henri. The personal experience of council members may well have played a part here: Venetian rulers weren't averse to a little chicanery of their own. Or perhaps another helpful source was called upon. *Il Catalogo di Tutte le Principal et più Honorate Cortigiane di Venetia (The Catalogue of the Chief and Most Renowned Courtesans of Venice)* was in common usage at the time. The register listed the addresses, charges and particular expertise of elite women whose sexual services were available.

From the Great Council's list, Henri chose one Veronica Franco as his companion. Some believe the two had already met. Henri, they claim, dropped by parties all over Venice and it was at one such gathering, hosted by Renaissance great, the painter Titian (Tiziano Vecellio), that the two first said *ciao*. Then again, it may be that Henri knew of Veronica and had long planned a catch-up, such was the fame of her charms. We can't be certain. History doesn't give up all its secrets.

But history does tell us that an attachment formed between these two most unlikely of lovers. Veronica later wrote to Henri, and dedicated two of her published sonnets to him. Henri, for his part, carried home an enamelled portrait of Veronica.

When Henri appeared outside Veronica's home the morning after their rendezvous, *mignons* and council members alike joined in applause. Here was proof that the about-to-be King of France could engage in sex with a woman. Children – future heirs and allies – were a possibility. A dishevelled Henri returned the greeting with a broad smile. Or so they say.

What a week. La Serenissima had excelled. Its reputation as the wealthiest, most fabulous place on earth was secure. More importantly, its military strength sat front-of-mind with France's new ruler. Relations between the two powers remained stable for two centuries until another Frenchman, Napoleon Bonaparte, oversaw the demise of the Republic in 1797. Napoleon's arrival, it goes without saying, was greeted with less enthusiasm than Henri's had been.

Fancy a little mischief yourself? Each August, to correspond with the anniversary of Henri's stay in Venice, there's a slap-up party at the Arsenale. An actor dressed as Henri mingles with the guests, and the menu, although not extending to a thousand dishes, is first rate. It's great fun, I'm told. The cost is 350 euro (A$700), and early bookings are advised.

And Henri? He waved *adieu* to Veronica and to Venice with sweet memories, bringing to an end the happiest week in his turbulent life. He returned to Paris to be crowned King of France, and married Louise de Lorraine-Vaudémont the day after his coronation. The marriage produced no children and there is no record of illegitimate offspring.

King Henri III of France ruled a country caught up in the turmoil of religious wars, an invidious position for any

monarch. To make matters worse, Henri fuelle
public discontent with provocative lifestyle choi
wheeling sexuality, and his love of fine clothin
facial cosmetics and expensive Italian imports
to turn public sentiment in his favour.

In 1589, fifteen years after his coronation,
murdered at the Chateau Saint-Cloud, near Pari

CHAPTER 3

VENETIAN DREAMING

*The only way to care for Venice as she deserves it is
to give her a chance to touch you often – to linger and
remain and return.*

Henry James, in *Italian Hours*

Sometimes I can snag a memory and reel it in out of nowhere.
I just need the right hook.

Flour rose in a puff as I slapped dough onto the kitchen
benchtop, then sank my knuckles into its cool sponginess. A
twig brushed the windowpane and I glanced up. Rain fell,
drops marbling the glass and dripping into diamond-shaped
outlines. I remembered the mullioned windows of Ca' d'Oro,
the fifteenth-century palazzo on the Grand Canal. It took
no more than that for my thoughts to spin off around the
world and across the centuries.

A month after returning home, Venice lingered at the
edge of my memory. It hovered as a half-remembered dream
might, flitting back in snatches to reach me as I went about
my after-holiday life. The very *idea* of Venice captivated me:
the notion of refugee settlers finding safety in a remote and

swampy wilderness, then building their city. And not just any city: from nothing but empty mud banks, those settlers – the first Venetians – created the most opulent place on earth.

I wished I'd known more about Venice on my last visit. I wished I'd been able to say to Jenny, as we stood lost in a *campo* at the edge of Venice: *This is where Casanova once waited for a lover. Right over there, beneath that statue of Bartolomeo Colleoni on his high-stepping horse. She was a mystery woman, this lover, and their trysts were discreet. Casanova referred to her only by her initials, MM. But I know who she was, this lover he met in such great secrecy. Shall I tell you?*

I rolled out pastry dough, then placed it over a pie dish and trimmed the edges. Grey clouds blistered, dimming the sky. My thoughts darkened with them.

I saw women – countless women, for generations, for centuries – pull their cloaks about them as they hurried along silent *calli*. I saw doubt shadow their faces as they drew alongside La Pietà convent, looking from the tiny bundle in their arms to a basket set into the convent wall. Had they delayed their decision too long? Would their baby still fit through the basket's covering? Its tightly meshed grate kept all but newborns from the safety of the cradle beneath. I watched as they juggled and pushed, wedging the infant into its new womb.

Then they turned away, these women, slipping back into darkness and I lost sight of them. Were their eyes shining with tears? Did they feel a sense of loss? Of shame? Or was there a feeling of virtue, knowing their child would not be among the nightly haul fishermen pulled from the lagoon?

My fingers smudged flour over a stack of CDs as I searched for Antonio Vivaldi's *The Four Seasons* and slotted it into the player. Vivaldi had been La Pietà's choir master when he wrote the concerto and, like much of his work, he wrote it to be performed by La Pietà's abandoned children.

The wind strengthened, dashing leaves against walls. White vinca petals dotted paving like debris washed up from a flood. My gaze moved beyond the rain-speckled windows and across the garden, but my thoughts stayed on the other side of the world.

I'd learned a lot about Venice in the last month. Books sprouted in heaps along the kitchen benchtop or rose in a listing tower beside my bed. The public library and the second-hand bookstore displaced the supermarket on my most-visited list. Hours slipped away as I pored over maps with the enthusiasm I once saved for best-selling novels. La Serenissima could have been my expert subject on *Hard Quiz*. I'd swotted up on everything to do with the thousand-year rule of the Doges and their Most Serene Republic of Venice. Splendour had been its hallmark, but it was stories of lesser glory that caught my attention. I delved into tales of the wacky and the wicked – tales of mischief.

There were plenty to choose from.

'Mad, bad and dangerous to know,' said Lady Caroline Lamb of George Gordon, Lord Byron. The poet's personal life in England was a catalogue of affairs, illegitimate children and debt. His marriage to Annabella Milbanke ended within a year amid accusations of mistreatment and cruelty. Scandalous revelations of a passionate affair with Augusta Leigh, his half-sister, and rumours of homosexuality turned public opinion against him and he fled England. Safely in Venice, Byron holed up in Palazzo Mocenigo on the Grand Canal, along with a large retinue of servants, six dogs, a goat, a fox and two monkeys.

Mistresses, prostitutes and one-off lovers too numerous to count joined Byron in his palazzo menagerie. For the length of his Venetian sojourn, the exiled English poet – dashingly handsome, although a little lame and short of stature – became the talk of the town.

But Venice had always attracted a rich blend of eccentrics and Byron was by no means alone in his exploits. Neither was misadventure solely an imported commodity: questionable behaviour within the ranks of the Venetian aristocracy had been whispered of for centuries. Doge Andrea Gritti was a stand-out.

The Gritti outfit were Venetian A-listers, linked through marriage to families able to trace their ancestry back to the origins of the Republic. But alas, unlike those great dynasties, no Doge appeared along the branches of the Gritti family tree. Andrea Gritti was to be Doge *numero uno*.

A bit of a rascal, was Andrea. His CV carried a long list of military and diplomatic accomplishments, all for the greater glory of La Serenissima, but his suitability to rule the mighty Venetian Republic came under challenge. In some circles his reputation nettled.

Andrea was an incorrigible womaniser. Remarked one detractor, perhaps with a touch of jealousy: 'We cannot make a Doge of a man with four bastards in Turkey.'

But make a Doge of him they did. Andrea continued his wayward habits, fathering numerous other children to different women, including the nun Celestina from the upper-crust convent of San Lorenzo.

Death mirrored his life of excess. One long-ago Christmas Eve, Andrea fell ill with a stomach ache and succumbed a few days later. He had eaten too many grilled eels, a traditional Venetian Christmas delicacy.

So many stories.

Each night I trawled through history's footnotes, yawns hollowing at the back of my throat, often awake when the morning newspaper thumped onto the front lawn. Time fell away as I followed up tales of the weird and the wilful, the near miss and the flawed. Tales of lives with rough edges and corrugated surfaces. And as I learned its stories, my feet grew into the Venice earth.

I wiped flour and pastry scraps from the benchtop and turned to the CD player. My arm brushed against books stacked ready for the evening's research, sending a papery waterfall crashing to the floorboards. Across the scattered pages lay a photo of the Basilica di San Marco; a typical-enough holiday snap, showing the famous mosaics glinting beneath the blue of an early-autumn sky. A bubbling cauldron of heads and selfie sticks oozed past the basilica's facade, while snaking lines waited for a one-way circuit around its interior. I'd taken the photo last year: Venice's foremost landmark, with its usual overlay of crowds and queues. All the appeal of a head cold in summer.

A different Venice; that's what I wanted. My next Venetian holiday would be about finding the hidden, private city, the Venice of the Venetians. I thought about an afternoon I'd spent in Rome's Trastevere district on the flight back to Perth, remembering the sense of community I'd felt in its cobblestoned *vicoli,* the sense of home, of being where I belonged. That's what I wanted in Venice. And I had an idea where I might find it.

I'd caught glimpses of Dorsoduro and its neighbourhoods during my visit with Jenny. On a day warmed by sunshine and possibilities, I'd gone off-grid to the city's western fringe, searching for Chiesa di San Sebastiano, the parish church and burial place of Renaissance master Paolo Veronese. I'd found San Sebastiano, and much else.

I'd found *calli* echoing with the shouts of children as they catapulted from doorways to their pavement playground. Boys rested their scooters against a wall to thread lights between the wheels' spokes before careening off, lights flashing on-again-off-again in red and green bursts. In the nearby *campo*, skipping ropes thwacked against stone and youngsters chanted songs in time with the twirls; the happy sounds of childhood. A little girl ran across the years to greet me: it was my younger self, on a scorching Perth summer's afternoon, skipping rope under the shade of a gum tree as playmates sang *Fly away Peter, Fly away Paul.* She made me smile, that little girl.

I'd found a vegetable barge moored in a canal. Venetian housekeepers pulled their shopping buggies away from pedestrian traffic and rested them against the canal railings, then leaned beneath the barge's canvas awning to assess the ripeness of tomatoes and the crispness of beans. The owner chatted without pause as he parcelled goods and handed them over the railings. I'd bought sun-warmed grapes and eaten them as I strolled off, humming to myself.

So Dorsoduro was the district – or *sestiere*, as Venetians say – where I wanted to spend my holiday month; a place where I might just find that other city and live, at least for a while, like a Venetian local. Now all I had to do was find an apartment.

❀

It was the perfect day for planning to be somewhere else. Perth springtime was a strange beast, I reflected, sitting with a cup of tea and watching storm clouds gather. A chameleon season, it borrowed from summer and winter. Here it was, early November, and winter had long outstayed its welcome.

I turned from the bleakness outside and switched on the computer, then pulled a notebook within easy reach. My thoughts went back to last year's online booking saga with Jenny – our relentless search for perfection; the scores of apartments assessed and dismissed before Campiello Riccardo Selvatico got the nod. Jottings and memos would cover many pages of that notebook, I guessed, before I found my Venetian home-for-a-month.

A month in Venice: my spirits lifted at the thought. It was enough time to revisit what I remembered and discover what I'd missed. Palazzo Gritti, for instance; I'd missed that. But it was easily put to rights. Doge Andrea Gritti's family residence was now a luxury hotel and accessible for a wander-through. Or perhaps even an aperitif, budget permitting.

Parameters keyed in, I pressed the search icon and watched the first image flick onto the screen. A photo showed views over two canals, crossed at several points by stone bridges. Small boats lined the canals, suggesting a residential neighbourhood matching the road-less-travelled flavour I wanted. In the background stood a church, its belltower rising above clusters of weathered roofs to shape the horizon.

I leaned in for a closer look. Below the photo, a description noted that this was the view from the apartment's kitchen and living room. *Not bad, not bad at all*, I thought, pinching my lips between thumb and forefinger, my standard you-have-my-complete-attention pose. The apartment met all my requirements; it was almost too good to be true. Like pigeons in the Piazza, my hopes winged skywards.

But wait a minute.

A hairline crack of uncertainty ran through the perfect picture. The apartment was not far from Piazzale Roma, the terminus for vehicles arriving in Venice. On one side the Tronchetto multi-storey carpark rose grim and grey, and across a bitumen desert, large buses transported passengers to and from cities throughout Italy. I didn't want the city's ragged hem. The Venice I had in mind didn't include a busy transport hub with the throat-catching smell of diesel. I was after moss-fringed canals and silent *calli*, not the noisy wash of the twenty-first century.

If it seems too good to be true, it probably is. I didn't fancy being holed up for a month, by myself, with *turistico centrale* right on my doorstep. A long search with copious note-taking loomed as the inevitable next step and I rolled a biro across the desk towards me, all set. That's when I remembered. Jenny and I had placed our trust in visitor reports; truthful, from-the-coalface assessments weighing up each apartment's merits. We hadn't been disappointed. I clicked onto guest reviews and found eighteen appraisals over three screens. How could people find so much to say about a one-bedroom apartment?

Five reviews in I found what I wanted.

Piazzale Roma? Not a problem, maintained this reviewer. She, too, had been concerned by the proximity of the apartment to a major tourist facility. But four hundred metres, a wide canal and public gardens separated the one from the other; the apartment turned its back, quite literally, on Piazzale Roma, facing instead a picture-book Venetian scene. What was more, she gave the property a five-star rating, as did all the other reviewers. It seemed I'd won a lucky dip.

Could it really be that easy, settling on the first apartment I came across? I scrolled back to the photo. Already the apartment felt like home. I could picture myself at the kitchen window, watching the sun rise over rooftops as the kettle boiled for my breakfast cup of tea. Or, prosecco in hand, gazing past the windowsill geraniums to the twilight activity on the watery T-junction below. It was all I had hoped for. I could be part of local Venetian life and connect with the city in ways I'd missed on previous visits. First apartment or not, somehow I knew it was the right choice. My confidence matched my anticipation as I emailed Sebastiano, the apartment's owner, and booked the apartment.

How lucky can one girl be? Next August would be spent in an apartment with a living room overlooking canals and bridges, where geraniums flowered on one windowsill and parsley grew on another. From my windows I would look out to a city of a thousand years and as many stories.

In a small way, I would be part of it.

CHAPTER 4

FELLOW TRAVELLERS

Tell me who I am, but not who I was.

Venetian proverb

I'm prepared to make this admission up-front. Sitting by myself on the train from Malpensa Airport to Milan I suffered a temporary loss of courage. Not quite panic, not yet, but heading in that direction. I tried to ignore my stomach as it crammed itself into my throat. For the first time, and rather late in the day, I wondered if this whole Venice thing might be a mistake.

The months since I emailed Sebastiano had passed in a whirl of activity. Venice existed between the pages of books; a tantalising prospect, but one dusted with a sense of the unreal. My real life, the here and now, kept me as busy as a kelpie in the shearing yards. With that same purposeful energy I ran between bridge games, social catch-ups and Pilates classes, finishing each day with a mental inventory of phone calls waiting to be made and household tasks still to be completed. On my overcrowded to-do list, doubt hadn't got a look in.

Now Italy was flicking past the train windows. Venice was three hours and two train journeys away and here I sat, alone, headed for one of Europe's busiest stations. I reached across to my bag on the seat beside me and pulled out a crumpled ticket, checking it for the third time. All was correct and in order, validated before boarding at the Malpensa Airport platform, meaning a fifty euro fine could be crossed from the list of potential mishaps. Other worries danced centrestage to replace it.

My previous travels, with friends or in groups, had not amplified a spirit of independence, and the one or two solo trips I'd made over the years had entailed little more than arriving at a beach somewhere, sitting on it for a week, then returning to the safety of home ground. Independence? The very word had a sophisticated, purposeful sound, suggesting depths of wisdom and worldly experience I'd never associated with my life. Independence was something at the end of a long, shadowy avenue down which I never journeyed.

Beside the luggage compartment my suitcase rocked on the floor in time with the train's sway. I'd heaved and hefted to hernia levels but still couldn't move it up onto the racks; even the lowest rung eluded me. How was I going to drag it along the platform at Milan? My muscles ached in anticipation. Chaos could be less than an hour away.

I rested my arm against the window and looked out, fighting down the first rustles of panic. Stations with drab, concrete platforms came and went. Between them the countryside was pleasant; soothing, even. Glistening veins of rivers wandered across farmland before cutting off into densely green forest. Dawn sunshine polished cornfields to a pale gold, and its warmth reached through the window to brush my arm.

The train slowed to a halt at Rescaldina, a township

of pink-painted houses sheltering beneath cypress trees. I watched the boarding passengers; only a few so early on a Sunday morning. An elderly couple edged along the aisle with their dog – an old spaniel, his adventures long behind him. The woman held her husband's arm to guide him, and I saw the wedding ring grown tight on her finger. Husband and dog plodded along, both of them hunched and arthritic, a matched set. Then soft thumps, the wheeze of upholstery. Safely seated. The deep gullies of the man's face smoothed as he offered his wife a fond smile.

Their dog sat in the aisle, ears twitched to the sound of their voices. The woman bent down and slid the dog's ears between her fingers, turning them almost inside out with the caress. The dog wiped her hand with a wet tongue and inched closer.

It was fatigue kicking in, I guess. Tears lined up behind my eyelids as I watched the trio. Their comfort with each other reflected the assurance of a known place in the world, whatever the size and scope of that world. And I imagined their world existed within one of Rescaldina's pink-painted houses.

My thoughts turned to another tiny patch of the planet. I'd never believed that living in a small place like Perth – or Rescaldina – led to a smaller life. For me, it had always offered contentment and security, a place of familiar boundaries in the grand scheme of things. Well into my middle years, I felt no wistful longing for a sprawling, complex life, for ambitious plans and extravagant optimism; things I'd never known. Like the couple sitting nearby, the security of an established niche – a place to call mine – was enough.

At Porto Garibaldi they stood to leave. The woman helped her husband to his feet. Beside them, the dog lifted itself onto its front paws before the hind legs followed in shaky imitation. Tail moving from side to side in time with his ageing gait, he crept along behind his creeping master. My eyes followed them along the platform until the swinging tail disappeared behind the station's concrete walls.

Fatigue taking hold, as I said. I remembered another swinging tail, another old dog; one who arrived from a rescue shelter, all tatty, skinny and unloved, then spent the next sixteen years rearranging my life and my household. Making it his own, as though he'd found his place in the world. I sniffed and ran a finger beneath my eyes.

Not far to Milan. The city's outskirts rolled past the window, a soul-corroding landscape of square apartment blocks stretching kilometre after dreary kilometre. Graffiti covered apartment walls and washing hung from lines strung over balconies. The apartments were constructed to house Italy's booming post-war population and urban beautification had not been a priority. At Milano Centrale, large areas of the railway yards were semi-derelict. Between disused tracks, weeds shot to the heavens like botanical fireworks and litter proliferated. Windows framed jagged, glassy spikes, mirrors in the sun.

Last year, Jenny and I had bypassed Milan. From the station's main hall – Mussolini's contribution to Italian architectural splendour – we'd caught just glimpses of the city. Some people loved Milan, others hated it. Milan Cathedral, for instance, divided opinion. One hundred and thirty-five spires crammed its roof and over three thousand statues freckled its exterior. Many Italy aficionados considered it among the nation's most beautiful buildings.

English writer DH Lawrence hadn't thought so. In a letter to Lady Cynthia Asquith, Lawrence wrote: 'I got to beastly

Milan with its imitation hedgehog of a cathedral and its hateful city Italians, all socks and purple cravats and hats over the ears.'

Quite the put-down, to both cathedral and citizens. *Milanesi* viewed themselves as the epitome of fashion flair and had a reputation for their enthusiastic patronage of Fendi and Versace. They saw themselves as different from other Italian citizens. Different from Romans, most certainly, who are known – envied, perhaps – for their earthy sensuality.

My thoughts drifted from Milano Centrale's grim surrounds to an autumn night I'd spent in Rome, homeward bound from a Tuscan holiday. Summer had departed Tuscany for another year, leaving behind grey skies, cold evenings and trees beginning to take on their winter bareness. But Rome was still hot and I sat outside on the Via Veneto for a late dinner.

Twenty-something I guessed she was, the young woman who walked along the pavement. Curling hair fell to her shoulders, pulled back from her face and secured in a high ponytail by two red marbles on an elastic band. It swayed as she walked. So did her hips. Pretty much everything swayed as she walked, and the dress she was wearing did nothing to conceal or discourage movement. It was a short, strappy number, unadorned by anything worn with it. On top or beneath.

She clipped along in her high-heeled sandals, the corners of her mouth turned up in a smile. She didn't contrive to make a statement. No eyes followed her, and she gave the impression of neither wanting nor needing anyone's attention. And that, I thought from my table under the trees, is the essence of Rome. Sensual. Self-confident. Not giving, not seeking approval.

Milan, on the other hand, is all about grooming, about one-upmanship in the undeclared war of being best dressed. The good folk of Milan undeniably win the style stakes. I think of the difference between Rome and Milan as the difference between a luscious, ripe mango and a highly polished, crisp apple.

The sound of wheels braking pulled me back from my thoughts. The train slid to a halt and doors whooshed open. Passengers straightened their clothes and gathered up belongings before stepping onto the platform and heading off on their different paths. Everyone had a destination and was in a hurry to reach it. The man sitting opposite me paused long enough to steer my case from the luggage racks to the platform before he, too, hurried away. I watched him disappear in the crowds; someone else who knew where to go and what to do. Not like me. There I stood, Alice on the wrong side of the looking glass.

Deep breaths, I told myself. In and out. *In*, hold, and *out. You can do this.* Noise racketed and crowds choked the platforms. Signs warned of pickpockets and the need for constant vigilance: in recent years, the separation of travellers from their cash and belongings had blossomed into a cottage industry. More deep breaths, more self-affirmation and off I trudged, threading my way through the crowds, tugging my overweight burden. The pulley handle felt like some strange outgrowth from my right palm. Surgery could be needed to separate us. Heaving and huffing, round-shouldered and tilted forwards, I made a slow advance along the platform. Then *thwack!* I ran up against a stretch of blue shirt. There stood a man, hands jammed flat in the rear pockets of his trousers, making his arms poke out like stubby, short wings. The apology forming on my lips turned to a gasp as he dipped one wing and grabbed at my suitcase. He didn't look official. An emblem of some sort was embossed on the left pocket of his shirt: perhaps it was the logo of Trenitalia or Milano Centrale. Or perhaps it was the logo of a local ice-cream company. Who knew?

He jerked backwards with a grunt as the full weight of the suitcase registered, then started off along the platform. *Stop that man!* But then again … little chance of a fast, Hollywood-style getaway with the load he was dragging. I tagged along until he pulled up beside an automatic ticket machine and propped my case against it. He raised his hand to eye level before opening it and then cautiously, one by one, flexing his fingers. Finding everything still intact, he turned to me.

'You go where, signora? Venice? Is thirty-seven euro, standard class.' His fingers flicked over buttons. 'Money in here.'

I pushed a fifty euro note at the machine and it gave me a ticket to Venice. '*Grazie mille, signor,*' I said, my fingers and palm again encircling the suitcase handle. I turned from the ticket machine to the platforms and the strangest thing happened. A caterpillar turned into a butterfly. The platform surrounds no longer spoke of decline and neglect. The Trenitalia carriages wore their red and green national colours with pride, as stylish as the *Milanesi* themselves. Once-dusty platforms shone. The beauty of the station's entrance extended right down here, to the ticket machine and the man standing beside it. A little kindness will do that.

'Signora, your change. Is here.' My blue-shirted helper nodded towards the coin return slot, then added, 'Platform ten. Twenty-five minutes, you leave.'

✺

Waiting on the platform that Sunday morning, I felt my body had arrived in Italy before my thoughts. Hours, places and people had merged and collapsed into a single hazy fuzz as I'd moved between worlds, encased in a metal cylinder. Now a white storm raged in my head; everything was blurred, a foggy window I was too exhausted to wipe clean. I needed two hours in the Italian countryside to recalibrate, to allow my mind to play catch-up.

Right on time, the Trenitalia train slid into platform ten. With a sigh of relief, I found the right *carrozza* and dropped into my seat. The part of the journey that had most worried me, getting from Malpensa Airport to a Venice-bound train, had been dealt with. The next two hours were mine to do nothing but relax; maybe snooze a little. I loosened my shoes, pushed hair from my face and unfolded the table between my seat and the two opposite.

A woman made her way down the aisle. She held an animal travel cage in both hands, cradling it to her chest in a protective embrace. An overnight bag swung from one shoulder, brushing against seats as she passed by. She scrutinised the overhead numbers, edging along, then came to a stop opposite me. A further check confirmed she'd found the right place. I watched her perch on the edge of her seat and reach across to place the dog, ensconced in its temporary home, onto the seat beside her. A marking in the shape of a W furrowed its brow, implying concern. The signora draped a white cloth over the cage and its folds whispered to the seat, loosening the fragrance of soap powder.

And then, as though it had been snuggling inside me all along, a memory wriggled free.

I remembered Mrs Cinanni, our Italian neighbour of fifty years ago, and my mother's admiration of her laundry skills.

Her sheets and pillowcases are so white, Mum would say, as though reading lines from one of the Omo advertisements I watched on our brand new, first-in-the-street, black and white television set. *How does she do it?*

Growing up in outer suburban Perth during the 1950s and 1960s meant I'd experienced first-hand the post-war immigration wave that swept thousands of people from their homes in Southern Europe to a new life in Australia. Four of them washed up next door. The children went to our school and, like us, pushed homework to one side to play softball in the Fergusons' vacant paddock. John – once Giovanni, I imagine – was a first-rate pitcher. Little sister Jessie was relegated to chase-and-return in the outfield. Together we resisted calls to homework, piano practice and feeding the chooks until dusk forced us inside.

And with dusk came the dinnertime smells of Casa Cinanni. I'd crinkle my nose as the unfamiliar scent of garlic and roasted capsicum, of olive oil and the sharp tang of parmesan cheese, drifted across a paddock in suburban Perth.

It was lamb chops and three veg at our place.

The fog in my brain began to lift. I let go of the memory and turned my attention to the woman opposite, watching as she opened the cage door and reached inside, patting and reassuring with soothing murmurs. She looked up at me and smiled in a way that invited more than just a smile in return. Anything less than a few words would have seemed churlish. The cage's small occupant presented an obvious conversation starter.

'Is your dog not well?' I ventured, embarrassed by my lack of Italian. So many English speakers have the expectation that all the world speaks English. And if they don't, then they should.

'My dog is well, thank you, but he does not like travelling.' The signora replied without hesitation, in accented but excellent English. She tilted her head over the cage, adjusting the cloth. 'I cover him so he cannot see around.'

A win for the dog. The twenty-hour flight had left me in less than showroom nick. Pockets of fatigue hung like hammocks beneath tired, watery eyes. A stain blotted my t-shirt, the result of an in-flight mishap involving yoghurt. No make-up. Finger-ploughed hair. The dog, covered and shielded, had got the better bargain. His less fortunate mistress viewed me from just a metre away, in the unforgiving clarity of morning sunlight.

The woman appeared unconcerned by my appearance and continued her story. 'If I am only going to be away overnight, I leave him at home. There he is happy. But I am visiting my sister and her family in Brescia for two days. He must be with me.'

Conversation paused for a moment as we showed the conductor our tickets. Then my companion chuckled and placed a proprietary hand on the travel cage.

'And the children love playing with him,' she said. 'They dress him in their old baby clothes and take him for walks in a pram.'

I turned that one over, remembering the furrowed W I'd seen on the dog's forehead. Perhaps he was less keen on the Brescia visit than his mistress. She chatted in her genial manner, and so at ease did I become that I told her about my own dog, Jake. A year after his death I still missed him.

'I've had a good number of pets in my time and loved them all,' I said to my friend of fifteen minutes. 'But that one: he was the pet of my life, you know?'

Again tears beaded my lashes. Again I blamed exhaustion.

With a cluck-cluck of her tongue, the woman leaned across the table, concern lining her face. She rested her hand on my arm and offered sympathetic, everything-will-be-alright pats.

'He was old, your dog? His death was expected, yes? Will you get another?'

And will you let children dress your dog in baby clothes and parade him about in a pram?

Our conversation shifted the day's equilibrium. If only in a small way, I edged from holiday-maker to belonging local. And, I thought, as I sniffed and our conversation moved on, hadn't that been my hope when I planned this trip? To slip beneath the tourist membrane and glimpse the lives of ordinary people, perhaps be a tiny part of those lives? Now I felt that might be possible.

We talked until the train pulled into Brescia. I gathered up the signora's overnight bag and carried it down the steps to the platform while she folded the cloth and tucked it under one arm, then devoted herself to her pet's safe disembarkation. We exchanged best wishes and said goodbye on the platform. She put the travel cage down long enough to shake my hand and speak a few of the Italian words she guessed I would understand: '*Allora. Grazie, grazie, signora.*'

The dog cast baleful eyes towards his mistress, then tucked his nose between his paws.

Back on the train, I settled lower into my seat and turned again to the window, watching as the outskirts of Brescia gave way to countryside. Corn undulated on hillsides, as though swept over by a hand, and clusters of farmhouses buttoned the fields. In the distance a monastery clung to a hilltop. Cypress trees dotted the slopes around it, with buildings nestled beneath their branches. No roads were visible and the buildings appeared as spots of human activity flicked over a green backdrop. It was all so different from a Western Australian end-of-summer landscape. No sunburnt country, this.

The train slowed, approaching Verona. Mind and body had been reunited and were now firmly in Italy. I turned from the world beyond the window and opened the book I'd brought to read, thinking a cappuccino as I flipped through its pages might be the go. My hands pressed on the armrests, all set to lever myself upright and head to the buffet.

As though someone had pushed the pause button, conversation around me halted. All eyes were trained on a young woman navigating the aisle's sway. She walked with a combination of easy glide and irrepressible bounce, carrying nothing more than her mobile phone and the demeanour of youthful optimism. Her clothing, too, was minimal: sandals, pink shorts and a top of insufficient fabric. In her wake, about-turned faces with mouths ajar suggested their owners' loss of coherent speech. Comment should be made, their looks implied, *needed* to be made, but was not immediately possible.

Indifferent to the hurricane of disapproval she'd triggered, the young woman dropped into the seat opposite me, vacant since Brescia. Twenty heads swivelled forwards as she disappeared from view. She looked across to me, flashed a smile that would open any door she ever chose to walk through, and announced, 'I'm Dixie. Hi.'

Dixie from Des Moines, Iowa, was young, Hollywood pretty and existed within an aura of total self-confidence. A curtain of hair fell to her shoulders and she scooped it backwards in a practised motion, trailing blonde tresses that returned instantly to their starting position. I'd come face to face with a junior Miss America.

I closed my book, leaving one finger inside as a marker, and returned her greeting.

'Are you going to Venice?' Dixie slithered across to the window seat, hair swinging.

'I am, yes. I've rented this *really* great apartment.' I felt the need to make an impression. 'Last year I was there for a week, with a friend, and I just loved it. So I'm going back.' I paused a moment, then added, 'For a whole month this time.' The last was just showing off, to be honest.

'Awesome. So cool. I've only got three days there, with my girlfriends.'

What was it about Italian train journeys that sanctioned communication between strangers? I'd never struck up a conversation with another passenger on the Perth to Fremantle line. I slid the book into my bag.

'We were in Verona together until last Thursday,' Dixie continued. 'They went on to Venice but I stayed behind.' A quirk at the corners of her mouth suggested there could be more to that particular story. She tapped the phone against her leg and the quirk blossomed into a private smile.

I didn't want to sound like Mother, calling for explanations, so my response was safely benign. 'I'm sure you'll have a wonderful time in Venice. I don't know anyone who's been there and not loved it.'

At the back of my mind another thought took up tenancy. Older generations sometimes didn't hear that inner meter telling them they were talking too much. Or if they *did* hear it, they chose to ignore it. On and on they'd talk, longer than even God herself could have patience with. I wasn't going down the path of offering advice on what to see and places to visit. Dixie was eighteen years old, or thereabouts, and her interest would be parties, not painters. As mine had been, at that age. In any event, a full account followed, without request.

'We just finished an intensive language course.' Dixie looked down at her phone, scowling at the blank screen. 'I start college this fall, and I wanted to do something different first, you know? Mom and Dad said whatever I did, it had to be, like, educational, and they could only afford a few weeks.' She draped her hair backwards, leaning over the phone to tap out a brief message. 'Anyway, I met this awesome guy, Gino ...'

Ah. I'd rather guessed there would be a fella involved somewhere. The smile had said as much. And what better place to discover a lover than in the city of Romeo and Juliet? In Verona, in summer and in love – I could almost feel envious.

'So I stayed on after the course, with him. So-o-o-o cool. I don't want to get old, like, into my thirties, and not have lived every experience that's been there for me. He's promised to come visit me for Thanksgiving.'

I wondered if Gino's Thanksgiving had already been and gone. Across the fold-up table I looked at Miss Pretty. What to say to a teenager from Des Moines, Iowa, who believes thirty is, like, old? I struggled to come up with an insightful comment or two. It's not as though I had much to do with eighteen-year-olds, and it'd been a long time since I was one. My mind remained as empty as the Australian outback.

Outback. The word rolled around in my brain, then took hold. A long ago something was again so close I could feel it as I had lived it, forty years before. Forgetting my resolve not to talk too much, words tumbled out, as heartfelt as they were unexpected. I hardly recognised them as my own.

'I'm with you. Totally. I felt the same way at your age. It's hard to imagine now – it seems like another lifetime.'

I shifted to a more comfortable position, then looked back at Dixie. Her eyes studied my face, flicked to full alert. 'I went to live in an outback town, thousands of kilometres from home. On a whim, just to do something different. In the end I stayed for two years, with my boyfriend. The two best years of my life, they were.'

Tick tick tick went the talking meter.

There was no stopping me. The intensity with which I remembered those distant events took me by surprise. 'We camped by creek beds. Swam in waterholes. I drove all across the outback with him. We had the best ever fun.' A smile, as I relived the memory. 'I loved that little town. Loved its big personality. Any adventure seemed possible, back then.'

The needle on the talking meter soared into the red.

Dixie listened, resting her cheek on her fingertips. The phone lay abandoned on the seat beside her. I watched a thought travel across her face, lifting the corners of her mouth.

'I could come back here and live with Gino, after college.' The thought settled, finding a snug home. 'You see, I had to take hold of the opportunity.'

Gino carried the great weight of Dixie's expectations, just as my long-ago boyfriend had been the centre of my universe. I guessed Gino was the reason for her anxious looks at the phone, but again I wasn't about to play Mother. And I didn't feel like Mother. Not at all. I liked the memories Dixie had kindled, the notion of possibilities, of adventure.

'Go do it now, while you can,' I said. 'Life's short and you can't squeeze the toothpaste back into the tube. The thing about ageing is that you gather speed as you go along. For me, it's all becoming one long, blurry streak.'

I doubted Mom and Dad back home in Des Moines would view things the same way. Gino would not be the educational experience they'd had in mind. But Dixie beamed an approving smile, curled her feet beneath her and turned to the view beyond the train window. We were approaching the industrial city of Mestre, the last mainland stop before crossing the lagoon to Venice.

'I so can't believe we're only ten minutes from Venice,' Dixie said, as we watched the progression of factories, warehouses and power grids slip past.

Heavy-duty enterprise rimmed Venice, stretching from Mestre to the port complex at Marghera. Like an ugly necklace, it encircled Venice, the jewel at its centre. Gone were the empty swamplands across which Venice's first settlers had fled to escape invading barbarians. Porto Marghera brought industry and jobs to Venice, but many Venetians held it responsible for the lagoon's pollution and for the damage to its fragile ecosystem. Looking at the smoke-belching furnaces, I found it hard to disagree.

I slid my thoughts to one side and watched with Dixie as the industrial world gave way to the waters of the Venetian lagoon.

'Where are you and your friends staying in Venice?' I asked Dixie as the train clattered onto the causeway. Behind her head, soaring gulls rowed the air with wings starkly white against the sky.

'Kelly found a hotel near the Rialto. We're right in the middle of everything. So cool.' Dixie turned to watch a gull drop to the water, then arc upwards and perch on a marker post.

Hmm. I'd chosen my Dorsoduro apartment to avoid places like the Rialto. Four centuries before Shylock, the Rialto was already the commercial heart of Venice, and four centuries after Shylock it remained one of the busiest places in the city.

Battalions of tourists surged across the famous landmark every day, buying trinkets from the Made-in-China markets and infiltrating the surrounding *calli*. The Rialto lay at the opposite end of the spectrum from the tourist no-man's-land I'd set out to find. But no need to mention that to Dixie.

Neither of us spoke for a few minutes, each absorbed in our own thoughts. Across the lagoon, the islands of San Michele and Murano appeared, one neatly encircled by its red brick wall, the other a clutter of pink and terracotta reaching down to the water's edge. Ahead lay a sliver of muted colour, wrapped in the blue of lagoon and sky.

Venice waited.

❋

We helped each other juggle our suitcases from the baggage compartment and onto the platform of Ferrovia Santa Lucia. Dixie had become rather subdued, in the manner of many people arriving at a new destination. I knew the feeling all too well. There's something unnerving about leaving the familiarity of a train or an aircraft in which you've been cocooned for a period of time and then, to all intents and purposes, being coughed up, spat out and abandoned to a new environment. Dixie's confidence was melting faster than a double-scoop gelato on a hot Venetian afternoon.

But it was more than just arrival anxiety and a cumbersome pink suitcase – the colour matched her shorts – that weighed on Dixie. Her phone remained silent. No amount of lifting and looking prompted a call or text.

I put a cheery ring in my voice. 'I'm going to buy a vaporetto ticket as soon as we leave the station. For a week.

But they sell them for a couple of days, too. It's the best way to get around Venice. There's a stop right near the Rialto.'

Dixie's frown moved from her phone to me. I nodded down to the suitcases. 'And for right now, it means we don't have to pull these along.'

A shrug. 'Whatever.'

Nothing more. Oh, dear.

We joined a river of humanity to trudge along the platform and into the station's main building. Then a frog croaked in Dixie's pocket. She came to an abrupt halt and, suitcase forgotten, grabbed with both hands for her phone. The suitcase rocked, then fell to the floor.

'*Pronto?*' Dixie said to the frog. Again the private smile as she dipped her head and spoke in exuberant spurts of Italian and English.

Was it Gino? Is a bean green? I smothered a snuffle of laughter and pointed to the entrance, indicating I'd wait for her there. Leaning against its glass wall, my eyes wandered over the part-forgotten, part-remembered scene. Nothing – not all the photos or films or paintings, not all the words of Henry James – conveyed the impact, the undiluted wow factor, of that first sight.

Venice stretched before me, an explosion of sunshine and water.

Dotting the Grand Canal was an armada of varied shapes and sizes. Water taxis carried pointing, head-swinging sightseers; sturdy, no-nonsense barges – this one transporting timber, that one delivering tomatoes – vied for space; families sat aboard launches or dinghies, enjoying their Sunday afternoon while the household dog kept watch at the prow. And through it all ploughed the determined vaporetti. Flat-roofed and sitting low on the water, they were filled to overflowing, with passengers oozing onto the deck space. I thought of an overstuffed sandwich and smiled. For that moment at least, exhaustion vanished and I felt carefree, lucky, grateful to life.

Dixie bounced up alongside me, beaming. She dredged back a handful of hair and looked out into the sunshine.

'Oh man,' she breathed. 'Awesome.'

I took this as reference to the sight of Venice, rather than the conversation with Gino.

We bought our vaporetto tickets – Dixie's for three days, mine for a week – and then walked to Dixie's platform. Our destinations lay in opposite directions along the Grand Canal; so too did our platforms. I plodded through the crowds, sweaty and silent. There didn't seem to be enough air in my lungs to manage the suitcase and a conversation at the same time. We came to a stop at the platform barricade. It was time to say goodbye.

'Enjoy Venice with your mates,' I said. 'It's been great meeting you.'

I meant it. Previous conversations with strangers had often proved hard work, something I wished I hadn't committed myself to. But not with Dixie. I was taken aback by the sense of exhilaration I'd felt as we chatted.

But now what I really wanted to say was *Gino? What's happening with Gino?* As if she had read my thoughts, Dixie smiled. 'Gino's coming to Venice tomorrow. We'll have the whole day together. At the beach, he said.' Doubt flickered across her face. She looked at the green water slapping against the canal's banks.

I looked, too. No place for a dip, that. But two centuries ago, Lord Byron hadn't minded. He once swam the length of the Grand Canal on a wager, and crowds turned out to cheer him on. More often, though, he freestyled along the canal to get from one romantic tryst to the next. Others relied on gondolas.

'The beach is out on the Lido,' I said. 'It's great. You'll love it.' That may have been overreaching: I'd never been there. But how many beaches were there in Des Moines, Iowa, to rate it against?

'And look after yourself,' I added, my first concession to Mother role-play.

'It was really cool talking with you,' Dixie said. She reached up, arms encircling my neck as her hair swatted my face in an almond-scented cloud. 'And thank you so-o-o-o much. For everything.' A second flamboyant hug followed. The Dixie of dash and flash again.

I started the hike to my own platform. No trees. No shade. The soles of my sandals gritted along the pavement and I felt heat rise through them. Could I have a man in a blue shirt, please? One to snatch the suitcase from my sweaty hand? But that sort of luck doesn't happen twice in one day.

My eyes watered and my mouth dried. My throat clicked when I swallowed. A spritz would taste so-o-o-o good and it waited just one vaporetto stop and a short walk away, beyond Piazzale Roma. I trundled on, dragging the stuffed-with-rocks suitcase. On impulse I turned and glanced back to Dixie's platform.

A young man stood by her side, lifting the pink suitcase onto the vaporetto's deck. Dixie beamed at him with the secret assurance, the private conviction, that nothing bad could ever happen to her, that the world would continue to offer one amazement after another. Such is the potent magic of young confidence. Dixie would always have someone to do her heavy lifting. Miss America deserved no less.

CHAPTER 5

MY NEW BEST FRIENDS

Not along the Grand Canal do you find the essential Venice. The beauty that is hidden away, not the beauty that is revealed, is the city's essence.

Max Beerbohm (Sir Henry Maximilian Beerbohm), English essayist, in *A Stranger in Venice*

I scraped off the *ferrovia* crowds like something stuck to my shoe.

Half an hour after farewelling Dixie, I sat at a cafe watching the comings and goings of my new neighbourhood. Beside me boats nodded at their moorings, so close I could reach down and touch them. In the centre of the canal a barge thrummed its way towards a bridge, workers squatting to guide the clinking load of soft drink bottles beneath the bridge's arc. Water splashed and wet stone gleamed. On the opposite *fondamenta* (the Venetian term for a canal-side walkway), a shop owner unfastened shutters and ratcheted them up, ready for post-siesta shoppers. Everything was as I'd imagined; better, even. Sighing my contentment, I leaned back in the chair, enjoying the sense of achievement that comes when an undertaking delivers the hoped-for result.

'*Prego.*' The waiter arrived to plunk a spritz at my elbow before he hurried back to the cafe, dodging pedestrians on the *fondamenta*. Afternoon trade was brisk. I pulled my suitcase towards me, away from traffic, then reached for the spritz. I've earned this, I thought, taking the first cold-sweet sip.

A cafe downstairs from my apartment was icing on the perfect cake. It offered front-stall seating for canal and people watching, and its fortunate position, I would soon happily learn, dished up sunshine for an early morning breakfast and shade from the strong afternoon sun. There and then I christened it Cafe Downstairs and never did learn its real name.

Ice cubes clinked in my empty glass. I pushed it onto the table, then looked up to see a man in shorts and an olive-green shirt scanning the crowd. His gaze stopped at the suitcase by my feet and he walked towards me.

'Hello. You are Margaret? I am a little late, I think.'

Sebastiano stood at my side, extending his hand in greeting. I looked into eyes that had smiled often enough to crinkle soft lines at their edges. A tanned face showed above a short-trimmed beard flecked with grey. *Very designer*, I thought, *very Italian*. And undeniably handsome.

'Have you finished your drink? I can take you to the apartment.' Sebastiano wheeled my suitcase to the apartment's street door and started up the stairs, continuing his easy conversation despite the weight of the suitcase.

'Today has been hot, hotter than usual. Tomorrow we expect cooler weather.'

'Right,' I said, just to make a sound. I needed all my breath for the stairs.

'Did you have any trouble finding the apartment?' Sebastiano maintained a steady verbal pace while I panted along behind. We reached the landing outside the apartment door and he paused to take keys from his pocket. I caught my breath while he searched for the right one.

'Finding the apartment wasn't a problem. Not at all. It's very easy to get here from Piazzale Roma.' I remembered my initial misgivings with a wry smile: the close-but-not-too-close proximity of Piazzale Roma had already proved its worth. Encouraged by Sebastiano's friendly manner I added, 'But I have been lost in Venice. Last year, going to La Fenice.'

The memory of that pre-opera adventure still lingered, a salutary reminder of the city's challenging geography. One missed *calle*, a turn to the left instead of the right, I knew the consequences. As an afterthought I asked, 'Do *you* ever get lost in Venice?'

Sebastiano smiled with 100-watt, Made-in-Italy brio. 'In Santa Croce and Dorsoduro, no. I have lived in these *sestieri* all my life. But walking around Castello is more difficult. Sometimes I take a wrong turn in all those small streets.'

Reassurance surged. A native Venetian, outwitted by his city's *calli*? My own navigational blunders could be dismissed as trivial, by comparison.

'But I soon know I am heading in the wrong direction. I turn around and walk back to where I started from,' Sebastiano continued. 'So I don't get lost.'

Curious. That hadn't worked for Jenny and me.

Key located, Sebastiano unlocked the door and stood aside for me to enter. I looked around, my gaze halting at the windows overlooking the canals. Gauze curtains stretched across them, puffed into scallops by the breeze. Through the curtains I saw pink geraniums in full summer bloom, and beyond them a tangle of rooftops.

'It's as open and sunny as my home in Perth,' I said, turning to Sebastiano.

He pulled my suitcase inside and balanced it against the sofa. He hadn't even raised a sweat.

'And it *feels* like home.' I delivered the final tick of approval.

'It was our family home,' Sebastiano told me. 'My wife Orla and I lived here after we married. We brought our first child, Conall, to this home following his birth.'

I knew then that I'd made the right choice. Family hustle and bustle had reverberated within these walls. Countless meals had been prepared and eaten; friends had been welcomed, perhaps as the bearers of good news, perhaps seeking consolation. Children had scampered across the floor, laughed as they were hugged or cried and been comforted. It was a world away from a tourist hotel. It was a world I wanted to be part of for the next month.

'Now we have two more children. Our daughter, Clodagh, is five, and she has a younger brother, Oisin, just three. We have moved to a bigger home in Santa Croce.'

No wonder. Those two flights of stairs. But for me the apartment was perfect: my Goldilocks home, not too big and not too small.

Sebastiano explained the details of the apartment and its maintenance. Rubbish collection at 8 am daily. No need to close windows unless rain seemed likely. (*Really? Venice was that safe?*) Water the geraniums daily, please. Housekeeping dealt with, our conversation turned to the visitor attractions of Dorsoduro and Santa Croce.

'I want to see the Scuola Grande di San Rocco,' I said. 'Tintoretto is my favourite Venetian painter. I planned to go to the Scuola last year, but time ran away from me. A week in Venice only stretches so far.'

Sebastiano nodded and took a folder from its resting place behind the toaster. He thumbed through papers with lists of emergency phone numbers and vaporetto routes until he found a map of Venice. He unfolded it across the kitchen bench and twisted it towards me. The scrunched edges and biro circles told me I wasn't the first tenant to use Sebastiano as a sounding board for sightseeing plans.

'The Scuola is not to be missed. We Venetians think of it as our Sistine Chapel.' Sebastiano reached across the kitchen bench to tap a well-marked spot on the map. 'Here it is.'

I traced a path from the apartment to the Scuola. Not far at all. Again I had the sense of finding the Venice I'd hoped for, and my thoughts went back to last year's visit. It wasn't only time constraints that had prevented a visit to the Scuola; the real decider had been its location in the maze of unfamiliar *calli* in a remote part of Venice. Now that remote part of Venice was my backyard.

'And the Frari, too. That's something else I missed last year.' I edged my finger to one side of the Scuola, to the Chiesa di Santa Maria Gloriosa dei Frari.

Sebastiano looked up. 'Orla and I were married in the Frari.'

His words rearranged my perspective. The church and its famous masterpieces took on a personal dimension, and a place that had existed in my mind as a sightseeing destination I now saw as part of a local community. This was how Venetians lived with the treasures of their city, I realised: proud of them, but not overawed. The richness of history was not isolated from daily life, it was incorporated into it.

I refolded the map. Sebastiano pulled out another sheet of paper.

'Here is my mobile number. I am only a phone call away if you need me.' He picked up his sunglasses and wished me a happy stay. I walked with him to the door and said goodbye, then watched as he bounded down the stairs two at a time, his hand barely touching the rail.

For the first time since leaving Perth I was by myself. Elation bubbled as I turned back to my sunlit home and walked to the dining table, pulling back a chair to sit for a while, arms folded and resting on the glass surface. I looked beyond the geraniums to canals and bridges and the rooftops of a medieval city. Just as I'd imagined I would.

It had been the dream start to my holiday, and a surprising one. Most often I deflected the attentions of co-travellers, disappearing behind a book the instant they leaned forwards and smiled in the happy anticipation of a chat. Long-haul flights in particular threatened endless, rolling breakers of aimless chitchat or, worse still, a leap into frankness with the disclosure of unasked-for and intimate confidences. All of which I must listen to. For a very long time.

Today changed the rules. I'd stepped outside my boundaries – to offer a greeting, to pursue a conversation – and I'd found it invigorating. Some of Dixie's exuberance had rubbed off and I felt a bit like a teenager myself; still young, just peering out from behind an older face mask.

Dixie-in-the-pink-shorts. I thought back to our conversation. *Go do it now*, I'd said, telling her how I'd gone to an outback town on a whim. It wasn't quite the truth.

What happened was this.

At the end of our nurse training, my two best pals struck out for London. I could have joined them. To think of it:

Ann, Debbie and me in swinging, 1960s London. Smoky bars and pulsing discos. Carnaby Street. Miniskirts and maximum mischief. The problem was I *did* think about it, and making my way in that larger-than-life metropolis quite overwhelmed me.

At heart I'm a small-town, keep-it-simple sort of person, not disposed to aim at high marks on distant walls. I frighten easily. Going to Darwin – a very small town, back then – had been less about making a decision than avoiding one. I'd loved my student nurse days; the work itself, but even more the sharing of life and living arrangements with other young nurses. I didn't want it to end, plain and simple. Darwin offered the same deal, with better weather and increased pay. What wasn't to like?

Nothing, as it turned out – in that I'd been truthful with Dixie. One adventure following another and then continued, post-Darwin, when I lived with my boyfriend on a tropical island. All in all, it was another of those chance events where somehow, with little effort on my part, all the ducks lined up.

Great memories.

By now evening sunlight angled through the apartment's side window, striking the chandelier above the table. Exhilaration lost its edge as fatigue stepped in, and I yawned into my folded arms. My eyes prickled with tiredness. I slipped lower in the chair, my head bobbing forwards on the cusp of sleep. A quick meal at Downstairs with an early night to follow seemed the best plan. Then tomorrow, Venice.

✹

I hadn't noticed before, as I'd puffed and panted along behind Sebastiano, that the stone steps leading from the apartment to the first floor were worn in the centre. How many footsteps over how many centuries had created those hollows? And polished the steps to their glassy smoothness? Clearly, these were not stairs to be messed with.

The cafe was as busy as it had been that afternoon, with patrons squashed around every table. I waited a few minutes for a vacant space, then took a seat by the water's edge. At the table next to mine diners shared large pizzas; cheesy, cheerful discs sliced into wedges. The smell of freshly baked dough reminded me I hadn't eaten since breakfast. And an in-flight breakfast at that – half a dozen plastic containers jammed onto their plastic tray, each one holding a bite-sized portion of something identified only by guesswork. Was it yoghurt? Or scrambled egg?

Pizza another time, I decided, and ordered the mushroom risotto. Five minutes later the waitress skidded it onto the table.

'*Buon appetito.*'

She must have been kidding. Perhaps the rice had once stood next to the mushrooms on a kitchen bench, but no more than that. Water-plump rice stuck to my tongue and clotted against my teeth. Sightseeing for the tastebuds this was not. Downstairs lodged firmly in the genre of casual cafe, and quick sustenance for undiscerning palates guided its mission statement. Next time I'd stick with pizza.

The cappuccino that followed was good, though, and served with just the right amount of chocolate. I ordered a second, lingering to watch shadows lengthen across the rooftops of Dorsoduro. Red bougainvillea trailed across the rafters of one second-storey balcony where a family sat outdoors with their dog, enjoying the evening cool. *This is bliss*, I thought – the perfect end to my first day in Venice. Coffee finished, another yawn, then I levered myself upright. Sleep beckoned. I turned from the rooftop family and walked to my apartment.

A man and woman stood at the building's intercom panel. Their fingers traced down the list of names and puzzled looks passed between them. I stole a sideways glance as I dipped into my purse for the key: a young couple on vacation, I guessed. They wore the universal statement of a casual summer day – t-shirts and shorts, a little crumpled. But for the concern etched on their faces, they were no different from other young people out walking the *fondamente* that evening.

'*Bonsoir, madame,*' the man greeted me as I arrived beside them. '*On cherche les chambres d'hôtes. Ces sont ici?*'

Huh? Did I look French? Was I yawning with a French accent? It had been thirty-five years since I'd spoken French with any degree of Serious Application, so I amazed myself by responding, *en français*, that the bed and breakfast accommodation they wanted was closed for the night. What awakened my long-dormant language skills I had no idea. Then I amazed myself all over again by continuing the conversation. The couple appeared to understand me – yet more amazement. They nodded their heads as I spoke, like people standing behind the prime minister on a television news report.

Linguistic lead weights fell from my tongue. Words magically connected. I suggested they try *l'autre côté du canal*, explaining there were numerous hotels and youth hostels *au quartier-là*. Then, to round things out, I added that if they couldn't find any accommodation they could '*restez avec moi, dans mon appartement ici.*'

Fatigue had taken over again. I'd just invited two strangers to stay with me. Strangers who spoke another language. To stay in an apartment that wasn't even mine. In a city where I knew no one. All smiles and thanks, the couple set off *à l'autre côté du canal* in search of a two-star hotel. I climbed the two flights of stairs to my apartment.

An hour passed. They'd found somewhere, I decided, and would not be returning to the dubious comforts of my sofa bed. A glance in the mirror convinced me it was all for the best. Crushed-strawberry eyes glared out from beneath hair resembling the shredded straw once used in packaging. No one should have to look at that. I pulled on pyjamas, turned down the bed quilt and fell headlong into sleep.

My dreams swirled with images. Crowded train stations; a blue shirt; swinging blonde hair. Two suitcases – one pink, both heavy. An old dog. A worried dog. I awoke disorientated when the intercom rang. My new friends were back. No accommodation was to be had in Dorsoduro or Santa Croce and, *s'il vous plaît*, might they accept my kind invitation of earlier that evening?

Still in a sleepy fog, I gathered up keys and started down the stairs. At the front door we said 'ello and introduced ourselves. I shook hands like I did this every day – greeting strangers in my Target pyjamas and with my hair a crinkled fan of straw. But Monika and Raoul didn't turn on their heels and run. That's how I knew accommodation in Venice that night really was at a premium.

With a spare key the pair set off again, this time to retrieve luggage from their car parked in the Tronchetto multistorey. Tiredness numbed my brain. I paused on my return to sleep just long enough to make up the sofa bed and leave what I hoped was a welcoming note.

Faites des beaux rêves. Dormez bien.

❉

Raoul, Monika and I sat at Downstairs, renamed En Bas for the next few days. Water splashed the *fondamente*'s sides as delivery barges commenced the business of making Venice a working city. Coils of flying rope settled around poles before the boats anchored to pass cargo over railings and onto the pavement. Grey and white squadrons of seagulls, already obscenely fat, screeched their wish to share our breakfast.

'We didn't book into the bed and breakfast because we didn't think finding accommodation would be a problem.' Monika broke open a bread roll, demurred over the choice of jams before deciding on strawberry, then wielded her knife to spread jam in one deft movement. I watched those fingers, imagining her at work for her employer, the high-end fashion house Hermès.

'Monika is a true artisan.' Raoul spoke with pride as he, too, watched Monika. 'She designs and makes handbags.'

'*Et vous savez …*' The sound of grating gears overpowered Monika's voice and we turned to the canal. With hesitant spurts and in a vapour of diesel fumes, a boat advanced from beneath the bridge, its driver bent forwards as though coaxing it to the canal's end. Monika flashed out her phone to record a holiday snap. I wondered what could be so special about a worn-out boat chugging along a canal.

'It has her name,' Raoul said, noticing before I did the lettering along the boat's side.

The boat and its namesake had nothing in common. The woman who sat beside me radiated youth and vitality: sun-browned skin covered a slim frame, and her hair was pulled back into a simple ponytail. I guessed her age to be late twenties; a mother–daughter split, near enough, with my sixty-four years.

As a couple, she and Raoul were magazine perfect. He was about her age, with good looks to match her prettiness. His hair, dark to her blonde, curled above a smooth brow. He had the calm, dark eyes of a man possessing wit and wisdom, and a smile that was broad and frequent. It was called into service now, as he attempted to explain to me, in a melange of French and English, the nature of his work in the finance industry. Most of it was beyond my grasp, in both the linguistic and the economic sense.

But two things I did understand. Hermès was selling lots of Monika-crafted handbags. And whatever locked Raoul into his world of graphs and computer screens for ten hours each day delivered financial rewards.

Monika picked up her phone again. Not to be overshadowed by her boyfriend, she tried a little English.

'Our home in Lyon. Two years, here we live.'

She pointed the phone towards me and scrolled through photos of a home Kevin McCloud would do well to consider, should he ever undertake a French edition of *Grand Designs*. I watched the screens flick by. Contemporary artwork and furniture highlighted white spaces in a triumph of minimalism. My face warmed with embarrassment. To think I'd taken it upon myself to tell them where they might find a two-star hotel.

Perhaps Raoul read my thoughts. '*Au cours de nos voyages, nous préférons le logement très simple. Notre argent est pour les choses importantes.*' (When we travel, we prefer simple accommodation. Our money is for important things.) Not surprisingly, these two French citizens nominated food and wine as *les choses importantes.*

We finished breakfast and Raoul went indoors to pay the bill. I watched a gull swoop and dip into the canal, sending ripples circling outwards. Light glanced off the water and onto the underside of the bridge, forming a wavy mosaic. I could forgive any number of meagre risottos, just to sit here in the sunshine. But Monika was speaking again, in French, and I needed to concentrate.

'We're planning to spend today on the lagoon.' She gathered up her phone and sunglasses in a manner as decisive as the first note of a concert. I guessed Monika was the duo's decision-maker. '*Surtout* Torcello,' she continued, 'because it is where Venice began.'

'*Oui, oui. Une bonne idée.*' I spooned the last of the froth from my cappuccino. Monika smiled at my endorsement of her sightseeing plans.

Surtout Torcello. I said the words beneath my breath, as much to myself as to Monika. I, too, wanted to connect with the very beginnings of Venice, to sit in its seventh-century cathedral where congregations had said the mass for 1400 years. '*Mais pas aujoud'hui, parce que ...*'

My French language skills were tested here. I spoke slowly, thinking through the words. Monika sat forwards, hands pressed together, making nods of encouragement as though willing the words from me. She reminded me of Mum, drilling me on my multiplication tables.

'... the only day mass is celebrated now is on the Feast of the Assumption. I want my visit to coincide with that,' I managed.

Untidy but comprehensible. Monika beamed her congratulations.

I had another reason for delaying my visit to Torcello. It might be a good idea, I reckoned, to give Raoul and Monika a bit of time to themselves. They hadn't sat in that stylish home in Lyon, travel brochures spread about, and said to each other, 'Okay, then. Venice looks good. And what would be totally awesome is a sixty-something lady to follow us around.'

No. Besides, I had stuff to do. There was no food in the apartment. I needed to find a supermarket and get things in order. For today at least, Plan Venice went on hold.

❀

'*Au revoir. À ce soir.*'

The door latch clicked behind Raoul and Monika. I walked to the kitchen and switched on the kettle, then searched through Sebastiano's papers for a biro. Organisation should start with a shopping list, and writing a list called for a cup of tea. Same as at home. Monika and Raoul would be back from Torcello this evening and we'd have dinner at a local restaurant. Sipping tea, I sat at the kitchen bench and collected my thoughts.

Bread. Milk. Coffee.

I glanced up from my list. Beyond the window, seagulls dipped and wheeled against a backdrop of blue sky and terracotta roofs. Downstairs staff unfurled umbrellas, raising them over tables as the day strengthened its hold. Oh, that view. In Venice it might not be exceptional, but it was mine and that made it special.

Eggs. Pasta. Salad.

My first day in Venice was far from what I'd expected. Never had I imagined sharing my new home and part of my holiday with two strangers I'd met by chance on the doorstep. But the funny thing was that Monika and Raoul didn't feel like strangers, not in the least. Sharing space and time with them seemed the most natural thing in the world. It wasn't that they felt like old, familiar friends. It wasn't that we had endless common interests, or even a common language. It just seemed right, somehow.

I turned from the window and walked to the door, then started my cautious trek down the stairs.

Life could lead you along some unexpected paths if you let it.

❋

I took extra care dressing for dinner that night. I didn't want to look like Mum out with the kids for a family catch-up. Scarlet nails flashed at my fingertips. A determined effort with blow drier and tongs had won the battle against Venetian humidity and my hair sat just so, disciplined and faultless. My favourite summer outfit, a short, white dress worn with flat shoes, hit the mark: pizzazz with just a little flash. Not too bad, I reckoned, nodding with satisfaction at the image in the mirror.

'Very nice, very pretty,' Monika said, approving my choice in her wonderful, accented English. For herself, Monika had decided on the classic French style statement: a liquid black dress poured over her slim figure and unadorned but for the sandwich-sized handbag she carried. Hermès, of course.

Off we set, chatting in our patchwork language, across the bridge at the end of the *fondamenta*, then turning right to Osteria ae Cravate. The front-of-house waiter showed us to a window table.

A difference in culinary attitudes was evident even before the food was ordered. Monika and Raoul studied the wine list as though all of life's secrets were contained within its pages. (*Une chose importante*. Of course. I should have remembered.) I wasn't too fussed, so long as what did eventually make its way to our table was well chilled. In the course of last year's visit, I'd come to believe that every restaurant refrigerator in Venice was an underachiever. Either that or people actually liked tepid wine.

I readied myself for a too-warm offering. 'I'd like some ice to put in my wineglass.' An easy phrase, straight from French 101, delivered with an improved accent, skilfully incorporating the use of conditional tense. I expected praise from Monika and Raoul.

Mais non. My new pals were aghast. They exchanged startled looks. With the speed of an icy pole melting in the Australian summer sun, I realised where the problem lay.

'It's not uncommon, in Australia, to add ice to white wine,' I assured them. 'It's because our climate is so hot.'

Raoul eyed me from above the wine list. Monika shook out her napkin with a brisk, snapping sound.

'*Vraiment?* Australians do this?' Raoul pinched his nose between thumb and fingertips, as if studying one of his graphs. Perplexity crinkled that smooth forehead. Beside me, Monika tapped starched linen against pursed lips.

The waiter sailed up to our table, a smile of smug assurance harbouring beneath the confident prow of his large nose. With much show of white napkin and corkscrew, he presented the bottle of pinot grigio that Monika had chosen. Then he prepared for battle with the cork.

The devil made me do it, I swear.

'*En Australie, c'est le cas ...*' With a gentle tease, I went on to explain that screw tops, not corks, most often secured Australian grape inside glass. Monika's back stiffened. Raoul lifted just one eyebrow. A second round of Looks passed over the cutlery.

Nodding towards the struggling waiter, I delivered my final, compelling argument. '*Et c'est plus facile, n'est pas?*'

Easier or not, Monika and Raoul were having none of it. *Mon Dieu. Quelle horreur.* Wine must come in a corked bottle; thus it had ever been. Modern technology be damned, some things were not to be altered and must remain constant in a changing world.

Raoul resorted to English in his effort to convince me. 'But the flavour ... how-you-say-it ... the aroma ... all this depends on the cork.' He looked to Monika for confirmation.

'*Oui, oui. Bien sûr.*' She echoed his conviction with an emphatic head tilt. Civilisation as we knew it was threatened if wine were stored other than in a corked bottle.

Raoul nodded, satisfied. If Monika agreed, then it must be so. He moved his glass towards the waiter and prepared to sample the offering. Somewhat prematurely, I thought.

White-knuckled with determination, the waiter struggled on.

New challenges arrived along with the menu. The debate that had preceded the arrival of the lukewarm pinot grigio now turned to the meal selection. 'Meat or fish, Raoul?' 'Pasta or rice, Monika?' 'Two courses or three, do you think?'

My eyes flicked over the menu I shared with Monika, barely registering its contents. For me the choice was as black and white as the dresses we wore. '*Je prends le poisson avec une grande salade.'* Keep it simple, I thought, stick with something I know. Something I trust.

Raoul and Monika continued their deliberations. *'Un plat typique de Venise,'* they at long last decided. Their traditional Venetian dish was a variation of *sarde in saor* – sole, sardines and scampi marinated with onions, pine nuts and sultanas. It was love on a plate.

'Ça été formidable.' Raoul finished eating and beamed down at a lone sultana sitting in solidarity with two onion rings on the shiny, bare surface of his plate. He reached for his glass, then leaned back in the chair and sipped the last of his wine. *'Oui. Ah, oui.'*

Monika agreed. *'Parfait, parfait.'* She scrunched the napkin and patted it to her lips, a delicate little movement that belied her robust appetite. I glanced down at her plate. As empty as last year's bird's nest.

I'd stuck with the salad and grilled fish. Its arrival at the table was announced with a theatrical flourish that rather overstated things, I felt. There on the serving platter lay the boniest little fellow who'd ever swum the Adriatic. Lemon slices ran in oblique alignment along his back and jaws gripped a wad of parsley.

I won't say my meal wasn't tasty. But separating small mouthfuls from those lethal bones demanded the skill of a surgeon. While my friends enthused over their *plat typique* I picked away in silence, focused on the project of getting enough to eat. When I finished my meal a curved skeleton, with the lemon and parsley business at one end and a pile of bones at the other, spoke of my struggle.

Monika had ordered dessert and turned her attention to the ricotta mousse while I rested up and chatted with Raoul, *sans dessert* like me. He could likely answer my question.

'How long does it take to become fluent in another language?' I said. 'Can a person *ever* become fluent in a second language, to the point of understanding cultural references and the like?' I managed the question in French, stretching my ability to its furthest boundary.

Five years earlier Raoul had left Portugal for France, leaving behind parents, siblings and a large extended family. He mentioned them from time to time, but hadn't said what prompted the move from his country of birth. And I hadn't felt comfortable asking. That's the thing of it, I thought, this whole second language business. My tenuous grip on the nuances of French ran the risk of making any casual inquiry come out sounding like an inquisition.

Raoul smiled at my determination to master French. '*Oui, mais ...*' Again I saw those graphs as he rubbed his forehead and considered. 'You must be surrounded by the language you hope to learn. For Monika, it was one year only to learn French. She lived in France and heard the language all the time.'

'*Oui, c'est ça.*' Between mouthfuls of dessert, Monika looked up and nodded. I knew she'd arrived in France from Poland a year or two later than Raoul but, unlike him, she made no reference to her family or the life she'd left behind. Did Monika's family accompany her to France? I had no idea.

My own conversation was sprinkled with family references, usually a stalling tactic while I cobbled together the words needed to complete a sentence. '*Ma mère a dit souvent que ...*' (My mother often said) prefixed numerous observations and probably led my friends to believe Mum held a strong view on just about every subject. My sister, *très intelligente, ah oui,* was invoked for the same reason.

But not so with Monika. Over the last spoonful of ricotta mousse, she put the migration and family issue to bed. *'Maintenant nous sommes français.'*

My eyes flicked to my watch. Two hours had passed since we sat down, and Signor Nose had poured the last of the pinot grigio some time ago. With commendable tact he had also removed my ice bucket. Watching from beneath my lashes, I followed his sorties through the restaurant. He passed by our table and paused, raising a fist to his mouth and hurr-umming with a see-here sort of cough before swooping on Monika's dessert plate and whisking the serviette from her lap. It was time to go.

Outside in the *calle* we paused for a moment, listening to laughter coming from behind the darkened buildings.

'Ah,' I said. 'Campo Santa Margherita. I passed it today, on the way to the supermarket. *C'était bon.* We could go there now.'

The *campo* lay close by – Dorsoduro's night-life central – the most hip and well-patronised destination in Venice. And the hippest place in the *campo* was the bar which bore my name. Margaret du Champs, claimed one travel brochure, 'keeps the *campo* animated well into the wee hours'.

Crowds increased as we neared the *campo*. We picked our way through people sitting on bridge steps, careful not to upset a drink or step on fingers. Young people were everywhere in this university precinct, mixing with the neighbourhood's older residents. I ducked around a group of students, then looked back at them. They leaned inwards; their conversation intense, gesticulating hands making a point. At midnight, on a bridge across a backwater canal in Venice. I smiled, recalling Max Beerbohm's observation:

essential Venice is not about what is revealed and known to everyone. The soul of Venice is hidden.

Raoul, Monika and I sat outdoors and took up the thread of our restaurant conversation.

'*Oui.* One year I am to learn French.' Monika spoke English with the same grammatical licence I brought to French. I watched her sip beer then run her tongue over her lips before replacing the glass on the table.

Raoul unlatched his hands from behind his head to reach for the Disaronno. I'd persuaded him to try my favourite Italian liqueur. *Pas mal*, he'd said. Not bad. His approval ranked lower than the fulsome praise he'd given to *un plat typique de Venise.* He ordered a second, to reconsider his verdict.

Monika continued her English workout, moving on to their travel program. 'We drive Venice. We look three weeks Croatia. Then home to France.'

Maintenant nous sommes français.

Whatever had led this couple on their separate paths to France, it now held their hearts and their future. I thought how much easier it must be to understand, even adopt, aspects of a country's culture when that country lay on your doorstep. So different from my own country, tucked away on the far side of the globe.

Monika finished her beer and reached for Raoul's hand. Finding it alongside her own, she lifted it, holding it to her cheek. She turned to him and they shared a private smile. And I felt a private hope. I hoped Monika would never master English. To listen to those fractured sentences delivered with that accent was a treat the world should not be denied.

Cafes hummed. Sounds floated around the *campo* and into the darkness. Essential Venice, and we were part of it.

On that summer's night, we shared Campo Santa Margherita with Venice's citizens. Three holiday-makers from two generations. Three people who called or had called five different countries home. Who between them spoke eight languages, but barely a word of the language spoken by the crowds around them. I don't know how long we sat there, but it was time enough for me to think that the world might be a better place if this happened more often.

※

A perfect morning. Cotton ball clouds bobbed across a blue dome of sky as I led the way to Chiesa di San Nicolò dei Mendicoli.

Run-down *fondamente* surrounded us. Windows went unrelieved by the cake-decoration trim of gardens. In a vacant allotment, waist-high weeds grew around slumped fencing, the neighbourhood's only concession to horticulture. We walked on, undisturbed by guides and their camera-clicking clientele. No tourist deal, this.

'It's the side of Venice I prefer,' I said, turning to Raoul and Monika.

Monika wrinkled her nose, catching the smell of mildew. She looked at me, then at Raoul. *Wears uncool pyjamas. Drinks iced wine and eats bony fish. Now it turns out she likes shabby neighbourhoods. What else don't we know?*

It was our last day together and we'd decided to see something of the historic hinterland behind present-day Venice. My favourite church marked our starting point. Its early parishioners – sailors and fishermen, mostly – were among the city's poorest residents. Some claimed the word Mendicoli meant beggars, others said it referred merely to poor folk. But one thing was certain, as we trekked past buildings where paint peeled like sunburnt skin: this was not the Venice of Grand Canal palazzi.

We reached the church's entrance. Monika and Raoul looked inside, eyes widening with astonishment. Morning sun struck the gilding and highlighted ceiling and wall frescoes. Overhead, San Nicolò busied himself with rescuing sailors and cutting down trees of pagan worship. In a painting on the left wall, Judas planted The Kiss on Christ's cheek. Impoverished though they were, the parishioners, known as the Nicolotti, had decorated their church with a generosity that belied their humble means. In this poor neighbourhood, Venetian opulence sparkled again.

I walked along an aisle, then slid into a pew at the front of the church. A statue of San Nicolò holding three golden balls looked down at me. Legend held that the balls were given to three maidens from the parish, providing a dowry for either marriage or convent admission. Thus were they saved from a life of prostitution.

Raoul picked up an information sheet and read aloud. 'Founded in the seventh century ...' He turned to me, a question forming on his lips. 'So this is the oldest church in Venice?'

'Almost. That honour, according to legend at least, goes to San Giacomo di Rialto. But I don't know of any other church older than this one.'

Monika finished her circuit around the aisles and walked over to join us. '*C'est belle, belle.*' She lifted her hands to encompass the church. '*Penses, Raoul, une noce ici.*' Many young women have felt the same way, and the church was in frequent demand for weddings.

Perhaps the church attendant understood Monika. He turned from the prayer books he was stacking on a table and reached up to a panel of switches. A series of clicks illuminated the interior. We took a final walk around the church.

'*Arrivederci, grazie.*' The attendant nodded as we placed donations in a box near the prayer books. He flicked off the lights as we left.

Outside the church, a group of today's Nicolotti had gathered to chat. Three women arranged themselves on a tree-shaded bench and placed string bags, knobbly with the day's shopping, at their feet. A man pushed his wheelchair-bound wife closer to the trio, and further into the shade. Were these folk descendants of the Nicolotti who once entertained the future King Henri III of France with a fist fight on the Ponte dei Pugni? Maybe. There was no reason why not.

The thought pleased me. It's what drew me to Venice: little stories attached themselves, suggested themselves, to everything I saw and each place I visited. The past was never really past. Sixteen hundred years provided a storybook few cities could rival. All those silent buildings – each had a life of its own, a story to tell, just waiting for me to listen. I loved it. All of it.

We left the glittering church and retraced our path through the run-down neighbourhood that surrounded it. The mild morning had become a sweltering afternoon and a refreshment stop moved to the top of our program. Gelato – what else in such heat? Not far away, a teensy gelateria opened off the *fondamenta*. We trouped inside.

And in that unremarkable, hole-in-the-wall gelateria, the attention Monika and Raoul gave to all things culinary resurfaced. Twenty ice-cream varieties beckoned from tubs beneath the glass counter. Monika and Raoul scrutinised them, heads drawn together in consultation. Double scoop, they agreed, meaning the possible flavour combinations were multitudinous. The shop's proprietor, a native French speaker, joined them in their deliberations. '*Et ici? C'est le citron?*' Monika pointed from one tub to another, rubbing her chin in contemplation between each question. The owner responded with enough hand-waving to send a worthwhile breeze through the shop's interior. Cruise missiles have been launched with less discussion.

At last, clutching our fast-melting gelati, we walked to Chiesa di San Pantaleone. Monika and Raoul wanted to show me their discovery.

'*C'est merveilleux. Merveilleux.*' Raoul assured me.

Marvellous? I was keen to see it. And to get out of that blazing sun.

To the passer-by making for the cafes and restaurants of nearby Campo Santa Margherita, San Pantaleone's austere facade did not invite further inspection. The treasure inside, and its quirky story, were missed by tourists seeking nourishment of the edible rather than the spiritual kind.

Raoul's enthusiasm centred on the nave's ceiling. Gian Antonio Fumiani had worked for twenty-four years, lying on his back atop scaffolding to paint his representation of the martyrdom and glory of San Pantaleone. Composed on sixty canvas panels, it was the largest single work of art undertaken in the seventeenth century. Even today it had a substantial claim to being the largest oil painting in the world.

I paced the church, looking at the ceiling. My head tipped backwards, almost touching my shoulder blades, and I wondered if I'd live the rest of my life with a crick in my neck. I wasn't the only one looking at the ceiling: Fumiani himself did so as well. He was buried here, after crashing to his death from the scaffolding *just as he applied the very last brushstroke to his life's work.* Fancy that.

The heat notched up. Sweat tracked across my face and down my neck. My hair stuck to my scalp and my scalp prickled. Monika joined me, wiping a hand over her face before taking my arm and pointing across the church.

'*Alors. Il y a plus.*' The French equivalent, apparently, of *But wait! There's more!* At the end of Monika's pointing finger was the Chapel of the Sacred Nail, containing a reliquary that once held a nail used in the Crucifixion. A swarm of cherubs guarded it.

Sacred scraps proliferated in Venetian churches. The Basilica di San Marco, for instance, contained a part of the true cross, a finger of Mary Magdalene, a phial of Christ's blood and one of the four authenticated skulls of John the Baptist. As well as the stone on which he was beheaded. And a knife used to cut bread at the Last Supper. To mention just a few.

Relics were popular all across Europe from the Middle Ages onwards. So sought after did they become that demand dictated supply, and overproduction went into overdrive. If all these relics were authentic, Mary Magdalene would have had six bodies and San Biagio, who has more official relics than any other saint, would have been a hundred-armed monster.

Monika stood near the chapel, her head tilted to one side. Did she share my cynicism? Catholicism flourished in her native Poland; perhaps she had grown up embracing the faith. Her face gave no clues and I was unsure what response she expected.

'*Merci, Monika. C'est incroyable.*' I spoke in a way that implied nothing, the matter-of-fact voice of someone delivering a weather report.

We bought postcards before leaving the church and starting homewards. I congratulated my mates. Fumiani's ceiling was indeed *merveilleux*.

'*Bien fait,*' I said, walking along between them. 'Quite a find.' Then, as I was pencilling a second visit onto my mental must-see-again list, a thought came crashing in.

I might never have met them.

What if I'd settled for a tourist hotel rather than chasing an apartment in Trastevere-like Dorsoduro? Would I have spent nights in my room watching CNN on cable television? Or perhaps ventured to the Piazza and sipped a thirty-euro coffee, wondering why Venice became so quiet after nightfall?

Random things, too, had favoured me. Like staying for a second cappuccino at Downstairs that first night. Living above a bed and breakfast that closed each evening. All chance. Small steps that had led me to this moment.

There was no doubt about it. Venice shone brighter because of a young couple from Lyon.

The cool of the apartment's air-conditioning welcomed us home. Monika pulled the clasp from her ponytail, gathered up damp wisps of hair and secured the arrangement higher on her head. She kicked off her sandals to walk barefoot on the cool marble floor.

'Never I am hot this way.' Red marks ringed her eyes where sunglasses had rested for the last few hours, and pinheads of sweat beaded her face. She paused at the kitchen window, shaking her head in disbelief. '*C'est impossible.*'

I bent my head and followed her gaze. On the bridge below, two men stood chatting, in no hurry to move out of the sun. Each was dressed in a business suit and tie, their shirts crisp and wrinkle-free. The women at their sides, likewise indifferent to the heat, sported long-sleeved blouses and pants. On a day when my skin screamed out for as little as possible to be placed on its surface, they flaunted chunky bracelets and necklaces like scaled-down motorcycle chains. Didn't Venetians feel the heat?

'*Oh, là là, là là.*' I squeezed Monika's arm and turned back to the kitchen. I stood longer than necessary in front of the open fridge, enjoying the chill against my legs as I took out leftovers and salads to put together a late lunch.

'Perth can be hot, too,' I said. A shadow passed over Monika's face, and I watched her mentally cross my hometown from her travel destination planning. 'But even by our standards, today would be bad.'

Bad. *Mauvais.* A spiritless word, but I had no idea how to translate 'scorcher' into French. I'd been speaking French with dogged tenacity, believing it might be another thirty-five years until my next intensive language workout. Little did I know …

Over lunch, I asked Raoul if they had accommodation booked for that night. Oh, dear. Was I starting to sound like Mother? Perhaps. Just a little. But Raoul and Monika mattered to me.

'*Oui, oui. Pas de problème.*'

So, I thought. There won't be someone, somewhere in Croatia, who'll return from dinner tonight and find a homeless young French couple on their doorstep. No one will be as lucky as I had been.

I remembered, then, the way I'd felt as I waited on the platform at Milano Centrale. It was the sense of disconnection, of mind and body arriving at different times. Back then it seemed as though I'd arrived in Italy before my thoughts; they remained behind somewhere, like pieces of forgotten luggage. Now I watched the sensation play out in reverse.

Monika and Raoul had moved on. Their thoughts were with the excitement of the trip ahead; the drive along the Dalmatian Coast, the adventure of discovering Croatia together. All that remained of our time in Venice was the walk to Piazzale Roma, where they would take the bus to Tronchetto for their car and set off on the next phase of their holiday.

We exchanged addresses. We promised to email. We said goodbye, not *au revoir*. No matter how keen the wish to stay in touch, the friendships formed during travel could be hard to sustain in the reality of busy, back-home lives. Which in no way detracted from their value, nor diminished their importance.

'I'll miss you,' I said, kissing them goodbye.

I walked home along the Grand Canal, then into the Papadopoli Gardens. Light filtered through the leaves of overhanging trees where tourists escaped the sun, resting on garden benches. It was on these benches that Monika and Raoul joked they might have spent their first night in Venice.

Beyond the gardens, heat rose from the *fondamente*. My sunglasses slithered down my sweaty face and the sun's dazzle hurt my eyes. I pushed the glasses back up my nose, reaching beneath them to wipe away a tear.

CHAPTER 6

LAGUNA (I)

I'm an old fan of the Veneto and it's here that
I'll leave my heart.

Ernest Hemingway, American novelist and Nobel Laureate

I planned an early start for my first solo day in Venice. A trip to the northern lagoon and the island of Torcello had always been a fixture on my holiday agenda, and I'd intended to link my visit with the Feast of the Assumption, which was still more than a week away. But somehow it felt right to make the trip today.

It wasn't that loneliness was sweeping through me like a desert wind. When I planned this holiday I'd counted on large amounts of time spent alone, and as someone who leaned towards solitude the thought hadn't troubled me. Sitting up until dawn, flicking through the pages of yet another book about Venice, I'd had no interest in anything except the words held on those pages. Companionship hadn't seemed important.

My days with Raoul and Monika had come as a windfall. Small, everyday happenings – the minutiae of life – had been shared, talked about and enjoyed. Now I missed my friends.

Three weeks in Venice stretched ahead and I wanted time out to think, to consider the next phase of my holiday. A day on the lagoon would be perfect.

But before that, something more physical. An hour's walk along the Zattere seemed like the plan – my trade-off before all that sitting on the vaporetto. I pulled on shorts and a t-shirt, smoothing out creases in a concession to tidiness, then double-knotted the laces on my sneakers. Those stairs still worried me.

The city I found that morning was unlike the city I'd spent the last five days coming to know. The *fondamente* were silent but for the screeching of gulls and the slap of water against canal sides. It was almost chilly. I shivered and fastened my pace, walking along *calli* and over bridges towards the Zattere.

A few minutes later, I crossed a *campo* and saw the Giudecca Canal. Adjoining it, and running its length on the Dorsoduro side, was the Fondamenta delle Zattere. *Zattere* means raft, and it was here that bulky goods arriving in Venice were once unloaded onto floating platforms. These days it's bulky *craft* that use the canal: enormous cruise liners, some carrying as many as three thousand people, sail along the Giudecca on their way to the passenger terminal, imposing themselves on the surrounding landscape. For now, at least, no ship cast its hulking shadow across the water.

Venice was easy to love that August dawn. The Giudecca Canal glinted under a sky crayoned red by the sun's fingers, painting a scene of watery peace. I paused to run a finger around the too-tight heel of my sneakers, then looked along the *fondamenta*.

An elderly man sat fishing. His legs dangled over the pavement's edge and he tapped them, first one and then the other, against the *fondamenta* walls. A weathered cap sat atop his weathered face; a landscape of folds and wrinkles signposted by a cigarette drooping from his lower lip. From it burned a long snake of undisturbed ash. He held the fishing line in both hands, and from time to time arthritis-crooked fingers jerked it towards his chest. I wondered what he hoped to lure from the canal's green depths. Perhaps catching fish was secondary to the peace of watching day break over the city.

I straightened and walked on, my pace slowing as the sun warmed. Further along the *fondamenta* another man set up his easel to record the sun's first rays, then laid out paints and unwrapped brushes with methodical care. A woman joined him; his wife, I guessed. Her interest lay only in the book she was reading. She sat alongside her husband, erect as a wind-up doll, while he bent to his work.

I stopped and leaned against a bridge railing to watch them. They conjured up an image of long-formed habits, of days begun according to known patterns. I wondered what routines guided their lives – modest lives, most likely, lived away from the hype of *Venezia turistica*. Ordinary lives and ordinary Venetians. They spoke of the other, hidden city I'd set out to find.

Just on from the pair lay the southernmost tip of Dorsoduro. I rounded it and looked ahead to the Grand Canal; tranquil in early morning calm, a scene borrowed from another age. Relentless activity would soon move it into the twenty-first century, but for now I could picture a time when the homes of great Venetian dynasties bordered its length. The merchants of Venice built golden, bejewelled palazzi to promote their status, to upstage their neighbours and to dazzle the world. For generations they were Europe's most affluent social grouping, made wealthy by their city's fortunate geography. Venice formed the maritime nexus between the European west and the Muslim east. Europeans, Ottomans, Muslims and Byzantine Christians flowed through Venice in a tidal wave of commerce that lasted for centuries.

But with time had come change.

Venice, the proud republic, the mistress of the eastern seas, was now a pale remnant of those long-ago days. The one-time economic powerhouse had become a cash-strapped, beleaguered city, where the whims of tourists rather than trade supremacy maintained its finances.

Sunshine glinted on water. I shaded my eyes against the glare and stood for a moment longer, wriggling my feet inside their tight casings. The blade of tenderness stabbing at my left heel could only mean the arrival of a new blister, probably a large one. Not the ideal start to the day. A glance at my watch showed it was almost seven o'clock, later than I'd thought.

Sore feet and running late: should I chance a map-less return trip through San Polo's *calli*? It was the shortest route home, but it was way outside my skill set. Becoming lost loomed as a real possibility, and all that chasing up and down *calli* took time. As I well knew. My plans for the day centred on an early start for Torcello, ahead of the mid-morning tourist crush, making tenancy of a prized seat on the vaporetto's back deck more likely. Early birds and worms. San Polo's *calli* went on hold for another day.

✺

Camera. Sunglasses and hat. Water bottle, money, keys, guidebook and map, vaporetto ticket. I ticked off the contents of my bag and placed it on the dining table, then added Panadol, just in case. In the kitchen, I lit the gas under the *caffettiera* and turned to look out the window.

Never I am hot this way.

Monika's voice whispered to me, and I remembered her standing here, strands of sweat-dampened hair coiled against her neck as she watched locals defy yesterday's withering heat. I wondered where she and Raoul were having breakfast this morning. A memory came to me, a mental snapshot of us sitting by the sunlit canal, chatting in a put-together language of ourselves and our lives. All at once the apartment felt too big, too empty. I flicked off the gas, gathered up everything I needed and walked to the door. Breakfast at Downstairs. The morning demanded it.

By 8.30 I'd finished my second coffee and was ready for the day. I set off towards the vaporetto stop at Piazzale Roma, reaching it in just a few minutes. *Grazie mille* to all those reviewers who'd pointed out the benefits of its proximity to the apartment. Easy access to transport in an overcrowded city wasn't something to be sneezed at, I'd discovered. *And* Piazzale Roma was a terminus, increasing the chances of getting a prized outdoor seat on the back deck. Another bonus.

For now I was the deck's sole occupant, but I knew that would change. Venetian summers and vaporetti were synonymous with crowds. Big crowds. Me-first-and-you-later crowds. I rested my carry bag beside me and my mind slipped back to another vaporetto trip.

It happened last year, when Jenny and I did our island-hopping day. We stood in the vaporetto cabin, rocking from side to side as the boat swayed across the lagoon. Every seat was taken, but no problem. We were casually dressed, wearing flat shoes and prepared for a day of standing and walking.

A bridal party boarded at Murano. All smiles, the groom walked his bride down the steps and into the cabin. No one smiled back at the smiling couple. No one gave them so much as a second glance. And not a single passenger stood for the young bride. Her special day was not special enough to warrant a seat on a vaporetto. Tottering on her wedding day shoes, she lurched her way across the lagoon to the island of Burano. Her brand new husband stood by her side, holding her trailing dress off the floor. All about them, seated passengers gazed straight ahead, absorbed in their own thoughts. Which did not include newlyweds.

From that couple I took a lesson: people have their own priorities and you may not be one of them. Get over it. Make the best of things. Above all, don't expect a seat on a crowded vaporetto just because you're special.

The vaporetto lurched away from the landing and I looked back at Piazzale Roma, pondering the cultural peculiarities of a country where a dog got a seat on the train but a bride couldn't get a seat on the vaporetto. Then I delved into my bag for a guidebook, flipped it open at the T section and settled back to learn more about my destination. With a population of just a dozen or so permanent residents, Torcello seemed an unlikely starting point for a republic that had lasted longer than a thousand years.

Unlikely now, but convenient back then. Torcello lay close to the mainland, making it the logical first port of call for refugees fleeing invaders. The surrounding waters were found to be rich in salt, a precious commodity at that time. Torcello flourished as a trading hub, initially for the other island settlements and later for townships along the length of the Dalmatian coast. Its population burgeoned.

But being close to the mainland carried risk. Incursions by marauding tribes continued along the Italian peninsula for centuries after the fall of the Roman Empire: the Visigoths, Attila, king of the Huns – an inventory of invaders. When the Germanic Lombards established themselves in nearby Ravenna in the ninth century, Torcello's residents were forced to rethink their future.

Increasingly, settlers withdrew to the better protected islands of *rivoalto* (high bank), a name later shortened to Rialto. The cluster of islands around the Rialto became known as Venice, taking the name from the ancient Veneti people who had inhabited the adjoining mainland in the tenth century BC. Venice became the centre of not only population but political power. As its importance increased, Torcello became a remote and forgotten island.

❈

Ripples broke over low shorelines. Grass-speckled islands rose bare centimetres above the lagoon surface, tattoos on a watery skin. On higher islands, buildings crumbled away the centuries, creepers spilling from their walls to the encircling mud banks. Overhead, gulls wheeled in sweeping arcs, silver arrows against an overcast sky. The vaporetto moved indifferently on.

The clear sky I'd woken to that morning now blossomed with bad-tempered clouds, and moist air wrapped around me in a suffocating blanket. I shifted in my seat, lifting one sticky leg and then the other. No breeze stirred. I clamped my hat down, casting shade further across my face. From behind my sunglasses, I watched the couple in the seats opposite.

From the time they boarded at Murano, the woman had bemoaned the heat. She punctuated her complaints with dabs at her face, patting beneath her eyes with a sodden hanky, then pressing it against her forehead and cheeks. Two deep lines curved in gullies from either side of her nose to her mouth. Sweat drained into them.

Alongside sat her husband, protected from the sun's full blast by a hat. Now and then he removed it to wipe the palm of his hand across his glistening forehead. One wipe too many ... His wife leaned towards him and muttered, thinning her lips in disapproval. The husband replaced his hat with a shrug and a put-upon expression.

As a travel activity, people watching had a lot to recommend it.

The cabin doors swung open. A man followed his young children as they clattered onto the deck. The woman opposite tucked her feet out of harm's way as the children stampeded past. Her husband gathered himself inwards, balling his hands into fists and tucking them between his knees. His hat rested on his ears and his eyes rested on the arrivistes.

No seats? Never mind, a photo then. Dad assembled his subjects, herding three unwilling youngsters into position against an island backdrop, sighing *poufs* of exasperation as the children denied him the smiling holiday snap he wanted. The eldest dug hands deep into his pockets and scuffed the toes of his sneakers on the wooden deck; backwards and forwards, backwards and forwards. His sister wound a strand of hair around her finger and looked at the deck, concentrating beyond all proportion on her brother's feet. The youngest of the trio eyed his father squarely above the thumb he was sucking. As the back deck audience watched on, the father coaxed without success. 'Aw, c'mon guys. Is a smile so hard?'

They tumbled back inside the cabin. I smiled down at my guidebook, remembering the innumerable family outings of my childhood. With my sister beside me, I would perch on the back seat of our family's Holden station wagon and lean forwards to my parents. Every few minutes, with bored resignation, I'd ask the same question: *Are we there yet?* I glanced again at the couple opposite and saw their frazzled, bad-tempered faces relieved by the upwards lift of smiles. Perhaps we shared the same memory.

Twenty minutes later the vaporetto pulled up alongside the platform at Torcello. Despite the heat, I liked the island. Insects chirred from the undergrowth and I heard the occasional throaty *craw-craw* of frogs. I walked towards the township, following a canal. Torcello's canals had added to the island's woes in the early days of settlement, silting up and causing several outbreaks of malaria. This, and the unsuitability of the land for large-scale farming, provided another reason to decamp to the *rivoalto*.

Beyond the canal, low trees and vines screened cultivated land and ahead rose the silhouette of the church belltower. The Veneto–Byzantine Cattedrale di Santa Maria dell'Assunta was first on my visitor must-see list. It could very well be last, too, as so little remained of the Torcello that once existed. No sign now of the eleven churches and scores of homes that once met the spiritual and shelter needs of twenty thousand people. I walked past overgrown blueberry vines wrapped around apricot trees – all that remained of an orchard – before low grey shrubs gave way to open farmland. A scattering of restaurants and guest houses completed the township, with the cathedral at its far edge.

The cathedral's interior was dark after the light outside and my eyes took time to adjust. I looked down to get my footing. Around my unsteady feet spread mosaic tiling stretching outwards to cover the entire floor. The intricate pattern-within-a-pattern had been designed and laid in the eleventh century, and one thousand years later the floor was still in near-perfect condition. Balance restored, I walked across it and slid into a pew. The ancient, chilly smell of stone hung in the air, clinging like wet gauze.

It led me back to another time.

For more than fourteen hundred years people had sat here, sheltered by this roof and protected by these walls. I could picture those early congregations, gathered here in their church in a lagoon wilderness, and feel the silent isolation that waited beyond its walls. The great noise of the twenty-first century halted and my skin prickled, so strong was the connection. Specks of brick dust drifted in the muted grey light and I looked to the right of the church. One section of wall crumbled, where a staircase once led to … what? There was no way of knowing. The ancient cathedral and its first parishioners kept their secret.

Torcello's cathedral was famous for its mosaics, considered second only to those of Ravenna. The most celebrated work, *The Last Judgement*, occupied the cathedral's rear wall. Grey and black colouring depicted the eternal gloom of hell, with lurid images of sinners burning as Lucifer watched. The mosaics extended to the ceiling, and I stood behind a Japanese tour group, joining them to crick my neck skywards and contemplate the bleak message. But even on this overcast day, the mosaics glinted in the light from high mullioned windows, making hell seem a little less gloomy.

Swathes of cloud decorated the sky when I left the cathedral an hour later. I backtracked to the green-shuttered Locanda Cipriani, sitting alongside the canal I'd followed into the township. The inn was the country cousin of the Giudecca Cipriani (think George and Amal nuptials), and many famous personages had signed in at reception.

Standing outside, I wavered. A scratchy dryness lodged in my throat, and from beneath the folds of my dress came the rumbling demands of an empty stomach. Lunchtime, most definitely. But wouldn't the Cipriani be up-market and pricey? *Too bad*, I thought, dusting off my dress and smoothing it down without the hoped-for improvement to my grooming, *I'll risk it*.

Inside the foyer, I again had the sense of stepping back in time. Timber beams crossed the ceiling and white-washed walls reflected light from the entrance doorway: the centuries-old style of an Italian country inn. In one corner a noticeboard caught my eye and I walked over to it. There were the photos I'd expected to find.

'*Ah signora, mi dispiace* ...' The front-of-house waiter appeared at my side, expressing his regret that the restaurant was fully booked for lunch. Again the language thing. It was high time I learned some more Italian, but for now English would have to do.

'Is a cappuccino possible?'

'Of course.' The linguistic shift was seamless. 'I 'ave a table available for a little while.' Noticing my interest in the photos, he nodded towards them. 'It is our record of famous people who have stayed here. Queen Elizabeth, as you can see, and Princess Diana ...'

'This card from Ernest Hemingway,' I began, pointing to the plain white card with the author's greeting. Written in Italian, it conveyed best wishes to all the Cipriani family and, in English, the message 'Hope to see you soon, from Ernest and Mary Hemingway'.

'And this photo.' I turned to the image of two men sitting behind a table of empty bottles and glasses. Winter-bare grapevines arched above them. 'Is the other man Guiseppe Cipriani?'

'Yes, it's a well-known photograph. The two became good friends. Hemingway stayed here for five months during the autumn and winter of 1948. The hotel was kept open especially for him.' A courteous smile accompanied the information.

I glanced at his name badge. Emile, said the black lettering, and I wondered if there might be a French connection. Perhaps I could try a little French, show I wasn't restricted to English? But that might be taken as showing off.

The opportunity passed as Emile continued, 'Hemingway worked on his novel *Across the River and into the Trees* while he sat in the garden.'

I knew the book well. It was among those I'd read in my pre-Venice research marathon, and it centred on wartime recollections. Hemingway had been a war correspondent and the novel, if not autobiographic, at the very least incorporated many places that Hemingway himself frequented in Venice.

Emile appeared in no rush to get back to his duties. I seized the chance. 'Is it possible to see where Hemingway sat to write? I suppose it's a strange request, but ...'

'Not at all.' Emile led me through the door and into the garden. 'There is hardly a day when someone does not ask the same question. Many Americans visit Torcello.'

We crossed a grey-pebbled courtyard. 'Hemingway sat in the far corner.' Emile pointed to a spot bordered by neat flowerbeds. 'In his time there were olive trees there, and a herb garden with rosemary hedges.'

My eyes moved across the garden. Tourist demands for prettiness and order had transformed the rambling gardens that once surrounded Hemingway. I stood beside the flowerbeds, imagining Hemingway at work. Had he looked up to those olive trees when the church bell announced noon; listening as it chimed just a single note, repeated over and over to spread across the lagoon? Did he glance up from his writing to the pink bricks of the cathedral and the terracotta walls of Chiesa di Santa Fosca? Perhaps he was distracted by the beauty of his workplace and glanced up too often. The reviews which followed the publication of *Across the River and into the Trees* fell short of the praise his previous work had attracted.

'Hemingway also worked late into the night.' Emile's voice ended my reverie. 'Each evening at 10 pm, he would retire to his room with six bottles of Amarone. It is a Verona wine. Hotel staff would find six empty bottles in the morning.'

I wasn't surprised. Hemingway's fondness of alcohol was legendary.

Emile looked at his watch. 'You would like a cappuccino? I'll get one of the staff to bring it to you. There is a table under the vines not yet set for lunch. It is where the photo was taken.'

I looked over my shoulder to where grapevines bordered a garden of roses and flowerbeds. A dozen or so tables waited under the vines, most of them already set with white tablecloths, crystal and silverware. At two empty tables, waiters shook out linens with a crisp, ripping sound and watched with professional satisfaction as they dropped into place. From the lawn in the centre of the garden, a bird pecked out its own wriggling lunch.

Emile returned to his place behind the reception desk. I took a seat, ready for some serious people watching, but instead my thoughts turned to Hemingway and the nightly half dozen bottles of Amarone. Now there was a man who enjoyed a drink …

As winter deepened, Hemingway left Torcello for Venice, where he found another corner to sit in. He became a regular at the Venetian–American watering hole, Harry's Bar, also owned by his old Torcello mate, Cipriani. Notwithstanding the jaw-dropping prices, Hemingway combined his two favourite pastimes, drinking and writing, while sitting at a corner table, away from winter sun reflecting off the Grand Canal.

'He drank industrial amounts of alcohol,' Cipriani told the UK *Independent* newspaper in one interview.

Hemingway liked his martini served as a Montgomery. This, Hemingway explained to the bar staff, was a martini made with the same proportions of gin to vermouth as the famous British general liked when he led his troops into battle: fifteen to one. Cipriani continued the tradition, and martinis at Harry's Bar still followed this recipe. Cipriani's fondness for Hemingway was apparent in another comment made during the same interview: 'He was generous to a fault, and filled more pages of his cheque book than those of a medium-length novel.'

I finished my cappuccino. Time was moving on, and I didn't want to repay Emile's kindness by holding up the guests he was expecting. Perhaps I'd call by Harry's Bar when I got back to Venice and see Hemingway's other workplace – maybe try a fifteen-to-one martini. Hang the expense.

The hot, sweet smell of baking followed me to the reception lobby. My stomach hollowed. Emile stood behind the desk, his head bent over paperwork. He looked up and nodded a farewell.

'Next time I visit Torcello, I'll book in advance. Then I can have lunch here. Or maybe even stay for a few days.' I still hadn't seen a price list, so that may have been optimistic. 'Thank you for taking the time to show me around.'

Emile offered another courteous smile. 'My pleasure.'

I wondered how that could be, if so many people asked about Hemingway. Emile concluded the conversation with a final observation. 'We did not rename a room for Ernest Hemingway. But at the Gritti Palace Hotel, where he stayed after leaving Torcello, a suite has been named in his honour.'

That was another snippet I'd learned from my research, along with the fact that the suite cost a cool 9100 euro (A$16 500) per night. And it was always occupied. I'd also read that Hemingway's contemporary, British novelist and short story writer W Somerset Maugham, was another Gritti guest to be honoured. The W Somerset Maugham Suite cost 8000 euro (A$14 000) per night and was likewise well patronised.

I stood aside as a couple entered, likely bound for the table I'd just left. Their lunch was a certainty, but what about mine? The cappuccino had done nothing to stifle the growls coming from beneath my dress. That's when I remembered. On my way into town I'd passed a restaurant with curtaining pulled back to give the impression of an Arabian tent. It might be reasonably priced, I thought. Or not. By now cost had become secondary, and I walked back to the Osteria al Ponte del Diavolo.

And oh-my-gosh. The tent theme continued inside a large restaurant, with drapes pulled back and secured against wooden poles to allow the lagoon breeze to circulate. It worked a treat. Cool air puffed against my skin and with it came scents of jasmine and honeysuckle. Beyond the restaurant I glimpsed a garden. *Mi sono cadute le braccia! Quelle surprise!* In anyone's language, I was astonished.

So much so that I didn't notice the waiter arrive by my side. I looked up to see a young man dressed in the white shirt and tie of his profession, his hair slicked back to form a plume behind his head. Despite the constraints of his dress code, he broadcast an air of nonchalant style. Just the faintest line creased his brow as he debated the language question. Which to use? He settled for a deep nod that was almost a bow, then beamed a high voltage smile.

'Signora?'

'I don't have a reservation, I'm afraid,' I said, returning a smile of equal wattage. That wouldn't be a problem, I knew, my eyes roving the restaurant. As many as two hundred guests could be accommodated around its tables – more than the total number of visitors on Torcello that day, probably. Lunchtime at last.

The young man's eyes twinkled with a long history of mischief. 'Is quite alright,' he assured me. 'I 'ave a table right by the garden. Is this way.'

I followed Ultra Cool to the rear of the restaurant. Off to the right, hidden from the reception area, a wedding party was in full, happy-ever-after swing, with waiters moving between kitchen and guests to serve meals from oversized platters. Tantalising aromas crossed my path and I found I no longer cared about cost. Or calories.

'A drink before lunch, signora?'

An aperitif seemed like the best idea in the world. 'A prosecco would be wonderful.' Then, as an afterthought, 'May I sit in the garden?' I was still stunned by my discovery.

'*Si, si*. Of course.'

Lawn stretched over half an acre, bordered by dense, high foliage. The tinny hum of insects returned, and beyond that the muffled sound of lagoon traffic. A small pavilion replica of the main building occupied garden centrestage. I crossed the grass and sat beneath its chandelier to speculate who among the rich and famous had been there before me.

My prosecco arrived, served in one smooth movement from tray to tabletop. 'And the menu, signora.'

Then, as if they were sitting alongside me, I heard Raoul and Monika.

Un plat typique de Venise.

I smiled at the waiter and handed him back the unopened menu. 'I'd like to try a traditional Venetian dish. Something you recommend. Perhaps you could surprise me, rather than having me decide.'

He dipped his head before making an elegant retreat. And so I sat, under a canopy of wisteria in full summer bloom, wrapped by draped curtains, wondering how many cheese-sandwich lunches would be needed to offset this extravaganza.

The first bridesmaid arrived as I sipped my prosecco. She skipped up to the pavilion and stopped to watch me, peeking from behind the overhanging wisteria. With hands pressed together over her chest, she drew up one foot and worked it in circles on the lawn.

'Hello, you,' I said to a cupid-like face that would crumble a heart of stone. She cast her eyes downwards, uncertain, then wheeled away, retreating to the safety of the wedding party.

I sipped my drink and felt a warm flush of contentment. It wasn't entirely the prosecco. *This is the stuff of make-*

believe. There should be fairies at the bottom of the garden.

As if on cue the bridesmaid reappeared, now holding the hand of a little friend. Leaning together, as if to give themselves courage, they slid into seats across the table, their eyes never leaving me. Entwined fingers rested beside white dresses. Then a sticky hand reached up to place a slice of wedding cake on the table, and another sticky hand pushed it towards me.

'*Grazie, grazie*,' I said, breaking off a piece and popping it in my mouth. Confidence grew, and chatter replaced shy stares. The safe harbour of childhood was established under the wisteria. Then giggles erupted, as we pushed the cake backwards and forwards across the table.

'For you,' I said, moving it in their direction.

'No, no.' And back it came, the finger marks in the icing deeper on each return journey.

But here came Mr Mischief Eyes to tell me that my meal was ready. 'Signora, please. I show you to your table.'

I said goodbye to the little girls, leaving them to play at the bottom of the garden, where all good fairies play. Low clouds gathered and thunder rolled in waves. The last of the day's warmth rose from the pebbled pathway and through my sandals as I walked to the table.

The waiter pulled back my chair and I settled in behind my *plat typique de Venise*. He had decided to educate my tastebuds with grilled eels from the lagoon, served with polenta. The taste was springtime in my mouth.

'That was delicious,' I said when he returned with the dessert menu.

Again the deep nod-bow. 'There will be rain now. Dessert perhaps, while you wait for it to pass?'

Another good idea, and I looked down the list of sinful possibilities as the first plump splats of rain fell. Across the room the bridesmaids returned from the garden and scampered around the wedding group, hugged and kissed at each stopping point on their circuit. The smallest climbed onto the groom's knee and he pulled her upwards, holding her as she laced her arms around his neck. He beamed at her, then at his new wife, and reached to brush hair from the child's face. His wedding ring gleamed.

I poured a glass of water, then slipped deeper into my seat and looked across the garden. Could there be a more fitting place in the whole world to celebrate the start of a life together than in this magical setting, on the island where a new and mighty empire started fifteen hundred years ago? *George and Amal, I think you've been upstaged.*

The listings on the dessert menu looked delicious. I ran my finger down the six offerings, wishing for the first time that a friend sat with me: we could share, and I'd get a double try. Monika never said no to dessert, I remembered.

Maybe the next three weeks would deliver other holiday companions like Monika and Raoul. Or maybe not. Would that be so bad? More days like today I could manage. A fisherman, a painter and a reader had connected me with the Venice-of-ordinary-folk, and an ancient cathedral had taken me back to where it all began. In the corner of a garden, I'd found Hemingway's workplace. And now this. I watched the rain gather strength, splashing diamonds on the paving and I knew that I, too – like Hemingway – could leave my heart here.

The waiter hovered, shifting from one foot to the other. I beckoned, ready to order dessert. And a Disaronno. Because it was raining. Because I might be there for a while. Because I'd travelled so far along the cost-and-calorie highway there was no point looking for the off-ramp now. I ordered chocolate and mint mousse.

'You will enjoy it, signora.' A chuckle bubbled. 'I could not have chosen better.'

Sometimes everything is perfect.

CHAPTER 7

SIGNOR NATALINO'S VENICE

*In Italy, the word government is synonymous
with corruption. The Italian way of life cannot be
considered a success except by visitors.*

Luigi Barzini, in *The Italians*

Yesterday's rain had brought an end to the stifling temperatures of the last few days. The city was cool and fresh, its *calli* and bridges washed clean of summer dust and the telltale evidence of its bird population. Here was Venice at its best, and perfect for the day's program. There was a painting I wanted to find: Jacopo Tintoretto's *Presentation of the Virgin*, hanging in his parish church of Chiesa della Madonna dell'Orto in north-east Cannaregio, some distance away on the far side of the city.

Total luxury, this; setting aside a whole day to do nothing other than track down just one painting. It wasn't something that would happen at home. Not on your life.

Time to myself, free from chores and with no one laying claim to it – that rarely happened. A day that could be planned according to how I felt when I woke up was unknown, as remote from my thinking as a career in astrophysics. Even a few hours of unexpected space – a cancelled appointment, an unavailable bridge partner – left me with a grab-it-and-run sensation: here was something precious, something I didn't want taken away. Something I didn't want to share. But holidays changed things, and I'd relaxed into a new kind of time.

I set off along the *fondamenta* towards the Ponte degli Scalzi (Scalzi Bridge), reaching it ten minutes later. At the top of the bridge I stopped, just as I always did, moving outside the traffic flow to look along the Grand Canal. Why be in Venice and hurry by without a second glance? Time was flashing past and the first week of my holiday already lay behind me. Back in Perth, immersed in plans and expectation, my stay in Venice had seemed boundless, as though time would somehow expand to accommodate all the things I hoped to do. Now I was forced to recognise the finite nature of four weeks. Every scene was precious. I leaned against the balustrade and focused on the morning's project.

Jacopo Robusti, called Tintoretto as a nod to his father's occupation as a dyer, was my favourite Venetian painter. Most of his work was to be found at the Scuola Grande di San Rocco, and a visit there had topped the day's to-do list. But perfect weather had changed my mind. The Scuola was close to home, in neighbouring Santa Croce, and could wait for another, hotter day when walking more than a hundred metres or so would become a sweaty affair.

Besides, walking matched my mood.

I rejoined the traffic to cross the Scalzi and start my trek through Cannaregio. Thousands of visitors swarmed here each day, trailing their suitcases from the *ferrovia* to the tourist mecca of San Marco. The area held premier ranking on my best-avoided list, but a walk to northern Cannaregio meant there was just no way of avoiding it. Ahead stretched a straight path to the Ponte delle Guglie (Guglie Bridge) and from there other straight paths took up the challenge of providing sufficient walking space for the millions of visitors who descended on Venice every year. Canals had been filled over, *calli* realigned and centuries-old landscapes destroyed to create these thoroughfares.

Retail outlets peppered their length. Faux-Venetian tourist trinkets proliferated: gondola ashtrays lay becalmed on a hundred glass shelves and fake Murano jewellery splashed in gaudy waterfalls over metal stands, or lay puddled in flashy gift-cases. The empire of kitsch had a firm base here.

Crowds churned around me. I tramped on, wondering how I'd feel about Venice if this were my first contact with the city. What would I do if I left the *ferrovia* and hauled my suitcase along Lista di Spagna, one tourist among thousands jostling for pavement space? Oh, I knew what I'd do, alright: I'd turn on my heel, head back to the *ferrovia* and catch the next train to somewhere else. Anywhere else.

Allora. I turned from the noisy pedestrian arteries into a series of smaller *calli*. Hustle faded behind me. Cannaregio's residential neighbourhoods lay close by these commerce and cafe strips; just a street or two away, day-to-day Venetian life continued untouched by *Venezia turistica*.

For the next hour I wandered, stopping in a small *campo* as the day warmed. I took a seat in the shade of its only tree and watched local life play out around me. At an upstairs window a soprano practised her aria, notes raining down to the pavement in a cloudburst rather than a light sprinkle. Children looked up from the chalked squares of their hopscotch ladder and giggled, fluttering play-gritty hands in a pantomime of imitation before reaching again for the marker to send another throw.

The genie escaped from the bottle and I remembered the games of my own childhood.

Winter meant tadpole catching. Creek beds and drains – puddles, even – provided wriggling black multitudes crying out to be resheltered in Mum's jam jars. First thing each morning I'd race to the jar collection, picking up one after the other and holding it to the light to see whether any legs had sprouted overnight. Very few of my charges made it to frog-hood.

Then summertime. I thought of sizzling afternoons and running over damp lawn beneath the arc of a garden sprinkler, back in a time when home swimming pools were unknown beyond the mansions of Hollywood film stars. Trips to the beach were a special treat. With a delighted, squealing daughter tucked under each arm, my mother would stand at the shoreline to assess the breakers, then wade out into the surf. Her safety directives were straightforward enough: *if a wave hits, hold your nose and sit down*. How many times did I squat beneath a crashing wave, fingers pinched to my nostrils, wondering if I'd ever draw breath again?

I looked again at the youngsters and stood to leave. This was the Venice I liked best: my Venice. No splashing gondola oars. No strutting, overfed pigeons. The other side of the coin from the image of Venice recognised the world over. The hoots of laughing children filled the *campo* and followed me as I walked away.

❋

My path to Madonna dell'Orto passed near Tintoretto's one-time family home. He lived in this modest neighbourhood with his wife Faustina and their eight children even after fame and fortune reshaped his life. So different from his high-living contemporaries, Titian and Veronese, and further grounds for my admiration of him. Give me the simple life, I'd always said. Not that I'd ever been offered the alternative.

Tintoretto never travelled unless Faustina accompanied him, and he refused numerous commissions in cities away from Venice, preferring to remain with his family. It's one reason why his art is seldom seen outside Venice. Another explanation lies in the fact that Napoleon didn't care for Tintoretto's work and so didn't expropriate it when he plundered Venice's art treasures.

I stopped near a bridge and looked across the canal to the adjoining *fondamenta*. Opposite me, at number 3398 Fondamenta dei Mori, stood a pink-painted house. I looked at the unassuming building, then noticed a plaque to the left of the building's front wall. Quite by chance, I'd found Tintoretto's home.

Casa Tintoretto. What a coup. I crossed the bridge for a closer look. And that's when I noticed the entrance to the adjoining building. It gave directly onto the *fondamenta*, its doors open. The owner would be sure to know about their neighbour but was I game to ask? Bailing up strangers to ask directions was one thing, accosting someone in their private space quite another. I hesitated. But yesterday, on Torcello, Emile hadn't seen my questions as overstepping boundaries. And this was Tintoretto's house. *Go do it now*, I'd said to Dixie. Putting on my please-can-you-help-me-I'm-just-a-tourist smile, I went inside.

Beyond the door was a shop selling Murano glassware. In the small space remaining after stock had been displayed and paperwork stacked, two men stood talking. One, a man of about my age, rocked from heel to toe as he leaned inwards to the conversation, hands thrust into the pockets of his denim overalls. From time to time his bespectacled face broke into a smile, furrowing crinkles at the corners of his eyes.

They turned to me as I stepped into the shop. Again I felt that reluctance to speak English. We exchanged the customary *buon giorno* and a further few words that established my language shortcomings. As it turned out, the younger man spoke English well. He introduced himself as Renato, an out-of-town visitor paying a call on his friend, Signor Natalino, the shop's owner. Beyond his greeting, Signor Natalino spoke no more than a few words of English.

I cleared my throat and took a steadying breath, unsure how to go about this. 'Um ... Next door is Tintoretto's house.'

'*Si, si*. Casa Tintoretto.' Like I was telling them something they didn't already know. They waited for my next insight.

'Who lives there now? Does *anyone* live there now?' I stumbled on, hoping the questions stopped short of intrusion. Signor Natalino and Renato smiled reassuringly.

Renato took up the dialogue, first in English for me and then in Italian to his friend, explaining our conversation.

'Oh, yes. The building is occupied. It is divided into several apartments. One is owned by an American lady. It has views over the canal and has been beautifully restored.'

From Signor Natalino came a comment that was not translated.

'Another apartment, on the second floor, is owned by an elderly lady,' Renato continued. 'It too has views over the canal and also has the use of a private courtyard. It is for sale at the moment.'

I stood, welded to a spot on the floor. I tried out a daydream.

The possibility of living in Venice had never occurred to me. I'd left Perth hoping to find a different Venice, the city away from the stereotype, and to become part of it for a month, as much of a local as I could. A temporary local; that was how I imagined myself. But as each day passed, I'd found myself more drawn to the city. Along with a growing familiarity with its *calli* and *campi*, with the best gelateria and the most convenient supermarket, came the notion of a permanent base in this magic city. Venice had become a present, wrapped and tied with sparkly ribbon, and I saw my name on the gift tag.

So what would it cost to live in this peaceful district? *And* in the one-time home of Tintoretto? I tried to remember to breathe.

Get a grip, girl.

I formed and exhaled the necessary words. A thin, barely audible rasp was the best I could do. 'It must be very expensive.'

'She says she wants one and a half million euro and when she sells it, then she'll go to live with her daughter. The apartment is too big for her,' said Renato.

'She has had it for sale before. The price is too high.' Renato translated Signor Natalino's contribution. 'She will never sell it.'

Air whooshed out of my lungs. Certainly she would never sell it to me. My address would never be 3398 Fondamenta dei Mori. Signor Natalino would never be my neighbour. In a perverse way I was glad the apartment was so far beyond my means. Had it been within reach, I might have been perilously tempted. As things stood, the purchase of

3398 Fondamenta dei Mori was a decision I wouldn't have to make.

Dust motes floated in the sunlight. I breathed in the papery smell of stacked folders as the chatter between us ebbed and flowed. Now and then I wondered if I had outstayed my welcome, but neither Signor Natalino nor Renato appeared in any rush to bid me *arrivederci*. Signor Natalino moved some folders and indicated I should take a seat. I was touched by his thoughtfulness, by the welcome it conveyed.

'Where do you stay in Venice?' Signor Natalino asked, via Renato.

'I've rented an apartment in Dorsoduro, not far from Piazzale Roma. I stayed in Cannaregio last year, but I wanted to see a different *sestiere* this time. And I don't like the crowds around San Marco.'

Signor Natalino shuffled the folders into their new position on an overflowing counter. A few sheets escaped to drift across the glass surface. '*Allora*. Have you seen Chiesa di San Nicolò dei Mendicoli? It is in Dorsoduro.'

'I have seen it, yes. I showed it to some friends a few days ago. It's my favourite church in Venice.'

Favourite church, favourite painter. What next? My favourite gelato combination?

'I grew up in that neighbourhood,' Signor Natalino continued. 'I played with my friends in the church's *campo* and swam in the canal. Swimming was permitted then, and the water was clean. The canal flows directly into the Giudecca Canal and the lagoon.'

Signor Natalino had a light, deliberate way of speaking that added fullness to his words. As I listened to Renato's translation, each word became a scene, dense with detail.

In my mind I saw youngsters leaping into the canal from a centuries-old bridge, squeals of delight accompanying the descent from railing to *rio*. Outstretched arms guaranteed maximum splash. For just that moment, they felt like my own childhood playmates.

Signor Natalino spoke again. 'San Nicolò was my parish church, where I was baptised and received first communion.'

A question sprang to mind, one Signor Natalino would be well-placed to answer.

'I know the Mendicoli were poor citizens,' I said. 'But were they beggars? Nothing I've read gives a clear-cut answer.'

Signor Natalino gave the rehomed papers a final nudge towards the centre of the counter and dusted off his hands. He looked up with a bemused expression. Perhaps he wondered at the unlikely odds of someone from the other side of the world sharing an interest in his neighbourhood.

'The Mendicoli were poor fishermen, yes, but they were also beggars. They requested permission from the Doge to beg as a means of earning extra money. The Doge allowed this.'

He leaned on the counter, hands knotted in front of his denim chest. 'And do you know about the rivalry between the people of my parish, the Nicolotti, and the Castellani? Once we fought to entertain a French king. On the Ponte dei Pugni. You have seen the bridge?'

I'd seen it alright. Monika and I had bought vegetables from the market barge moored nearby, mingling with local domestic-goddess signore. That shopping trip marked the beginning of my realisation that what I call dressing up is what Venetian women do whenever they leave the house.

'Oh, I know the bridge *very* well,' I answered with a triumphant, been-there-done-that smile.

'And the footprints painted on the bridge's paving? They marked the starting point for the two leaders to commence hostilities. You will have seen them, of course.'

Oops. Caught out so easily. I coughed into my hand – no, I hadn't seen the footprints. They were walked over by thousands of people each day; their gaze directed, as mine had been, towards a quaint canal rather than the feet at their feet.

New questions sprang to mind even as the previous one was answered. I mentioned the account I'd read of San Nicolò and the three golden balls given as dowries for either marriage or convent admission.

'This was a common theme.' Signor Natalino rubbed at a point just above the middle of his glasses. 'Prostitution played a significant part in Venetian history. Its importance cannot be ignored.'

I popped this nugget in a side pocket of my memory, to take out if ever a future conversation turned dreary. Similar glints of information sprinkled our talk, making it difficult to muster up the determination to leave. Signor Natalino struck me as someone who liked to chat and I wondered if he might be willing to share other insights. We could be talking about my new hometown, after all.

My request brought a nod and a smile. No problem at all, much like Emile yesterday. Such friendly, obliging people. I'd feel comfortable here. If Venice became my new home.

'But now you will come with us for a drink,' said Renato.

We headed out the door and into the sunshine. Not far away was a stall, about the size of a Mr Whippy van, surrounded by its entourage of umbrella-shaded tables and chairs. Defiant of its modest surrounds, Mr Whippy strove for style.

Shaded by an awning, we sipped our drinks and looked along the *fondamenta*. Signor Natalino's shop was visible from where we stood, but still ...

'You didn't lock up,' I said, looking over my mint drink and back to the shop, 'or even pull the door closed.'

Signor Natalino gave a relaxed shrug. 'In Italy, thieves only take the big things. The little things are safe.'

❋

Oh my, what had I done?

One thing had led to another. A chance encounter, a bit of chatty exchange – I'd got caught up in the current of goodwill and swum out beyond my depth. Suggesting a catch-up to talk about Venice went way beyond asking Emile a few questions about Hemingway. Besides, I usually did my best to discourage conversations with strangers, resorting to pretended other business whenever they threatened. Yet here I was, instigating a *meeting*. Who did I think I was? Joanna Lumley on a field trip?

And where would I find a translator? Renato was returning to Treviso. Sebastiano would be busy with work and family. I needed to reschedule my visit to Madonna dell'Orto until I'd thought this one through. Developed a strategy. Of some sort. Sitting with a cappuccino seemed a useful starting point but finding a cafe in this road-less-travelled neighbourhood seemed about as likely as a UFO sighting. Deserted *fondamente* stretched before me and behind me.

'The hotel is here, sir. I will take your luggage?'

I hadn't noticed the water taxi pull up to the landing. Nor had I noticed the red awning and twin potted trees – always a giveaway – that bracketed the hotel's entrance. Right here could be my best hope for a cappuccino. I trotted along behind the arriving guest and walked straight into the unexpected. In this unlikely place, I'd stumbled across a hidden gem.

A re-purposed seventeenth-century palazzo, no less, waited behind the potted trees. Along the length of the salon, oversized mirrors reflected a scene of understated but unmistakable luxury and off to one side a black grand piano stood ready for the evening's action. Paintings and frescos provided additional polish. I felt rumpled just looking at it.

Beyond the lobby, a garden continued the theme of restrained abundance. I followed white pebbled paths further into the garden, listening to birds chirrup in the tree canopy: real birds, not just tourist-fed pigeons on leave from the Piazza di San Marco. Or ever-hopeful seagulls, like the ones who monitored my every mouthful when I ate at Downstairs. At the far end of the garden, a boathouse looked across the lagoon to Murano and I went over to it, hoping to find a vaporetto stop close by. But no. The exclusivity of Hotel Boscolo Venezia (now known as Venezia Grand Hotel Palazzo dei Dogi) was maintained by not having access to public facilities. Of course.

I made my way back through the *giardino segreto* to where topiary squares enclosed tables set for afternoon tea. Not your Mr Whippy experience, this. The waiter, too, had a decidedly up-market approach.

'My name is Matteo. You will be comfortable sitting here?' Matteo extended his hand in greeting.

I'd never shaken hands with a waiter before ordering a cappuccino. It crossed my mind he'd mistaken me for someone else. Someone of note, as distinct from someone

wandering around northern Cannaregio looking for a cup
of coffee.

'I think I've found paradise,' I said to my new mate. Did
he tire of people making the same comment? He gave no
sign of it.

'It is the largest private garden in Venice, madam.'
I registered the use of *madam* rather than the more
casual *signora* I had become accustomed to. 'It is over
three thousand square metres, and we have a large
gardening staff.'

I wondered. Could I afford to stay here? I liked the idea
of sitting beneath a Murano chandelier, sipping a cocktail
while I listen to the grand piano. The price of the coffee
was reasonable. A one-night sleepover might be doable;
there was no harm in asking. I stood to leave and Matteo
farewelled me with another handshake. *Who did he think
I was? It had to be someone important. Joanna Lumley,
even?*

I stopped at reception on my way out, waiting as a
handsome young man spoke to his colleague in rapid-fire
Italian. Why was everyone in Italy, men and women alike,
so darn good-looking? It wasn't the first time I'd noticed this
apparently national characteristic. The current object of my
admiration turned to me.

'*Buon giorno.*' His speech was more measured, but Italian
still. This was another thing I'd noticed. More and more
people addressed me in Italian, asking for directions to the
ferrovia or the nearest vaporetto stop. Could I possibly –
hopefully – look like a local?

'*Buon giorno.*' The usual embarrassment followed, then,
'I speak only English, I'm afraid. I was hoping to see the
accommodation price list.'

'Of course.' Without hesitation he switched to English and handed me a hotel brochure. I glanced down at his name tag.

'Pablo. That's a Spanish name, surely?'

'Yes, indeed. But I am a Veneto resident for several years now.'

I offered up my most engaging smile. I'd found more than a cup of coffee.

✷

Pablo and I listened as Signor Natalino spoke about his life in Venice.

'I met my wife Elena in 1974, and we married the same year. Her family were from Cannaregio, and so I moved here from Dorsoduro. This shop was once a fruit store, owned by her father.'

Signor Natalino gestured to embrace the huddled interior. I twisted on my stepladder seat and glanced around. I couldn't imagine it other than just as it was.

'Lena and I were married at Madonna dell'Orto. It is not far from here. Lena did not work outside the home after we married. She looked after our children, two sons and a daughter. She raised them well. Her work was as important as mine.'

He paused while Pablo translated. I bent over my notebook and scribbled down his words, then looked up at Signor Natalino's next comment. It seemed to come with an exclamation mark at the end.

'Family is the cornerstone of Italian life.'

My mind slipped back to Luigi Barzini's book, *The Italians*. I'd read it as part of my pre-trip research. The strength of family, Barzini believed, underpinned Italian society, carrying its citizens through the daily trials of living in their ineptly governed country. It was not the most tactful observation to share with Signor Natalino.

'And your children? Do they live in Venice?' I asked instead.

'Enzo works for Alilaguna, in an administrative position. Do you know Alilaguna? They transport people across the lagoon from the airport. It is a secure government job. A good thing. Unemployment in Italy is high, more than ten per cent. In Venice it is even higher.'

So not something to be shrugged at, I thought, shifting to make myself comfortable on my perch.

'And your two other children?'

Signor Natalino looked down and the corners of his mouth tensed. 'Our second son, Marco, died in a boating accident when he was twenty-four.' He nodded as first Pablo and then I expressed condolences, but said nothing further. A pause followed before he spoke again.

'And we have a daughter, Elizabetta.' Signor Natalino's smile returned as he spoke of his daughter and her achievements. 'She graduated from university with a degree in languages. She can speak five fluently. But even so, the only work she could find after university was in a boutique. A sales assistant. She could not start a career in Venice and she moved to Paris. Now she has a senior position with Christian Dior. Elizabetta will never come home to Venice.'

Beyond the personal loss, it spoke of a wider problem. Little work was available in Venice outside the tourist industry. Each year, keen young graduates headed off to Milan or Rome – or overseas – with their freshly printed degrees. Venice lost its best and brightest.

Those without tertiary qualifications also faced an

employment dilemma. Signor Natalino waited as I wrote, then continued. 'This is not a new problem. For many years, offices and industries have transferred to the mainland, to Mestre or Padua. Once Giudecca Island had many factories. One by one they closed. In the last thirty years it has become much worse. I will give you an example.'

His voice rose as he made the point. 'The Molino Stucky building. A flour mill once, with hundreds of jobs for unskilled workers. It is now the Hilton Molino Stucky. The jobs have gone. Where do those people find work?'

I was surprised. 'But what about Porto Marghera? That's a huge industrial complex. Surely it provides employment for Venetian locals?'

'Porto Marghera did not help Venice. But the man who developed it, Guiseppe Volpi, it helped him. The national government gave him money. Public money, our money. For a private undertaking.'

I made a noise that could pass for cynical acknowledgement. 'How convenient it must be to have friends in high places.' Pablo translated my tongue-in-cheek comment and Signor Natalino directed a long, noisy breath at the ceiling.

'Venetians do not cross the lagoon each day to work at Marghera. Most who found work at Marghera left Venice to live close by, on the mainland.'

It fitted with my reading of Margaret Plant's research. The city's depopulation presented a major concern. Those remaining were older citizens, by and large: the average age of Venetians was now the highest of any major European city, with thirty-five per cent of residents over the age of sixty-five. The demographic tragedy of the historic city had caused one local observer to comment that 'this is the end of Venice as a city for Venetians'.

I followed another thought. 'So could Venetians commute to Marghera?' I asked. 'Some town planners think a rapid, underground train network linking Venice and the mainland is the answer.'

'There is no money.' Signor Natalino spoke without hesitation. 'Money has been spent – *wasted* – on many things. Especially it has been wasted on MoSE.[2] And many people think it would be madness to interfere with the city's foundations and the lagoon.'

That made sense to me: the lagoon's delicate eco-balance was already under threat. I paused from my writing and looked up to Signor Natalino.

His features hardened. 'No one can agree what is best for Venice. There is always talk. Just talk. Nothing happens.'

Gondolas adrift on backwater canals, I thought, remembering numerous initiatives that had been suggested to halt the city's declining population. One such vision saw science, the internet and associated new technologies as providing employment and retaining citizens; financial incentives would attract large firms to develop Venice as the Italian answer to Silicon Valley. But finance was the operative word. There wasn't a lot available. The plan's movement from drawing board to reality stalled.

Another, more radical proposal envisaged the European Commission taking charge of Venice, the underpinning belief being that the Italian national situation had impeded rather than facilitated the preservation of Venice as a viable, working city. This could be achieved by the formation of a separate state within Italy, based on the model of the Vatican city-state. It seemed as unlikely as every other proposal.

---

2   See Author's Note on p355.

I straightened my shoulders and looked back at my notebook. So where to now?

Signor Natalino offered his suggestion. 'Some people see Venice as a centre for higher education. Our university is well regarded, especially for architecture and languages. The future might lie with this.'

I thought of Oxford and Cambridge universities in the United Kingdom, and the Ivy League universities of North America. They presented formidable opposition in what has become an international competition to attract fee-paying students. Gaining a foothold in this lucrative market would not happen overnight.

It was hard to be positive, so I said nothing. But I couldn't help thinking how at odds with the usual perception of Venice all this was. Most holiday-makers associated Venice with gondolas and fairytale palazzi and knew little of the problems besetting the city. I turned to Signor Natalino and Pablo, who were deep in a conversation. Their talk had moved to the one problem people did associate with Venice.

'It was the *acqua alta* (flooding) of 1966 that really convinced people to leave,' Signor Natalino said. 'They just didn't have the heart to start again. Our homes are already old and fragile. The flooding weakened them even more.'

He was eager to talk, taking up the conversation so promptly after Pablo's translation that their words often overlapped.

'The homes of people who lived on ground floors were completely destroyed. Furniture, everything. People were dispirited, left without hope. Many decided to move to the mainland where the housing is modern and there is good transport. And, of course, it is dry. People abandoned Venice.'

I bent my head and scribbled away. I knew the statistics. Before the calamitous 1966 *acqua alta*, the worst in the city's history, Venice had 120 000 residents. A decade later, the population stood at just 70 000. For the city, it was a life-destroying exodus. In the following years the population had declined at a constant but slower rate, to around 55 000.

And I knew about *acqua alta*. It resulted from heavy rain and strong winds that prevented water from leaving the lagoon at low tide. With no exit route, water flooded back into the city. Venice had been subjected to flooding for centuries, but on 3 November 1966, these circumstances were worsened by an earth tremor. The ensuing tidal wave, pushed by strong sirocco winds from the south-east, caused the lagoon water to rise two metres above its average level overnight.

In 1966, Signor Natalino was a young man in his early twenties, living with his family in Dorsoduro. Fifty years on, the memory remained. I kept my eyes on his face as he spoke, pen and notebook forgotten in my lap.

'The wind and the rains started during the night. All night, howling winds and pelting rain. The electricity went out. It was dark, so at first we didn't know how bad things were.'

Signor Natalino paused a moment, remembering. Then he continued, his voice steady but intense. 'We are a city born from the sea, forever linked to it. Most parts of Venice are only one metre above sea level. *Allora* ... by morning, when dawn came, we saw no *calli*, no *fondamente*, only water. Wherever we looked, water. It remained high for two days. There was no electricity, no telephone. Just filthy water. Rotting seaweed. Rotting animal bodies. Oil from broken storage tanks. All of it flowed into our homes.'

I tried to imagine the scene facing Signor Natalino that morning. How would I have felt, waking on a cold, late-autumn morning to find water creeping beneath the doorway of my home? Then watching as it continued to gush in, destroying everything I owned? What would I have done? I tried to imagine. I couldn't.

'I got out my boat. With five friends we spent the day helping people move their belongings to upper floors. The whole day. We didn't stop, there was no time for meals. We drank a whole bottle of grappa, to keep us going.'

It was soon after the flooding that Signor Natalino considered emigrating, before meeting Elena and deciding they would make a life together in Venice. He didn't regret his decision to stay.

'I am a proud Venetian, happy that I live in Venice.'

Signor Natalino faced me and tilted his chin upwards. I guessed the nature of his next comment ahead of Pablo's translation.

'But I am angry that the government did not do as they said they would, following the *acqua alta*. The government promised to help all Venetian citizens re-establish themselves, but that didn't happen. It was all talk, nothing but talk.'

He adjusted his glasses, then stuffed his hands deep into the pockets of his denim overalls. 'I was a glassmaker. I installed expensive chandeliers in government-owned palazzi. That money should have been spent repairing homes.'

At this point, Pablo added to his translation. 'He wants you to be sure to stress that, if you do write your book. It's something he feels strongly about.'

With a stern face, Signor Natalino watched Pablo relay the information. I looked up from my notebook and nodded my understanding.

He had good reason to be upset. *Il Comune* (Venetian local government) made grand promises in the wake of the flood. Architecturally significant buildings would not be preserved for tourists to marvel at, they vowed, while at the same time local housing remained in a state of disrepair. People would be the priority.

But they weren't. Buildings that housed art treasures were deemed more important than buildings housing people. Some new housing projects were undertaken, then and later, but these few showcase pieces masked a disheartening reality. Very little new housing has been provided since the 1966 *acqua alta*. Town planners insisted then, as they do now, that improved low-rise, low-cost housing in suitable locations would not impact the city's historic ambience. And such housing is sorely needed if Venice is to halt its population exodus.

Signor Natalino spoke again. 'My family was lucky. Two of my brothers were tradesmen. We were able to repair the lower floor of our home in a few months. But other homes were never repaired, despite all the promises. People were forced to leave Venice with whatever they had. For them the government offered no help. Nothing.'

I stopped writing and looked over at him. He shook his head and studied the backs of his hands. Pablo stepped in to lighten the mood, asking Signor Natalino to join him for a beer the following day.

Signor Natalino smiled again. '*Si, si.*'

Time had passed unnoticed in the little shop on Fondamenta dei Mori. Sitting on a stepladder, I'd listened to the story of an ordinary Venetian who had lived through an extraordinary event. But it was time to go. I gathered up notes and packed them into my bag. I had a final question.

'What would you most like me to say about the Venice you know?' I asked Signor Natalino.

He thought for a few moments, then reiterated that he was a proud Venetian. 'But tell the truth about Venice,' he said. 'That is the important thing.'

Tell the truth about Venice ...

Venice is incomparable. The Basilica di San Marco, the Palazzo Ducale and the cliffs of palazzi lining the Grand Canal are images recognised the world over. The sight of gondolas sliding through placid water, the sound of bells ringing through the mist or in the sunshine – these speak of nowhere else on earth. But the city faces challenges. It would be dishonest to speak of Venice as an art-filled haven and an architectural wonder without noting the bleaker realities.

We shook hands. Pablo and I moved towards the sunlit doorway.

'I have enjoyed talking about my city,' Signor Natalino said. 'My life has been a simple one. I lacked a good education, and I am pleased my children have done so well.'

With complete sincerity I responded that his life seemed to me to be one of great dignity.

His reply was as wise as it was gracious. 'There will always be dignity in truth.'

CHAPTER 8

MADE TO ORDER

Venice is not something one can explain. You need to see it, feel it, and experience it from the right point of view.

Massimo Cacciari, former Mayor of Venice and Professor of Philosophy, University of Venice

Have you ever stepped onto a set of talking scales and heard the computerised voice tell you only one person at a time can use the machine?

I searched through the wardrobe for the dress I wanted: a pale green Audrey Hepburn-style number. Neat and unfussy, it suited today's plan. I pulled it from the hanger and dropped it over my head, frowning when its encounter with my hips cut short the descent. It used to fit perfectly. Either it had shrunk without cause or reason while hanging in the wardrobe, or a week of pasta and pizza indulgence had taken its toll.

I'd known this would happen. Stepping outside my dietary no-go zone always carried unhappy consequences. At home I munched my way through one righteous salad after another, summer or winter, determined to maintain the weight I'd kept for two decades. All my life I'd been slim, at times even skinny. In my twenties, I remember, I'd stood before mirrors and cried in despair at the sight of my slender frame.

Then came a surprise. Middle age rolled around and all those kilos that had eluded me in my youth rolled around with it. And they didn't land in the places where I wanted them. Food treats – things I'd eaten without a second thought, not even considering them treats – moved to the banned list. No cake. No ice cream. A tiny biscuit now and then, but only when it appeared in the saucer beside my cappuccino.

Middle age is a cruel time.

But, I'd reasoned, holidays change all the rules and I'd fallen – *jumped*, you could say – from the diet wagon, hitting the ground in bouts of joyful excess. More pizza! Bring on the double-scoop gelati! I don't typically do moderation.

Now I stood halfway into a dress that gripped where it needed to give, facing a wardrobe of slacks that had lost their slackness and tops that had become too tight. A day of calorie control was in order.

And, truth be told, I needed a break from all the back roads, going-where-no-tourist-has-gone-before business. If only for a day, I wanted the pointy end of the aircraft, something first class. *And* something that would take my mind off food at the same time. Two birds, one stone, et cetera. I knew what to do.

I turned to the steadying force of retail.

A final, sharp tug and the dress settled into position, clamping my thighs in its tight wrap. But something loose and casual just wouldn't do. Morning tea – Russian Caravan, two cups, black, nothing more – at the Hotel Danieli, one of Venice's plushest five stars, would kick off my program. Charles Dickens had once been a Danieli guest; so, too, had Madonna. Now it was my turn. I smiled at my lumpy reflection, anticipating a day of up-market action.

An hour later, the vaporetto thumped against the platform at San Zaccaria. I reached into my bag for a pair of high heels and slipped them on, poking the sandals they replaced into the bag's depths. The Danieli called for fancier footwear.

Once inside the hotel, plush-hush replaced *fondamenta* noise and I cast an appreciative look about. A staircase hugged one wall, rising four levels above the reception atrium, and Moorish arches cut into the encircling grey marble. Much of the interior remained true to its Gothic ancestry. Like many hotels in Venice, the Danieli started life as a rich man's castle, commissioned in the fourteenth century by the Dandolo clan, a family of great wealth and influence. Doge Enrico Dandolo, although blind and eighty years old, had led his troops in the Fourth Crusade, capturing Constantinople on the way (1204). Five hundred years later, in 1822, the palazzo was purchased by Friuli businessman Guiseppe Dal Niel, known as Danieli, who rented it out for several years before transforming it into what is today one of the city's most prestigious hotels.

I took a seat in the reception lounge alongside a fireplace big enough to hold a party in. The Dandolos had enjoyed a reputation as lavish entertainers, so the fireplace would have been in constant use during their palazzo get-togethers. Small wonder the forests of the Veneto were all but wiped out in the Middle Ages.

A waiter glided to a halt beside me; good-looking, of course, like every other waiter in Italy. Was it part of the job description? I sat straighter and arranged my ankles in a position that mimicked elegance.

'I'd like tea, thank you.' So-o-o-o handsome. It crossed my mind to flirt with him.

'Of course, madam. Just one moment.' He inclined his head and withdrew.

On ya, girl, I thought, inhaling up-market ambience in deep breaths; a delightful change, this, and a wise choice – more sensible than making my inaugural venture into the confusing *calli* of San Polo. With my days in Venice slipping past like a series of swiftly dealt cards, I still pushed back at the challenges of San Polo and eastern Castello – the neighbourhoods I most wanted to see, along with Dorsoduro. Their complex geography unnerved me; made me think of Hansel and Gretel, that sort of thing.

The waiter reappeared, driving a tea trolley. He parked alongside me. 'Madam, your tea.' A white napkin, crisp as a new snowflake, flipped over my knees before he lifted a silver pot from its silver tray and poured a cup of tea, placing it on the table. Now came the dangerous part. A sinful selection of Danieli delights waited trolley centrestage: sandwiches sliced to the thinness of a wasp's wing, dainty cakes in pleated-paper cradles.

'You can't expect me to eat all these.' I flashed my best smile. I could easily have eaten the lot. In one go.

'Some different tastes for you to try, madam,' he said, striking the right balance between deference and friendly professionalism. More a diplomat than a waiter, really – a great loss to the UN.

I sipped tea and continued my appraisal. Signor Natalino had told me he worked at the Danieli for a period in the late 1980s, during a business downturn. He recalled it as being the first time he realised how many Americans came to Venice. If he sat beside me now he would see little change. For the most part, the language I heard was English, the accent American.

Rich American. Finely dressed couples sat about the lounge, greeting friends and planning outings. *We're expected at the Cipriani for drinks first. I've ordered the launch for midday.* A woman strolled through the lobby, chatting over her shoulder to the porter who carried her logo-emblazoned shopping bags. It might have been the scene from a movie. The verdict of success, of wealth, was in the air; rising above the murmuring voices to hang beneath the gold filigree ceiling in a halo of self-approval. The irrepressible confidence of life in the dress circle.

My waiter returned and poured a second cup of tea, then pushed Temptation in my direction. I felt obliged to try a sandwich. Just one. So as not to cause offence. A cake soon followed, for the same reason.

Did luxury become habit-forming? I wondered, sitting in my swank surroundings. I could see the appeal. I could also see the bill my waiter had placed under a napkin on the table. A glance at its lower right-hand corner convinced me I had little chance of ever resolving the luxury-and-habit question. *That* much? Ruinous. And before the tip, even. But today wasn't about so-so. Today was about so, so good.

The Danieli met that measure, alright. I took one final, wistful look at the cakes I mustn't eat and the posh I couldn't afford, then stood to leave. Outside the revolving doors I leaned against a wall to change shoes, then set off to cross the Piazzetta, avoiding the two columns near the waterfront. For centuries this spot had marked the site of public executions. Hanging, decapitation or burning were the preferred methods for dispatching wrongdoers, but small refinements were sometimes invoked. Three fifteenth-century traitors were buried alive, head down, in this place. Superstitious locals still considered it unlucky to walk between the columns. I skirted to the left. No point taking unnecessary risks.

Ahead lay the Piazza di San Marco. Late morning in Venice drew people to the Piazza in numbers that rivalled the Melbourne Cricket Ground on AFL Grand Final Day. The air filled with the sound of a thousand voices speaking at different pitches – an orchestra tuning up. A forest of selfie sticks rose above bobbing heads. Pigeons cooed and pecked.

The Piazza was undeniably grand. It was the only open space in Venice to be called a piazza, the belief being it was way too grand to share the title with lesser spaces. An English child in Venice, on seeing the Piazza for the first time, is said to have asked, 'Mama, are people allowed to see this every day, or only on Sundays?' More worldly visitors have been likewise impressed. Napoleon famously described the Piazza as 'the most beautiful drawing room in all Europe'. And then set about demolishing large chunks of it.

Behind the Piazza lay Rio del Cavalletto, *gondola centrale* for visitors wanting to round out the Venice experience. More crowds. More voices braided together, rising in a single drone. Then a voice pierced the hubbub, stopping me in my tracks.

Holding a microphone close to her teeth, a tour guide mustered her charges. 'Stay near the canal. Don't block traffic.' Her orders rippled the air in a voice that crossed octaves, screeching upwards one minute then lowering to a raspy growl the next. I watched her, noticing the telltale tuck at the corners of her mouth. She enjoyed this.

'Six people to each gondola. No more. Form into six now.'

She lifted the glasses dangling from a chain around her neck and inspected the queue of sixty or so prospective passengers. Her forehead puckered. 'Make your group ready now,' she snapped at a few brave souls who had broken ranks to take holiday snaps. Like a cattle dog mustering the herd she circled them, growling.

Her voice ranged upwards again. 'Back in line. Ten gondolas coming soon. Then we go.' Behind her glasses, a bright-eyed intensity signalled her determination to get the herd afloat. I turned away, leaving her to sell the dream of a gondola ride along a Venetian canal, a dream that to me looked more like a nightmare. The last of her ten commandments boomed along the canal as I walked off.

'And no ice cream in gondola.'

But I suppose we all enjoy Venice in our own way.

Now down to serious women's business.

The Mercerie, where I was headed, had for centuries been the retail heart of Venice. Such was the quality and beauty of the goods displayed in its *calli* that seventeenth-century writer John Evelyn described them in his Diaries as '... the most delicious streetes in the world ... and with that variety ... I hardly remember to have seene the same piece twice exposed, [with] innumerable cages of nightingales, which they keepe, that entertain you with their melody from shop to shop ...'.

Not anymore. Crowds had replaced nightingales and pricey, one-name designer shops had ended variety. Fashion heavyweights stood shoulder to shoulder in defence of modern consumerism, many of their entrances attended by black-suited security guards. I moved with the human tide from one *calle* to the next, past shops displaying goods identical but for the logo they bore. Then, from between jostling bodies and swivelling heads, I spied something different. Elbowing my way out of the traffic, I nudged up for a closer look.

My breath hit the air-conditioned glass in a misty O shape as I peered inside the shop. Style icon Fendi flew the banner of consumerism with bold originality. Every item in its window bore a cat motif; some small, others large enough to attract the attention of a passing dog. Intrigued, I pushed open the door and entered the rarefied world of Fendi.

A young assistant was immediately by my side. She smoothed back imaginary wisps of hair, patted the neat, complex bun anchored at the nape of her neck and prepared for engagement.

'Do you like our new designs, madam? Sweeter even than Space Monkey, don't you think?'

Her tinselly voice posed the questions with practised charm. She continued her sales patter, the words flowing over me as I trawled the dark recesses of my brain. *Space Monkey? Who was Space Monkey?*

'I am so thrilled with them.' Her gesturing hand indicated we were back with cats. 'Look at this bag. It is very different, don't you think?'

I did think it was different – a green and pink affair with a whiskered cat's head trimming the front panel. Ms Fendi brought the bag down from its shelf and passed it to me with the reverence she believed it deserved. I held it aloft at arm's length, turning it this way and that while making clucking sounds of admiration, hoping for a glimpse at the price tag. There wasn't one. Fendi's clientele had no need to concern themselves with the cost of a trinket.

I hesitated. 'So pretty ...'

'The cost is three thousand euro, madam,' she cooed, her voice achieving the same pitch as the pigeons outside in the *calle*. 'Look, I, too, wear the design.' She twisted the scarf encircling her neck and from between its folds another cat looked at me, awaiting my decision.

Three thousand euro. My hand shook. At least it won't break if I drop it, I thought, handing back the costly cat.

'It's ... hmm. Yes. Thank you. *Grazie, grazie mille.*'

I edged towards the door, aiming for a gracious getaway. But the signorina proved a determined advocate of all things Fendi. She moved between me and the door, holding kitty up for my reconsideration. 'And these bags are available now. There is no waiting list.'

I smiled until my cheeks ached, nodded until my head felt loose on my shoulders. But I was every bit as determined: the only handbag I would be leaving with was the one I'd walked in with. Whiskers would not be joining me for the trip home to Perth. She would never be left lying around on a sofa, making my dog feel displaced as the household pet. I searched for a polite, noncommittal remark to end our encounter.

'So many fashion houses in Venice ...'

'Oh, yes. And Fendi is in cities all over the world. Having many addresses adds prestige to our label.'

With hopes of a sale fading, Ms Fendi decided to educate me. Major fashion houses, she explained, bought retail property in Venice because it improved their image in, say, New York. By and large, the goods sold in Venice were the same as those sold in every other city. It hardly bore thinking about. All those cat handbags and scarves, popping up across the globe. And Space Monkey, still out there and circling.

More smiles and nods followed before I pushed open the glass doors, exchanging the world of Fendi for the stifling, cramped *calli* of *sestiere* San Marco. Too many people. Too little space. My thoughts lay thirty-five years ago...

... when I'd wandered through the near-deserted Mercerie, finding a shop the size of a thimble set into a leaning wall. Through the doorway, I'd watched a man adjust his apron and draw his tools closer, then bend over the hide he was working on. His wife showed me the shoes I pointed to, and I sat on the shop's single chair to try the size. Children ran inside from the *calle*, giggling and pinching one another's arms.

I never imagined the years would not bring change. It was the dimension of that change, the discrepancy between my recollections and the present-day reality, that stunned me. Nothing aligned with what I remembered. Small artisans like the shoemaker family had disappeared, forced into other *sestieri* by high rents following the designer-label takeover. The magic I remembered had gone. In many ways, this holiday had centred around revisiting the past – not only the stories and buildings of a long-ago Venice, but the places I remembered from other visits. Now I realised that sometimes the past is best left alone.

The day was reshaping as an endurance test. True to form, the mild morning had been overtaken by a pitiless, moist heat. Sweat trickled between my shoulder blades and down my back. My tongue stuck to the roof of my mouth. By now one *calle* looked very much like another and I wasn't interested in walking down any of them.

I wanted a drink and I wanted lunch. A salad would be okay, surely, a restorative pick-me-up, and well deserved after a morning of jostling crowds and crunched toes. I slipped beneath the green awning of a trattoria and was greeted and seated with the speed of a rescue mission. The waiter delivered a spritz; olive neatly speared, orange slice afloat, ice cubes clinking. Above its frosty rim I looked out at my patch of *sestiere* San Marco.

A middle-aged couple shuffled into view. Their faces glistened and their shoulders drooped under the weight of shopping bags: Gucci, Armani, Dolce & Gabbana – a road map of their morning's travels. They halted at the trattoria's menu stand.

'Here? This one okay?' The husband spoke in a gruff voice, as though repeating a question he'd asked several times.

'I guess so, Earl. I need to sit a piece.' His wife's voice had a bristly edge to it, the sound as wiry as her hair, which the humidity had frizzed into a tight ball. She pulled out a chair and her husband joined her. Under the green awning they sat, ready for lunch.

'Oh, Lord, my feet are on fire.' The woman slumped low in her seat and pushed a swatch of frizz from her gleaming face.

'It's those durned shoes you're wearing. I warned you before we left the hotel.' Disapproval laced Earl's voice as he pointed to his wife's footwear. She anchored the stray hair and turned to face her husband, studying his face as if trying to make up her mind about something. *Will I argue or won't I*? *Can I be bothered*? Then she pulled her lips together in the pained, virtuous look of a martyr and made no reply.

I peeked under their table. The woman's feet were encased in heeled shoes above which ankle bones jutted like doorknobs from tight, swollen skin. The memory of last year's pre-opera detour and my own suffering feet came back to me. I felt her pain.

Earl had his own issues. He rubbed his back and jiggled about, scowling his annoyance.

'Dammit. This chair hits my spine in just the wrong place.'

He grasped the table edges to lever himself into a more comfortable position. A sigh followed, the sound of someone hanging on to the last shred of patience.

'And wouldn't you know it, the table rocks.'

Earl juggled the table backwards and forwards, this way and that, along the pavement in search of a level spot. At last satisfied, he turned his attention to the pizza menu, rubbing at the bridge of his nose with thumb and forefinger as he considered the offerings.

'There isn't a single pizza here that I want.' He flicked the menu onto the table.

Earl was not one for making the best of things, I could tell. In a grumbling voice he commenced an inventory of his travel disappointments, documenting one by one the travesties visited upon him. The traffic in Rome had been dreadful. The leaning tower of Pisa didn't lean as much as he'd expected. Gondoliers charged the earth and still wouldn't sing. And now this: on a list of twelve pizzas, not one appealed.

Tipping his head back, and with a wave of his hand, he beckoned the waiter. The young man arrived, smiling, pencil poised above his notebook. Earl stabbed at the menu with a blunt forefinger. 'I'll have the margherita and the pepperoni combined.'

The waiter looked at him and blinked. The pencil halted on its path to the notebook.

'Yes, that's right. No olives or anchovies. Instead I'll have extra capsicum. Just a few mushrooms. And I like the crust well baked.'

Confusion lined the waiter's forehead. No one had told him to expect this.

Unfazed, Earl continued. 'Now for my wife, the rustica without the bean sprouts. With a side serve of ketchup.'

The waiter's eyebrows rose to a what-on-earth level.

Earl misunderstood. 'You don't know ketchup? Why, it's kinda like a sauce ...'

I watched the disgruntled duo sort through the pizza conundrum. I watched the personable demeanour of the young waiter change to one of irritation. And through the woolly layers of my mind – I'd ordered a second spritz – an old joke resurfaced. The one about a tourist in Florence who asks at every street corner for directions to the Renaissance. Now the joke became the possible. I could picture Earl and Mrs Earl in their suburban sitting room, talking of their time in the Beautiful Country. 'Well, it was okay,' Earl might say, 'but the hotel rooms didn't have bar fridges. Everywhere we went, there were these really old buildings. And we never did find that durned Renaissance.'

Perhaps a morning of retail disappointment lay behind my uncharitable thoughts. Beyond the awning waited still-bustling *calli* – the shoppers of *sestiere* San Marco didn't slacken the pace for siesta. This was no Trastevere, no Venice of the Venetians. So what was I doing here?

An up-market shift. A Weight Watchers' reset. Handy reasons, drawn from a ready stockpile of rationales aimed at transferring my San Polo visit to another day. I'd wanted to stay with what I knew. Or thought I knew. A power outage, so to speak, as had happened on the train to Milan.

Condensation trickled down the side of my glass as I ran through my options. If I caught a vaporetto along the Grand Canal I could make my way home through San Polo. So what if I got lost? I wasn't in a race with the opera's opening curtain.

I left the shade of the green awning and walked between buildings, passing from one scalding wedge of sunlight to another. A final hurdle blocked my escape from the crowds: the San Marco vaporetto platforms, hot favourite for the worst-place-in-Venice trophy, challenged only by the Lista di Spagna in Cannaregio. I shuffled forwards as the vaporetto heaved up against the platform. Fifty people shuffled forwards with me, making way for the fifty people shuffling to disembark. Heat and damp bodies. Still, thick air.

From nearby came an American voice, female and vaguely familiar in its assertive self-confidence. Dixie? *Dixie?* But no, of course not. By now Miss America Junior would be unpacking her pink suitcase at home in Des Moines. I turned to find a sturdy and sunburnt woman of indeterminate age.

She spoke in the vernacular Dixie had so liberally deployed. 'I so-o-o-o think this place is totally overrated.'

Sweat trickled under my sunglasses and down the sides of my nose. My dress stuck to my thighs and my thighs stuck together. The tops of my sandals disappeared as my ankles melted over them.

Overrated? Right at that moment, I so-o-o-o had to agree.

✳

A little sprig of hopefulness budded.

I left the vaporetto and walked through a web of *calli* towards Campo San Giacomo dell'Orio. No crowds buffeted me. I gave my shoulders a shake, adjusting to the changed tempo, and turned into a small *calle*, then into another, smaller again. The bud of hopefulness blossomed into full flower.

A bridge intersected my path. Buildings flanked the canal, crossed in the distance by another bridge. A woman leaned from a window, steadied her laundry basket against a ledge and pegged washing to a line. Further along the canal, greenery spilled over a terrace garden, reaching down the wall to the window below. The only sound was the grate of my sandals on paving.

'Do you speak English?'

A sharp voice came from behind me, cutting through my thoughts. I turned to find a middle-aged woman, hands on her hips, waiting for my answer. Her yellow bermuda shorts, bright and sunny, belied her disposition. Above the shorts, a t-shirt provided free advertising for a designer fashion house. VERSACE, her bosom screamed.

I gulped a breath, startled. Given more warning, I might have smiled and turned my palms upwards in a display of incomprehension. Instead I stumbled into a rushed reply.

'Yes, I speak English. Can I help you with something?'

'Which way to San Marco? We want to go to San Marco.' She pressed her eyes and mouth into three straight lines and tugged at her straw hat, pulling it downwards, helmet-style, over her brow.

I looked from the woman to her teenage daughter who stood nearby. She, too, wore a designer t-shirt, draped over jeans as tight as sausage skins. Long hair, licorice-stick straight, flicked her wrists as she held a mobile phone close to her face. She had no interest in going to San Marco. Twitter held greater appeal.

How on earth had the pair ended up in this cluster of alleyways? It was off the main thoroughfare of an area that was itself away from the usual tourist trail – the Venetian equivalent to the middle of nowhere. If they had set out with the intention of becoming lost, their success could not have been more spectacular.

'San Marco is on the other side of the Grand Canal,' I said, taking out my map and unfolding it square by square. 'This is us, up here in the left-hand corner, and ...' Across the map's full extent I traced a line '... San Marco, way over there on the lower right-hand edge of the page. It's more than a kilometre away.' I wanted to impress on her the scope of the challenge ahead.

Her eyebrows quirked in annoyance as she peered at the map. Then she looked up at me. *Glared* up at me. Total meltdown was just one snapped nerve away.

'No,' she said. 'No no. No.'

She spoke in the clipped, peremptory way of someone for whom English is a second language. Adamant and defiant, this was one thorny lady. She nodded in the direction of a man who was disappearing along the *calle* like he'd been shot from a cannon.

'I asked that man the way to San Marco. He said it was straight ahead.'

Ah. *Sempre diretto*. Straight ahead. The phrase carries two meanings in today's Venice. It may be a simple direction, or it may be a direction to simply get lost. Locals have grown weary of assisting the millions of tourists who flood their city. The expression derives from the city's long history of preserving its lagoon sanctuary and, like so much else in Venice, it's a mixture of legend and fact.

It goes like this.

In the year 810AD, the armed forces of Pepin, son of the mighty Holy Roman Emperor, Charlemagne, arrived on the mainland near Venice, intent on conquest and destruction. But the lands were empty and the farms deserted. The settlers, seeking safety from the coming onslaught, had decamped to the lagoon islands. No one remained but for one old woman, tending her fields.

'Which way to Venice?' Pepin demanded of her.

Raising a bent old finger, the woman pointed *away* from Venice, to a shallow and marshy part of the lagoon. '*Sempre diretto,*' she instructed the invaders.

And straight ahead charged Pepin's forces, only to become bogged in mud and ambushed by the Venetians.

So think twice when a Venetian tells you that your destination is straight ahead. In today's Venice, the invading forces come armed with selfie sticks rather than swords, but the intent behind the direction is unchanged. Get lost.

And I so wished she would. With a deep breath, I summoned up the most gracious response I could manage. 'It's probably best if you catch a vaporetto to San Marco. I can take you to the nearest stop.' The cut-off point in my willingness to help loomed close.

Mother VERSACE glowered from beneath her helmet, a protest forming on her lips. Then she thought better of it. Her mouth snapped shut and she wheeled about, ready to follow me. Daughter lifted her head from the mobile phone, blinked at her surroundings, then trailed along behind us.

We passed a moored gondola. With his oar pulled up beside him, the owner made the most of lengthening afternoon shadows, enjoying a nap. Not for much longer.

Mother looked back over her shoulder. 'That man in the canoe. He can row us to San Marco. You can come with us and share the cost.' She was off in an instant, zoning in on her target like a mini guided missile.

Now it was the gondolier's turn to be startled. He woke with a jolt and lurched upright. 'No, signora,' he said to Mother's strident demand. 'No, no.' He didn't want to go to San Marco any more than I did. But he hadn't reckoned on the determination of this little lost lady.

No. His voice lifted and reverberated from building walls. *No.* His arms wheeled, slicing the air beside his head. *No.* His shoulders rose to his ears in an I-don't-care-what-you-say shrug.

Mother stayed the course. What persistence the woman had. She wheedled. She cajoled. I watched on, transfixed. It was like the circus had come to town. Then she removed her hat, flapping it about to emphasise her resolve. Above her brow, helmet-hat and afternoon sweat had plastered her hair stiffly against her scalp. At the sides it poked outwards in frenzied tufts.

She reappeared at my side. 'He said no.'

She brushed off her hat and replaced it, covering the hairstyle from hell. Still no closer to San Marco. What now? Her eyes widened as a new thought entered her head. Hands fell from hips and her mouth stretched sideways, implying a meagre smile. 'We'll walk with you to San Marco, then,' she said.

I shook my head. I cleared my throat and prepared my best listen-to-me-carefully voice. 'I'm not going to San

Marco. I'm going in the opposite direction.' I spoke ve-ry slow-ly, to get the message across. Of all the places in Venice I wouldn't be going to, she'd picked *numero uno*.

She looked at me in disbelief, as though I'd arrived from another planet. Her mouth opened and closed a few times.

'Why aren't you going to San Marco? Everyone goes to San Marco.'

That's right. Everyone does go to San Marco. I'd spent a miserable few hours discovering exactly that. I was fully over this woman.

Now look here, lady. I'm not going to San Marco. Got that? I'm not going to San Marco because I have to queue for a one-way shuffle through the basilica with a thousand other people. I'm not going to San Marco because I don't like pigeons. I don't like crowds. I don't want to be dripped on by melting gelato. But most of all, most of all, *I'm not going to San Marco because it's full of people just like you.*

No, I didn't say that. Instead I took a steadying breath and forced myself to stay calm. But I did have to work my mouth a minute or two before the next words formed. 'I really think the vaporetto is the best way for you to get to San Marco.'

Mother pulled at her hat and gave me a final scowl. *What a waste of time you were. No help whatsoever.* Impatient to be on her way, she snapped an order over her shoulder at Daughter. She didn't discriminate when it came to awarding her bad temper. Everyone shared.

At last the pair turned and headed off. Daughter raised her phone to its position under her nose and pecked away at the keypad. Mother strutted out in front, like Pepin on his high-stepping horse, following the directions I'd given her. *Sempre diretto.*

✻

I walked into Campo San Giacomo dell'Orio, hidden in a spaghetti tangle of canals and dead-end *calli*. Finding it had been tricky, but not as hard as I'd imagined.

And worth the effort, I thought, sliding onto a tree-shaded bench. Bands of sunshine stretched across the *campo* to its ninth-century church. Its rebuilding over the next five hundred years saw the addition of two large columns to support its ship's-keel roof. The columns were plundered from Constantinople and brought to Venice by the fleet returning from the Fourth Crusade. That was Doge Dandolo's crusade, I remembered. I'd had a cuppa at his place this morning.

The fleet was a floating treasure trove of riches, looted without conscience following the Venetian conquest and destruction of Constantinople. The ruination of mighty Constantinople was truly a thirteenth-century version of shock and awe. Even Pope Innocent III thought it was all a bit off. Stealing from Muslim heathens was one thing, but sacking Christian Constantinople was quite another matter. He scolded the Venetians in the strongest possible terms, threatening a papal interdict (the prohibition of sacraments) against the entire city. Did the Venetians care? Not one bit.

Shade quivered around me and I leaned back, looking across the *campo* to where neighbours chatted and children played. Young boys raced after a soccer ball, oblivious to any heat save the heat of their contest. A dog broke loose from the cluster of gossiping adults and bounded after them. Fortune had smiled on him, and he wasn't about to miss his chance. Hind legs met back legs in leaps of pure joy as he joined the youngsters: no more watching from the sidelines, now he was part of the team. With his lead trailing behind, he played to be best-on-ground. A shouting, gesticulating woman chased after him.

Another dog sat nearby. She watched on with a sniffy dignity, her head shifting to and fro as she followed the action, held tethered by a jewel-studded collar and lead. I imaged her name would be Princess.

I glanced at her owner. A distinguished-looking man in his middle years, he sat at a cafe table, knuckles resting at his temples as he studied the pages of *Il Gazzettino*. The dog whimpered and folded her ears back, inviting a pat. *Il signor* obliged, reaching over to ruffle the ears back into their upright position. He didn't need to reach far. The dog sat on a cushioned chair pulled up alongside him. I guessed he preferred her company to that of an overly talkative spouse or a fractious child.

Church bells rang, a reminder of passing time. I stood to leave, looking again at the tucked-away *campo* where a woman chased a dog who chased young boys who chased a soccer ball. I thought of the soprano and the laughing children who mimicked her. I thought of Renato and Signor Natalino and a little shop on Fondamenta dei Mori. Away from San Marco there was another Venice, another world. A world like this one, where the last hours of a pleasant day could be savoured or the day's disappointing edges filed smooth.

This Venice called my name.

At the end of a *fondamenta*, across the next bridge, I could slip into the cocoon of local communities. Somewhere to come home to. A place where life moved at a slower pace; a balancing out of the frenetic activity of the Piazza. It was all at a piece with the warp and weft of Venice.

CHAPTER 9

MY OWN BACKYARD

A man without money is a corpse that walks.

Venetian proverb

I woke to the sound of morning explorers on the *fondamenta*, a drift of voices reaching in through open windows. Sunlight fell across my feet and the terracotta glow from a wall across the *campiello* slanted through the window with the promise of another hot day. I yawned and turned over, searching for a cooler spot on the pillow. It couldn't be time to get up, not already. My eyes fell on my watch: after nine o'clock. I lay a minute or two longer, listening to the screech of Dorsoduro's seagulls before I cranked myself up onto one elbow and launched upright to shuffle off along the hallway and start the day.

In the kitchen I opened the refrigerator door. An uninterrupted view of its white interior greeted me, as empty as if it were displayed on a showroom floor. Then I remembered. Last night I'd stopped for a bite at Downstairs and ordered a second glass of wine. Next thing I knew, continuing on to the supermarket was just too darn hard: a leisurely stroll over hot coals seemed a more attractive proposition. So I'd stayed put, shaded and cool and lulled by the hum of mingled voices. There's something soothing about listening to conversations without understanding the words being spoken, I'd thought, looking at the world through the bottom of my wineglass. Talk became pleasant background music.

Across the canal, the rooftop family and their dog sheltered beneath bougainvillea branches to enjoy the last of the day, just as they had on that first night when I'd watched them from this very spot as I tackled my mushroom risotto. Seeing them again, I felt the same reassurance as I had that first time: a trust in the future; a belief that whatever lay ahead would turn out for the best.

I'd had that belief when I retired. Plagued for months by a will-I-or-won't-I prevarication after returning to nursing twelve years earlier, I'd deferred my decision until a busy, understaffed Friday night shift at last convinced me it was game over. I woke the following afternoon with an image lodged cerebral centrestage: more of the same, not just for the coming night but for countless other nights stretching into a future only I could change. *That's it*, I'd thought, pouring a second cup of tea and watching Jake finish his Weet-Bix. *I'm done*. A five-minute conversation removed my name from the on-call roster and ended a forty-year career.

All I could think of was freedom.

With a delighted Jake beside me I'd driven to the beach. Jake stuck his head out the window and barked himself hoarse, his tongue flapping about like a length of red flannel. Don't tell me that dogs aren't aware of what's going on around them – and that holds true as much for a worried Italian dog on a train trip to Brescia as for a barking Australian dog on his way to the beach.

At Dog Beach, he'd dug a hole to settle alongside me and together we watched the sunset. An easterly started up, carrying the smell of barbecues and cut grass. It was the Saturday between Christmas and New Year, and I thought of that evening as a belated Christmas gift. And the start to lots of happy new years.

How satisfying, to leave behind something that had defined my life for so long. Knowing it had served a purpose, but that circumstances had changed and there would be no going back. Time had moved on and consigned some things to the past.

But pleasant reminiscing meant the fridge had remained empty. A trip to the supermarket would be today's first post-breakfast task, then a walk around the parts of Dorsoduro I still hadn't explored. Campo San Barnaba ranked top-of-the-list. It lay not far from Ponte dei Pugni, the one-time site of mass punch-ups between the fishermen Nicolotti and their cross-town rivals, the Castellani.

The bells of San Nicola da Tolentino clanged to life as I took up my canal-side position at Downstairs and watched the mid-morning bustle. Barge drivers pulled up alongside the *fondamente*, tossing coiled ropes over mooring poles. Rolls of insulation foil, glinting in the sun, joined open-slatted wooden crates to pass from one pair of hands to another, relayed across railings and onto the pavement. Bags of cement lay on the deck, stacked against the mixer and ready to be unloaded at the next stop.

So local. So everyday. So not *sestiere* San Marco.

Grazie, Venezia. I stretched my arms behind my head, enjoying the moment, then reached for a book tucked into the shopping buggy at my side. I'd always considered shopping buggies totally uncool, an accessory for the elderly, but in

Venice they made sense. How else to get the shopping home in this car-less city? Sebastiano kept one in the apartment, and towing it along marked me out as a local. At least that's what I told myself.

The sun's warmth fell on my shoulders and I settled down to the book. Donna Leon's *A Noble Radiance* had been among Sebastiano's collection of holiday reading material bequeathed to the apartment by departing guests. I leafed through the pages, noting the message scribbled on the cover sheet: *Sebastiano, you must read one of these books about your city.*

Millions worldwide have done just that. Ms Leon's fictional Venetian, Commissario Guido Brunetti, has been the subject of more than twenty best-selling novels. So famous has Guido become that a mini industry has sprung up around him, with tour companies offering a 'Brunetti's Venice' sightseeing package focused on his local haunts. By my reckoning, Guido lived in a fifth-floor apartment on Calle Lunga San Barnaba which adjoined Campo San Barnaba, the *campo* topping my must-see-today list.

The San Barnaba neighbourhood interested me for another reason, one pre-dating Guido by several centuries. I'd read about the Barnabotti, the noblemen–paupers who once called this district home. I could go there now, I thought. It was no more than a ten-minute walk away, a mini detour en route to the supermarket. Holidays allowed for diversions and distractions. I'd start with the Barnabotti's backyard, a little pocket of my own backyard, and delay domestic tasks for a while.

❀

They came from once-wealthy families, these Barnabotti, but by the mid-eighteenth century, the fortunes of many aristocratic Venetian families were sinking faster than a punctured gondola. The blood in their veins ran richer than the deposits into their bank accounts. No longer able to afford their swank addresses, they moved to less affluent neighbourhoods where rents were lower.

In and around the parish of San Barnaba – hence the term Barnabotti – they gathered, eking out a living from their dwindling incomes. Family possessions were sold off, piece by precious piece, to meet everyday expenses. Quite extraordinary, the dispersal of Venetian riches. Of all the moveable treasures in Venice at the beginning of the eighteenth century, it has been estimated that only four per cent remain in the city today. Napoleon, of course, must shoulder a fair share of responsibility for this state of affairs.

So. The Barnabotti. What were they to do? Their possessions were gone. They were forbidden to earn an income by running a shop or practising a craft. Impoverished or not they remained aristocrats, and the governing council deemed these occupations beneath the dignity of a nobleman.

The Barnabotti came up with an alternative money-spinner. They sold their council voting rights. While they might be sliding down the aristocratic totem pole, other nobles, rich and ambitious, were looking to fast track their rise to power. Extra voting rights allowed them to step up to the smaller councils, the inner sanctums of power. They were keen to purchase the Barnabotti votes. Everything in Venice had its price and its purpose.

But the Barnabotti couldn't take a trick. The final irony came when the Great Council insisted they wear silk, as befitted the nobility, never mind their inability to pay for such finery. Travellers to Venice often remarked on the incongruous sight of these shadowy figures, flitting around the *calli* of San Barnaba, clad in their tatty silk rags.

❉

I walked into Campo San Barnaba and looked around. Not a silk-clad pauper in sight.

The *campo* had a slightly dank, worn-around-the-edges feel. A musty, wet-cement smell hung in the air, and no trees studded the pavement, as they did at Campo San Giacomo dell'Orio and Campo Santa Margherita. Even so, cafes spilled across the paving, doing a brisk trade. Around the tables clumped smartly turned-out seniors and their equally well-groomed dogs. I'd need to make some changes, should I ever call Venice home. Even the dogs were better dressed than I was.

My eyes fixed on an empty seat and I picked my way between tables. A wiry little terrier, outfitted in a tartan collar and matching coat, nudged up to me as I sat down. *A coat? In this weather?* My eyes traced back along his lead, a silvery umbilical cord attaching him to his owner. The woman at the other end smiled.

'Is 'appy.' She nodded at the dog, then leaned forwards to pull a wrap over her shoulders before turning back to her friends. Venetians had a whole different understanding of heat, I thought, reaching down to rub the tartan back.

I'd found a seat just in time. A young man, possibly still in his teens, jumped onto the *campo*'s wellhead. He stood for a moment to steady himself, then tilted his body back, his feet somehow finding support on the well's curved surface. He took out a flute and played, sending music into the sunshine as he looked heavenward with a face as untroubled as a statue. At the end of his performance he moved between tables, seeking donations. Perhaps he hoped to further an education in music, or perhaps he hoped just to meet day-to-day needs. The women at the next table interrupted their talk, reaching into purses and fumbling for coins. *Grazie, grazie* flowed back and forth.

The dog-owner lady caught my eye and tapped her watch. 'Is 'ere most days. This time.'

I pushed back my chair, ready to leave. The dog twitched his eyebrows and gave me a puzzled look – *leaving so soon?* I wondered what his name was. MacDougall? Or Jock, perhaps? Scottie? That could work. I gave him a final pat before he waddled back to his owner.

Calle Lunga San Barnaba ran along the far side of the *campo*, carving a neat swathe through the neighbourhood and making it ideal for a stroll-and-explore. I checked my watch; just after 10.15. Plenty of time. Who hurries on holidays?

And that's when I spotted it. Seduction, lying right in my path. Whichever way I walked along the *calle*, I'd have to pass the Grom gelateria. I hesitated a moment, then decided: if there was a queue in the shop, I'd walk past. I looked through the windows. There was a queue. I didn't walk past. Yesterday's surge of good intentions surged right on past. Mango and pistachio this time, double scoop.

Dribbles of green and orange trickled down my fingers as I stood in the *calle*, focused on eating it before it melted. Next door a jewellery store displayed its own confections: gold and silver metal draped over scarves and gloves. I looked at a gold disc with clusters of oversized, pearl-like beads. Gorgeous. And its neighbour was keeping up with the

Joneses. A collection of grey wire rings in a reverse pyramid shape stretched from collarbone to mid-chest – a statement piece. *Buy me*, they whispered. This was a place to come back to when I had clean fingers. I caught my reflection in the shop window and smiled. Yesterday I'd gone shopping to stop myself from eating. Today eating was stopping me from shopping.

I licked the last icy sweetness from my fingers and wandered off along the *calle*. Shops offering all nature of merchandise dotted the bordering stone walls. *They can't exist by just selling to locals*, I thought, *tourists must reach this neighbourhood and shop in these shops*. But I preferred to imagine Guido in his living room five floors above me, feet on the sofa and relaxing after a day spent investigating the misdeeds of errant Venetians.

None of this was getting the grocery shopping done. I retraced my steps along the *calle* and then back through Campo San Barnaba. On the corner stood Signor Blum: a shop, not a bloke. How had I missed it before? Brightly coloured wooden toys lined shelves where Pinocchio reigned, his nose overlooking trains, jigsaw puzzles and building blocks. I went inside.

In the corner perched a parrot. Its colours of orange and green, red and yellow could rival any Australian bird. *And* they were the same mix of colours as an advertising print I had at home. I'd bought the print thirty-five years earlier in New York and it was an established part of my household. The parrot would fit right in. I leaned across for a better look.

'*Buon giorno, signora.*' The proprietor spoke in a soft voice. I knew I liked her, even before I turned around.

'*Buon giorno.* Love the parrot.'

The following smiles and nods established that I didn't speak Italian and she didn't speak English. But language limitations have never stopped a serious salesperson. She reached into a cupboard and emerged with other members of the flock, arranging them so different sizes and colours roosted along the counter.

'Hmm. No, *grazie*. I like that one best. I'll take her, *per favore*.' I nodded to Polly on the stand. Then a thought struck me. Just yesterday I'd turned up my nose at a pink and green cat. Today I was buying an orange and green parrot. Some people might see a certain inconsistency there.

Polly was settled into a nest of tissue paper, then an outer nest of bubble wrap before being passed to me.

'*Grazie mille*. Thank you,' I said, placing Polly into the shopping buggy.

The proprietor looked at me, doubt scribbled across her forehead. Did she wonder if Polly was going to a good home? She reached into the buggy's canvas depths and took out Polly, sitting her back on the counter. Speaking with a note of firmness, she nodded towards the shopping buggy. If I had to guess, she probably said: *Signora, I am Venetian. I, too, have one of those. And I know what you will put into it. Cartons of milk. Fish. Overripe tomatoes. Allora. Accidents happen. So let's keep everyone happy. You and me and the parrot.*

She dressed Polly in another layer of bubble-wrap clothing, then reached for a cardboard box. A new, safer nest. Doubts allayed, she placed the package back into the buggy. '*Arrivederci, signora*.'

What a kindly, helpful woman. I'd known I liked her, even before I turned around.

Next stop, supermarket. Definitely. As I'd planned. I trundled through Campo Santa Margherita, staying under the cover of restaurant awnings. Heat sluiced over me. I passed Chiesa di San Sebastiano, sitting on the far side of a canal and stopped, shading my eyes against the sun's glare.

Memories flooded back. I remembered the day last year when I'd set out to find this church and seen most of Dorsoduro before I did. At every corner I'd opened and closed the map, folding and refolding it like a piece of origami. Sunglasses had been swapped for reading glasses, then back to sunglasses. With steely resolve I'd paced the *fondamente* of western Dorsoduro until I looked up and saw San Sebastiano, Veronese's parish church and burial place, just over the next bridge. Now I passed the church every day on my morning walk. It had become known territory, as familiar as my own backyard.

I knew that behind San Sebastiano was Chiesa dell'Angelo Raffaele, the church at the centre of Salley Vickers' novel, *Miss Garnet's Angel*. Her book had joined others on my bedside table as pre-holiday groundwork, so I was keen to see it. The supermarket had waited this long, I decided, it could wait a little longer. The *thwack thwack* of buggy wheels against stone counted out my steps as I crossed the bridge and made for the church.

It was cool inside. I ran my hand along the back of a wooden pew and the scent of dust reached me. Sunlight flooded in through high windows and glowed on walls the colour of fading gardenias. Organ music whispered. *I'll remember the softness. The stillness, the peace.*

Above the side altar, a marble likeness of the Angel Raphael led Tobias by the hand while the little dog looked up from their feet. A series of paintings on the church's rear

wall depicted Tobias' journey under the protection of the
Angel Raphael. I didn't need to understand the complex
tale. To sit alone in that rich glow was enough.

I left the church and walked to the adjacent *campo*.
Paint blistered from walls and most windows remained
bare of flower-box gardens. A lizard basked on the *campo*'s
wellhead. I could picture Miss Garnet living here, imagined
character though she was. She would feel at home, sure of
her place, in this unassuming neighbourhood. It captured
the Venetian soul that delighted her – the Venice of
ordinary folk.

Midday came and went. I stood in a sliver of shade and
transferred the shopping buggy from one sweaty hand to the
other. Would it be better to stop for lunch now, before going
on to the supermarket? I couldn't stop for lunch *after* the
supermarket – this heat would melt everything before I got
to the orange at the bottom of my first spritz.

Across the canal, a row of umbrellas shaded tables where
napkins sat ready in wineglasses and bread sticks waited in
baskets. That settled things – it was no more than a brief
side excursion in a day already running behind schedule.

I picked up speed and made for the umbrellas, taking
a canal-side seat. The menu offered thirty-nine varieties
of pizza – enough, surely, even for Earl and Mrs Earl. No
torment of indecision faced me; I'd decided to try as many
as possible. So far I hadn't journeyed beyond number four.

I twisted to watch the comings and goings on the local
waterway. The canal suited its neighbourhood. It buzzed
with the activities of a lived-in locale, much as it had done
since the sixth century when it became home to a community
of poor fishermen. Dinghies weaved between delivery barges
before turning into smaller waterways where brackish, green

water wrinkled, barely moving. Miss Garnet would have approved my choice.

The pizza rustica arrived. I sliced into the crunchy dough and smelled the baked-apple aroma. How. Totally. Wonderful. Only yesterday I'd vowed off pizza and now here I was, sitting behind one, knife poised and ready to go. *But you're in Venice. You should eat pizza. You have a responsibility to eat pizza.* That little voice again: I heard it often, whispering from somewhere close to my heart.

I didn't argue. Dieting could wait until I got home.

Home. It was not something I wanted to think about. A change was underway; a change I could neither deny nor ignore. For the last fortnight I'd detached from my Perth life; the familiar, satisfying life I'd spent years constructing. It waited on hold while I stepped into something different – something I didn't want to end. With each day my time in Venice became more than just an interlude; a book read then abandoned, absorbing while it lasted but left behind without regret. I felt linked to the city in ways I hadn't expected and couldn't explain. Away from the tourist circuit, in neighbourhoods like this one, I enjoyed life's pace. The absence of cars slowed things, removed the rush factor. And Venetians seemed happy with the leisurely flow of events. Channelled into small *calli* with their fellow citizens, they were connected to one another, always ready to chat or call a greeting. I thought again of Miss Garnet. She'd found the same thing, and left her home in London to start a new life in Venice.

I caught the waiter's eye and signalled to pay the bill.

'*Arrivederci*, signora. You will be back?' His eyes held mine in a friendly grin.

'*Si, si.* I promise. And next time I'll try the casanova.'

I mean, why wouldn't you?

A breeze fanned the Giudecca Canal when I turned onto the Zattere, at last within sight of the Conad supermarket. I glanced across to Giudecca Island, where afternoon shade stretched over *fondamente* to touch the water's edge. Pulsing blue and silver lines danced on the canal, the light of a Venetian summer afternoon, and gulls soared overhead. Plan Venice included a trip to Giudecca at some stage, and right now a walk along those shaded *fondamente* appealed more than a sun-baked homeward trek pulling a load of groceries. And a little exercise after a lunch of doughy indulgence might not be a bad plan, either. *Allora*. Decision made, I boarded the next vaporetto with its prow pointing towards Giudecca.

Inside the cabin I spotted a seat next to a woman already lifting her bag from it. I inched towards it. The buggy followed, bumping knees and rolling over toes before I slid into the seat and pulled it inwards out of harm's way.

'You right there? Not much space, I know.'

The woman angled her knees to make more room. Her voice had a cheery ring and there could be no mistaking that accent. I turned to face an Australian woman of about my years, her face framed by a greying fluff of curls. A talkative Australian woman, as it turned out, as ready to chat as a Venetian in one of those small *calli*.

I think I would have started a conversation even if she had not. Some people just reach out to you.

By the time the vaporetto thumped against a platform ten minutes later, we had moved past introductions and the polite, hostess-type questions that are part of forming an acquaintance. Mary was running me through her morning at the Palazzo Ducale.

'All those tour groups, I'm telling you. Fascinating, though. If not for the crowds I'd rate it a ten.' She paused, and her laugh came as a sequin fizz. I fancied she laughed often. 'It's like I'm giving out gold stars, I know. Too many years in the classroom will do that. I only retired last year.'

'I'm retired, too,' I said. 'For me it's been a few years. And my sister is a teacher, although more an administrator these days.' I hesitated a moment, still feeling – as I first had with Dixie – the need to keep conversation at the safe level of one remove and not start along the path to incautious, tell-all chatter. Besides – unlike Dixie – I'd be farewelling Mary in just a few minutes. I went with the obvious.

'How long did you teach?'

'All my working life. And my husband, too.' She turned from me to gaze through the vaporetto window, laughter giving way to a long moment of silence. The slope of her shoulders hinted at some deep, unspoken regret. Then she spoke again, her voice even. 'He died not so long ago, following a heart attack. Too much stress, too little exercise. You know the story.'

'I'm so sorry for your loss.' I took shelter behind the customary platitude; an inadequate response for the pain I'd glimpsed in Mary's eyes. I imagined her husband as a kindly man, bespectacled and cleft-chinned, devoted to his work and his students. I imagined their home, filled with books and chatter and laughter. I imagined they loved each other.

The vaporetto's grating gears saved me from further comment as it slewed to a halt. Mary stood, hooked her bag over one shoulder and waited for a family group to pass. 'I'm getting off here. I thought I might walk to the Redentore. How about you?'

Right at that moment I knew I was going there, too. I followed Mary from the vaporetto and onto the shaded *fondamenta*, then set off towards the church. But now a problem. Pinned to the church door was an authoritative little note, handwritten on a scrap of torn paper. *Oggi la chiesa rimane chiuso.*

'Closed. Damn.' Mary pushed her glasses up her nose and frowned at the note. 'Someone needed the day off, I imagine. But we could walk along the *fondamenta*.' She nodded to our left. 'Along there, away from my hotel.'

Her suggestion matched my thinking. I took off my sun hat and raked a hand through my damp hair. Mary strode off at a brisk pace, indifferent to the heat. 'I'm a Queenslander. We're used to it.'

Chatting of this and that, we continued along the *fondamenta* until it came to an abrupt halt, blocked by a no-nonsense wall with no way through it and no way around it. Mary frowned again, this time in disapproval of Venetian town planning. She turned to look back along the *fondamenta* for the nearest vaporetto stop. 'I'd best head back to the hotel, I suppose.'

'Okaaay,' I said, wavering. I'd enjoyed Mary's company, brief though it was, and I cast around for a way to avoid saying goodbye. That's when I noticed a path leading off to the right. I pointed towards it.

'What about that? It might cut through to the lagoon. We could give it a go.'

Alright, I'll admit it. I'd become a detour junkie. Signor Natalino, Pablo, the largest private garden in Venice – they'd all waited at the end of an unplanned side trip. This morning's roundabout walk to the supermarket was further proof of the riches delivered by diversion. I'd found a parrot I couldn't live without. A church where a little boy and his dog followed an angel. A pizza that ticked the must-come-here-again box. So it goes without saying that I had no qualms leading Mary off along a no-account laneway and, as it turned out, straight into the gardens of the Hotel Cipriani.

'Oh, yes. Nice. And so like my garden at home,' Mary said.

We walked beside white climbing roses coaxed into symmetry on trellised walls. Colour coordinated begonias flowered beneath them, every leaf green and glossy, every bloom perfectly shaped. A bee crawled along, buzzing contentment. Ahead, lawns dotted with cushioned seats unfolded towards an orchard of pomegranate and apricot trees where a herb and vegetable garden thrived. To one side, cleverly placed grapevines concealed a hen house. The sight of this evening's dinner still pecking for its own dinner might offend the sensitivities of guests.

On we went, past more designer-inspired horticulture. Mauve hydrangea blooms set the background for vividly purple impatiens. Archways of yellow roses led to flowerbeds of pink roses. Would it never end? And then it did, at a portico entrance to the hotel. I looked at Mary. Mary looked at me. Then I pushed open the door and we walked into Europe's most sumptuous hotel.

I've made better entrances. Venetian humidity had turned my hair into a bloom of frizz, savagely indented by the crown of my sun hat in a personal adaptation of Mother VERSACE's ringed, sweaty hairdo. Aesthetic failings continued to a dress that had given up any claim to freshness hours ago and now clung where it should have hung, attaching itself in a damp hold to underlying body parts. Quite possibly I smelled.

And behind me, pulled along like a naughty child, was the shopping buggy. Its wheels whooshed over the marble-tiled floor. From his perch at the reception desk the concierge looked up, perhaps mistaking the sound for the arrival of a suitcase-trailing guest.

'*Buon giorno, signore.*' He cast a professional glance over us before turning back to his computer and clicking to the next screen. Mary and I exchanged conspiratorial smiles and continued through the interior and out to the terrace. No puzzled looks followed us across the foyer. Our ruffled appearance did not rate so much as a second glance.

'It's all a bit creepy, don't you think?' I said. 'Too perfect. Too quiet. Too *empty*.' We circled a table, unloading hats and bags onto its white-tablecloth surface. I patted my hair to settle it a bit, then sat down. 'We could be the last people left in Venice.'

Ahead stretched the lagoon, with the Lido blurring the horizon. A breeze carried the scent of honeysuckle. *Not bad, George and Amal*, I thought. A nice spot to be married.

'Sometimes I wish I *was* the last person left in Venice.' Mary's observation ended my wedding-venue appraisal. 'I never expected these crowds. Although my daughter Cathy did warn me. She and Marcus stayed here last year, on their way to Aberdeen.'

I remembered Aberdeen. Bleak and discouraging, with grey stone buildings and an overcast sky in both summer and winter. I'd been there years ago, visiting my husband's family.

'Why Aberdeen?' I asked Mary. I couldn't imagine anyone going there willingly.

She looked at me for a moment without speaking and I saw the same steady gaze I'd noticed on the vaporetto. For a chatty person, she sure knew how to use silence to advantage. Had she read my thoughts?

'The countryside is very pretty, though,' I offered. Just in case.

Mary spoke in one sharp burst. 'It was on the cards for months. I just hoped it wouldn't happen. Marc works in the oil industry, and they transferred to Aberdeen not long after Cliff died. I lost my husband and said goodbye to my only child in the space of six months.'

The words came without self-pity; a simple statement of fact. No hint of bitter resignation lingered in their aftermath. I felt a wash of admiration for Mary, for her strength and courage; her practical, straightforward nature. And for the optimism that underpinned so many of her remarks. I watched as she sifted through the contents of her bag, searching for her camera.

Mary stood and pointed her camera towards the Lido, speaking from behind the lens. 'Now I'm wondering if I really need to stay in Australia. Since I've retired, I mean.' *Click. Click.* 'This Aberdeen business is a sort of test run. To see how we all get on.'

She turned to the gardens of the Cini Foundation across the canal, repositioning her camera. *Click.* 'Their first baby is due in November. I guess I just don't like the idea of my grandchild – *grandchildren* – growing up on the other side of the world.' She laughed with the same bubbling energy I'd heard before. 'They'll wonder who the strange old lady is who keeps on coming to visit.'

My laughter joined hers. 'I've never had children, so I can't offer any insights on parenthood.' I stretched back in the chair and followed Mary's gaze across the canal, remembering my married days. 'I'd expected to have children, though. And my husband wanted a family. Quite a large one. But I found having a nice husband and living in a nice home was enough.'

Mary rejoined me at the table and I tacked off on another course. 'I remember a friend from years ago. She had a party each Mother's Day and invited everyone she knew who'd never had children. Her own mother used to fly over especially. A New Zealand lass, she was.'

'Ah, well,' said Mary, 'New Zealanders.'

We sat in the fragrance of honeysuckle and talked about children. About the batting order of the Australian cricket team and the best recipe for zucchini soup. Then we talked about meeting up the next day.

'I'm leaving tomorrow night,' Mary said, lifting her bag to her shoulder and taking a final look around. 'So it's my last chance to see things. I'd like to get out to Murano. And Burano, too, if there's time.'

Murano suited me. I wanted to revisit the island and to do so with Mary would be a definite plus. The likelihood of our paths crossing had been remote; the chances of an acquaintance more so. It had followed from no more than a greeting, a casual remark and an impromptu conversation. Even then, I could have farewelled Mary, wished her a happy stay and remained on the vaporetto when she left.

The serendipitous nature of life. I stood to follow her from the terrace. My stay in Venice was turning out differently from what I'd expected. Differently and better.

We recrossed the reception area. The concierge remained head bowed, transfixed by his computer. Silence followed us through the gardens and down the laneway.

Reaching the *fondamenta* was like walking back into life. Babies cruised in their strollers, pushed by parents or grandparents out for an afternoon stroll. Children raced past like scraps of paper blown by the wind. The Giudecca Canal sparkled and flashed, scattered shards of a broken mirror.

Near the Cipriani laneway was a cordoned-off section of pavement, all rather impressive with red velvet chairs and leafy plants. I'd noticed it before, when Mary and I followed the path into the hotel gardens. I'd assumed it belonged to the floating restaurant close by. But no, the roped off area was part of the Hotel Cipriani. Then came another surprise: the restaurant, too, belonged to the Cipriani. Both were as busy as the terrace and gardens had been empty.

Mary and I took seats, ready to order a spritz. Across the water Venice baked in afternoon sunshine, with the majestic dome of Santa Maria della Salute dominating a shimmering skyline. I could never think of Venice without thinking of the Salute. Baldassare Longhena designed his seventeenth-century masterpiece when he was just twenty-six years old, and a grateful city built it to thank the Virgin Mary for delivering Venice from the 1630s plague. The fact she allowed the plague in the first place and then only 'saved' Venice when fully one third of the population had succumbed was never mentioned. Those Renaissance Venetians were a mighty forgiving bunch, I thought, again feeling linked to the city and its stories.

'I totally don't get it,' I said now. 'Why come to Venice and then remove yourself so completely from it? Getting away from crowds, that I understand. But the Cipriani is in another bubble.'

Mary put her bag on an empty seat and fossicked for her sunglasses. 'I'd never stay at the Molino Stucky again.

It's been like travelling halfway around the world to get somewhere and then stopping just short of your destination. I bet other people feel the same way.' She nodded towards the tables around us. 'That's why everyone's out here and not inside.'

Then, as if to pick up her drink, she leaned forwards and bobbed her head to the right, indicating a table not far from where we sat. 'I'll bet you my weight in chocolate they're hotel guests,' she said through ventriloquist lips. 'And I bet they didn't get here on a vaporetto.'

I hadn't missed the eye-searing razzle-dazzle a few metres away. Two women lounged in chairs, relaxing after their retail workout, a flotilla of oversized shopping bags anchored beside them. They were well beyond full bloom, these ladies, with the petals starting to brown at the edges. But undeterred by age, or perhaps in defiance of it, both were dressed to make a head-turning statement. Sequins splashed over jackets. Lurex encased legs. I looked at my own crumpled dress and felt a grudging admiration.

The volume of their conversation guaranteed eavesdropping. Mary and I put our own chat on pause.

One woman drew her coffee cup towards her and sighed, the sound wrenched from her chest. 'I don't think marriage should be as common as it is, you know what I'm saying? It should be the exception rather than the rule. I mean, it's all well and good ...'

What followed was lost beneath the crash of bangles sliding down her arm as she raised the cup. A manicured hand, unconquered by the burden of gold jewellery it bore, hoisted it to her lips.

The second woman slipped deeper into her chair and sent two long streamers of smoke from her nostrils. She listened, watching the hand holding her cigarette as though it were a foreign object. Diamonds glared from her fingers.

'Oh, for Lord's sake.' She leaned towards her friend and spoke, holding the words behind her teeth and letting them escape through the thinnest possible opening of her jaw. 'Herbie snores. He's so old he snores even when he's awake. And he twitches.'

We learned about Herbie's sleeping habits. Flatulence was a problem, too, apparently. But was Herbie husband or pet? I couldn't be certain. The litany of complaints kept flying off in all directions.

I risked a glance at Mary. She raised her eyebrows so high that her forehead resembled corduroy. From behind her hand she whispered, 'They look like human disco balls.'

A chortle bubbled in my throat. The slide into cascades of breathless laughter was only seconds away. I shielded my mouth, ready.

Stop that right now.

Hey, what? That voice again. It could pop up anywhere. Last time I'd had a message was at lunchtime. *You have a responsibility to eat pizza.* I'd liked that. I didn't like this.

When did you become the arbiter of good taste? You've got a few mistakes hanging in the wardrobe, you know. Like that green and black miniskirt you insist on wearing. At your age? It should have gone in the Good Sammy bin years ago.

I only ever wear it with black tights. It's cool. Totally.

You reckon? And that senior citizen thing you're dragging around – we won't even go there.

My shopping buggy? What the—

Tell me something. The young woman you admired that time, walking along the Via Veneto in Rome. You remember the one? Hair swaying, hips swaying. Not seeking anyone's approval, you said. So what's different for these women? Is age the issue? I wonder what you'll be doing in your ninth decade. Sitting with a mate in a cafe across the water from Venice? You should be so lucky.

What could I say? I pressed my fingers against my lips and winked at Mary. Then I moved the shopping buggy closer to another table, like it wasn't mine.

'I'm so glad we met,' I said. 'And I'm looking forward to tomorrow.'

From the next table came a little laugh, marinated with scorn. A sigh followed.

'Fickle? *Fickle*, you say? That man put the word in the dictionary.'

❋

Coolness washed over me and my dress gave up its sticky grasp on legs and shoulders. The supermarket's air-conditioning murmured as I moved along the aisles, placing groceries into the shopping buggy. One way or another, I'd spent more time with it in a day than I'd spent with some of my closest friends in a month. I looked up and glimpsed the pink-gold light of sunset reflected on the canal outside.

A glimpse of water. Maybe sparkling, like now, or grey-green in evening shadow. Unexpected things, suddenly there. I could find a bridge leading to somewhere unknown, then lose it again as the city closed around me. Marcel Proust had best summed up things, I decided. 'It was very seldom that I did not, in the course of my wanderings, hit upon some strange and spacious piazza of which no guidebook, no tourist had ever told me,' he wrote. So it was for me.

My days were often dusted with a layer of the unforeseen. Days like today. I hadn't reckoned on a *campo* with a flautist and a multicoloured parrot. Or a church which told the story of an angel and a little boy and a dog. Most of all, I hadn't reckoned on a talkative Queenslander.

I left the supermarket and started homewards, passing Palazzo Ariani. Even on the brightest days it seemed forlorn. And more so now, in lengthening shadows. For me the palazzo mirrored the travails of its fifteenth-century owners, the wealthy land-owning Ariani family. I paused to look across the water and remember another story.

The family's tenure as high-flying Venetian aristocrats was cut short by an accusation of fraudulent bankruptcy and they were stripped of their noble status. For many years, and by all possible means, they tried to regain their patrician rank. But no luck. Even large sums of money promised to the Venetian Treasury were to no avail – a surprise for Signor Ariani, as enough money usually secured anything in Venice. Defeated and despairing, he eventually threw in the aristocratic towel. Marco Ariani abandoned Venice, his palazzo and his family. He moved to Ferrara and became a monk.

I continued along the *fondamenta* at a leisurely pace, enjoying the familiar sights of my neighbourhood. My patch. My backyard. No wonder contemporary authors set their stories here, in this *sestiere*. Dorsoduro had so many of its own stories to tell.

Children on scooters flashed along the *fondamenta*, past the wooden doors at number 2590. The garlic-and-onion fragrance of evening meals drifted from apartment windows. Tourists in motor launches returned to their cruise ship, taking sunset photos of bridges and half-hidden gardens. No one pointed a camera at number 2590. But if walls could talk …

… they would say this was where Veronica Franco founded her refuge.

With her days as Venice's premier courtesan drawing to a close, she established a home for prostitutes wishing to leave the industry. The home's chapel, Santa Maria del Soccorso, still stood at number 2590. I looked at those doors. Each morning I passed them, wondering if I would ever find them open.

Fragments of history, part of the everyday. History didn't form a design around the edges of Venice, a ruffle of interest at the margins. The past held its place in the present, the two as interwoven as the city's *calli* and canals.

Evening tightened around Dorsoduro. Doors blinked open, then blinked shut again. On Fondamenta del Gaffaro, Downstairs' staff worked around stragglers, packing chairs and furling umbrellas. The shutters of the bed and breakfast were closed for the night. I opened my street door and lifted the buggy onto the first step. It was the right choice, this apartment – a perfect fit for the holiday I'd planned and the Venice I'd hoped to find.

On the landing, I juggled out another key and slotted it into the lock. From the doorway I glimpsed *fondamente* and canals, darkening now, pin-pricked with lights. Windows stood open and a breeze puffed the curtains. Notes lay scattered over the dining table, and I watched a sheet of paper float downwards and skitter over the floor. I walked across the room, picked it up, then turned on lamp switches.

It felt like home.

CHAPTER 10

LAGUNA (II)

Fortune is like a cow: to some she shows her good side,
to others her backside.

Venetian proverb

The morning was cloudless perfection. I waited for Mary in the reception area of the Molino Stucky. Sunlight washed down from the atrium windows, warming my face as I gazed upwards. Metal poles, skeleton-like remnants of what once existed, supported heavy timbers that formed a ceiling two floors above. Industrial heritage met 21st-century chic in the flour mill turned five star.

Mary walked towards me, smiling as she glanced at her watch. 'Hi, Margaret. You're right on time. I'm just going to finalise my account before we leave. How about a coffee?' She pointed in the direction of the guest lounge.

Fine by me. I tip-tapped across the marble floor and, for the third time in as many days, settled into five-star comfort. Not that the Molino Stucky screamed its up-market status; far from it. Original brick walls remained, their curved architraves forming an unexpected geometry with the sharp lines of modern artwork. Understated furnishings complemented an air of restraint.

I turned as Mary slipped into the armchair opposite.

'I've just checked with reception,' she said. 'Today's going to be a scorcher.' Her dress puddled about her – a loose, teepee affair with a knee-skimming fringe. Queensland hot-weather gear, I imagined.

We sipped cappuccinos, the flow of our talk matching yesterday's easy pace. Half an hour later we walked outside to the *fondamenta*. Mary paused in front of a stone tablet set into the wall.

'It names the mill's employees who died in World War I. I like the way the hotel has retained original structures. It shows respect for the past.' She rested her lands on her hips and nodded approval.

I looked at the engraved names. I thought of the thousands of similar tributes around the world and of the cost war imposed: the loss of life, the sorrow of those remaining. I thought of families torn apart, and life never quite the same after as it was before. Then a thumping sound brought me back to the here and now as a vaporetto churned towards us. Sitting low in the water, it made no more than a puncture-mark impression on the city that formed its backdrop.

'Let's go outside,' I said as we boarded. 'This early, there may not be anyone on the back deck.'

We had it to ourselves. I settled my bag on an empty seat while Mary reached for her camera. Mary liked taking photos.

'Perfect,' she said. 'This doesn't happen often. Yesterday morning, on the Grand Canal ...' Her voice drifted as she repositioned the camera. 'I sat outside to get some shots. Everyone else had the same idea. It didn't matter that there were no seats left. People just stood there, determined to photograph every single palazzo.'

I laughed. 'That's happened to me, too. I've finish up photographing someone's waistline.' Or more interesting anatomical parts, I could have added, depending on the height and gender of the interloper. And all from alarmingly close range.

'Anyway,' I continued. 'Today it's the Cannaregio Canal. I want some photos of the Palazzo Labia, especially the facade on the canal. Now there's a palazzo with a tale to tell. I'd say—'

'Oh, I know the story.' Mary-the-history-teacher looked up from her camera, overtaking my student-style commentary. I guessed it was hard to change the habits of a lifetime just because you'd closed the door on the classroom.

'And I can promise you I'd never try that hard to make an impression,' she finished with a wink.

※

Venice was running out of money.

Waging wars and running an empire had taken its financial toll. Outgoings were mountainous and the income side of the ledger wasn't keeping up. Venice had prospered from its domination of Mediterranean trade but now international commerce was undergoing a seismic shift, with Atlantic Ocean trade routes carrying more traffic and generating far greater wealth than those of the Mediterranean. Venice declined as the hub of world trade. As the seventeenth century entered its early decades, Venetian Treasury coffers were in a sorry state.

But Venetians were a canny lot. They had survived for centuries by adapting to change and turning it to their advantage. Now they pulled another rabbit from the hat. They reopened the *Libro d'Oro (Book of Gold)*.

That was some trick. The book registered all the noble families of the Venetian Republic. From within its pages, and *only* from within its pages, were drawn the rulers of Venice. The *Libre d'Oro* had been slammed shut in 1297. *Finito*. End of story. Not registered, never rule.

But never say never. The Republic needed revenue. And so it was that new families, those prepared to pay exorbitant sums of money to the Venetian Treasury, could now have their names inscribed in the book's hallowed pages. They could buy blue blood and join the aristocracy. They could rule the Republic.

Enter the Lasbias family (Labia was their Italianised name), Spanish merchants who moved from their homeland to Avignon in France, and then on to Italy. They settled first in Florence before establishing themselves in Venice in the mid-seventeenth century. Their enormous wealth guaranteed some acceptance into Venetian society, but clan Lasbias wanted the peaks, not merely the foothills. Now the very pinnacle – the ruling aristocracy – was available. They seized their chance.

The parvenu Lasbias were among one hundred and sixty families who entered the aristocracy around this time (1646). Their payment to the Venetian state coffers was the sum of three hundred thousand ducats, about twelve million dollars in today's money. The usual price for admission to the *Libro d'Oro* was one third that amount. The Lasbias' extra payment was a donation to support the Venetian war against Crete; a generous gift and representative of the extravagant gestures for which the family became famous.

So. Now an aristocrat and ruler, Giovan Francesco Lasbias set about building a palazzo worthy of his position. He directed his fortune towards the construction of a building whose opulence would impress not just Venice but the whole world. Later family members shared this mindset, extending the already huge building and commissioning frescos by Giambattista Tiepolo, the must-have artist of the day and essential kit for the up-and-coming aristocrat. Nothing but the best for brand Lasbias.

Extravagant banquets were commonplace. Arrivistes among families who could trace their Venetian lineage back a thousand years, the Lasbias needed to make their mark. And so, at the end of each banquet, Signor Lasbias would stand on a balcony and throw all the gold and silver used during the festivities into the canal below. Spur-lash. Guests watched the performance open-mouthed. As you would.

'*L'abbia o non l'abbia, saro sempre Labia* (Whether I have them or not, I will always be a Lasbias),' he declared, hand raised to his heart.

Awestruck, his guests headed off home in their gondolas. *What a gesture! What a fortune the man must have!* They busied themselves with plans to spread the word about the city's new aristocrat. And in his opulent palazzo, the good Signor Lasbias was busy, too. He wasted no time dispatching servants to reel in nets hidden beneath the canal's surface and recover the tableware.

❊

The vaporetto thrummed along the Cannaregio Canal, passing Palazzo Labia. I focused my camera for a last shot, then pointed to the dozen or so balconies on the palazzo's facade.

'Which one do you think he used? A different one each time, maybe?' The activities of the rich were more fun to contemplate than the ordinary details of life.

Beside me, Mary bent down and slid her camera away. 'There was another fascinating owner, you know. Some mega-rich South American bloke. He bought the place as a derelict heap, two centuries after the Lasbias. Completely restored it. Gave parties and invited Sophia Loren.'

She settled into her seat with a smug expression. The tiniest poke of irritation took hold – Mary had one up on me. And after all my research. I weighed back in.

'It's impossible to get inside to see the frescos. I've asked at reception, but the ballroom is being renovated. *Seven years* it's been closed. Nothing happens quickly in Venice.'

I imagined Signor Natalino at my side, nodding agreement. Then I served up my ace. 'The palazzo is owned by Italian Radio Television. They plan to transform it into an exhibition space.'

'Hmm,' said Mary.

Advantage Mrs Cameron.

The wealthy South American was in fact Mexican–French Carlos de Beistegui, fabulously wealthy indeed, and intent on continuing the Lasbias tradition of party giving. He lived in the palazzo for many years and, when not partying, furnished it with eighteenth-century antiques and priceless art objects. None of which were thrown out the window.

The day warmed. Passengers crowded into the vaporetto's cabin. At each stop, the door to the back deck swung open and hopeful faces searched for an empty seat. I settled further into mine, putting its tenancy beyond doubt. On the opposite side of the canal, beyond the *fondamenta*, a collection of taller buildings clumped together.

Touching Mary's shoulder, I pointed. 'That could be the Ghetto, just over there. I've never seen it, but I'm pretty sure it's around here somewhere. And there are the tall buildings …'

Mary looked towards the *fondamenta*. 'It's still early and we've got all day to see Murano. What d'you reckon we get out and have a look?'

Anticipating my response, Mary was already on her feet and moving towards the cabin door. I rose to join her. A scuffle followed as other passengers rushed to claim our prize seats, bottoms lowered in readiness. Once inside the vaporetto's cabin, we angled first this way and then that, struggling to infiltrate the human blockade. Voices rose in a woven mass through air thick with the smell of moist bodies. My mind reached back to the schoolrooms of my childhood and hot summer afternoons, just after final bell.

From the vaporetto we walked along the *fondamenta* before turning into a narrow *calle*. I felt a distinct otherness, a stillness at odds with the surrounding bustle. I had no idea what to expect. Near the entrance to the Ghetto we stopped and looked up at another stone tablet. This was no Molino Stucky honour roll. Set into the wall of number 1131 was an inscription detailing the penalties – torture of assorted variety and death by hanging – for any Jew engaging in activities reserved for Christians. Despite the heat, I felt a chill creep down my back, and I had an inkling of how bleak life had been for citizens living on the margins of society.

Once inside the Ghetto, however, any sense of foreboding lifted. The area opened almost at once onto a large, sunlit *campo*. Mary and I stopped for a while, taking seats on a tree-shaded bench. Stretching my arms above my head, I looked upwards. Snatches of sky peeked through leaves, a mosaic of green and blue, shifting with the breeze. Morning sunshine hung like a warm blanket. Across the *campo* two men, black-coated and black-hatted, disappeared inside a shop bearing Hebrew signage. A laughing child ran from a doorway, dark locks flying as he scurried across the pavement.

I found it hard to conjure up the scene of cramped deprivation that had once existed. For centuries, Jews were confined to this area, guarded by Christian watchmen whose wages they were forced to pay. The location itself was ideal for segregation: a natural island, isolated by encircling canals and at some distance from the city's political and commercial heart. And to the location can be added a further distinction, one forever linked with ostracism.

Venice has the dubious honour of giving to the world the word *ghetto*. It derived from the Venetian word *getto*, an implement used in metal smelting, and the area in Cannaregio where the Ghetto was established had been the site of bronze foundries.

Set apart within the Ghetto, Jews could mix with other Venetians only during daylight hours, and then only to engage in certain restricted activities. Three occupations were open to Jewish participation: moneylending – in any case forbidden to Christians – trade in second-hand goods and, surprisingly, the practice of medicine. When they ventured outside the Ghetto, Jews were forced to wear red or yellow hats, allowing the Christian community to keep an eye on their movements. Jewish moneylending was essential and Jewish medical expertise valued, but Jews themselves were feared and disliked.

The laughing child returned, now clutching an ice cream. Melting chocolate dribbled over chubby fingers, spotting

the pavement. He pushed open an apartment door and I
glimpsed the shadowy dullness beyond. A slam, and the
door closed on the near-deserted *campo*.

I had to remind myself, sitting with Mary in this tranquil
setting, how different life had once been. The Ghetto's early
residents would not have passed their time resting on a bench
in dappled sunlight. They would not have looked from the
doors of their cramped buildings to watch a child running
across an empty space. At its peak in the mid-seventeenth
century, the Ghetto's tiny area housed five thousand people.

A city within a city, I thought, looking again around the
campo. But disadvantaged though they were, Venetian Jews
were still more fortunate than their fellows in other parts of
Europe. And so, in the centuries following the establishment
of the Ghetto in 1516, persecuted and exiled Jews from
across Europe sought refuge in Venice. Housing this influx
of new citizens proved impossible within the existing Ghetto,
and its area officially expanded in 1541 and again in 1633.

A tour group of a dozen or so walked from a nearby
synagogue into the *campo*, making it feel all at once cluttered.
I wished they would leave me in tree-shaded peace, and to
the quiet of my imaginings. Beside me, Mary twisted to look
at the Ghetto's mini-skyscrapers. 'Those buildings. Are they
still occupied, do you think?'

I lowered my sunglasses and followed her gaze towards
the buildings. Electric cables hung like decorations from the
walls and mildew-streaked window frames. The windows
themselves were closer together than in other Venetian
buildings. For good reason.

Over time, the Jewish population outgrew even the
expanded Ghetto. Venetian authorities refused to further
enlarge the area. Buildings could not spread outwards, so

Above: Me and Jenny on our Italian holiday in 2014.

Right: Venice in a picture: Sebastiano and his dog set off across the lagoon, with Santa Maria della Salute – an iconic seventeenth-century landmark – quietly magnificent in the background. The building's massive weight is supported by one million wooden pilings driven into the muddy soil beneath.

My beloved corner of Venice, from the windows of Sebastiano's apartment in Dorsoduro. The bridge and palazzo (top left) have provided the backdrop for many wedding photos.

Right: I couldn't resist capturing a memory of the *ristorante* in Campo Santa Margherita bearing my name, where Raoul, Monika and I ended our first day together. Below, in one of my favourite photos, you can see why they became my new best friends!

A Tale of Two Venices. Above: Window box flowers always spoke to me of quiet summertime in this city. Below: Typical gondola traffic in the canals and at the boarding area near San Marco. Not nearly the tranquil vista one imagines when they think of a romantic gondola ride!

On the island of Torcello, in the northern lagoon, the beautiful garden at Locanda Cipriani where Hemingway sat to write was inspirational for my own writing – I finished my novel in a nearby garden. Below is a gorgeous canal-side *ristorante* on the island.

Above: Laundry day in Castello!

Left: The man I met at the bus stop, Brian, and me at a restaurant near Campo Santa Margherita.

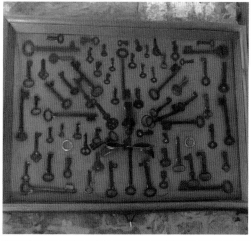

Above: The Casin dei Nobli is among Dorsoduro's best restaurants. In the seventeenth century it was a brothel, and the original chart detailing services and prices still hangs on the wall. Beside it are the keys used to lock women in their rooms each night. (Photos courtesy David Hannaford.)

Below: The Palazzo Loredan Vendramin Calergi, where Richard Wagner died in 1883, is now the Municipal Casino...

Above: Rossano and me at Ca' Leon after a concert.

Below: This photo of my friend Domenico (right) with Signor Natalino was taken during the visit when Antoinetta invited me to see her – and Tintoretto's former – home. A full-circle moment in so many ways.

they had to move upwards, and structures with as many as seven storeys resulted. A problem arose here. Building regulations stated that heights in the Ghetto could not be greater than one third above the rest of Venice. Storeys were therefore made as shallow as possible, low-ceilinged and cramped, to squeeze in the maximum number of levels.

Mary turned from the buildings to me, expecting an answer. A memory flash came to my rescue. I recalled that in Salley Vickers' novel, Miss Garnet had a young friend who lived in the Ghetto. Thank goodness for all that pre-trip, uni-grade research. No beating it.

'I imagine they are still occupied, yes. But probably not by Jewish people. Only about five hundred Jews live in Venice now, scattered across the different *sestieri*.' My gaze wandered back over the empty *campo*. 'It's hard to imagine how crowded it must have been,' I said, trying to do just that. 'Seventy shops and businesses once ringed this area.'

Poverty and deprivation continued for centuries. As late as the nineteenth century, Théophile Gautier described the Ghetto in his *Voyage en Italie* as this 'fetid and purulent district … [where] the alleyways got narrower and narrower, the houses rose like towers of Babel, hovels stacked one on top of another to reach for a little air and light above the darkness and filth'.

So here's a thought. As Signor Lasbias, newly and proudly registered in the *Book of Gold*, threw his tableware into the canal, was he aware of the suffering that existed within sight of his grand palazzo? Would he even have cared? Extremes of wealth and poverty were not unique to Venice, nor to this time in history. Perhaps my reaction had to do with the proximity of the one to the other. Or perhaps the sunny day emphasised the bleakness of Ghetto life in past centuries, and a sense of that lingered. Whatever the reason, I found it confronting.

❋

It was late morning by the time we reached Murano. Another stifling summer's day. More swarming *fondamente*. I recalibrated my mind from the Ghetto to the retail experience.

Murano's glassmakers attracted millions of tourists each year. Most of them had chosen today to visit, if the crowds bustling from one shop to the next were anything to go by. Although Murano glass was sold throughout Venice, the island remained *the* place to go, with its furnaces turning out more glass per square metre for the serious shopper. Furnaces were banned in Venice, and had been since 1292. An official decree moved the industry away from the crowded city, where the fire risk was high and the potential consequences disastrous. Murano prospered as a result. Its glassmakers gained a reputation as purveyors of superior glass goods, a worldwide pre-eminence that remained intact for more than seven centuries.

A useful thought to keep in mind, I reflected, as we strolled along, glancing into one shop window after another, all stocked with souvenir trinkets. Menageries of green and red glass animals pranced across shelves, vying for space with miniature gondolier figurines.

Mary scowled at the animals. 'Teeth curling stuff, that.'

I snuffled a laugh. 'But really, it's no joke. All these shops, stuffed with stuff. Most of it's no more made in Murano than I am.'

The Made in China revolution had hit town in a big way, forcing many artisan retailers, unable to compete with low-price imitations, to close their doors. I thought about it as we ambled along.

'It's not all bad news, though,' I said. 'Lots of people *do* still want the original, not the cheap imitation. I know I do. It's just I can't afford …'

We drew level with a jewellery store. Lozenges of threaded glass formed necklaces or dripped into stylish, look-at-me earrings. I pressed up against the window and tried out some mental arithmetic.

'Well, I might be able to afford a little something. Just this once.'

We opened the door and went inside.

'*Buon giorno, signore.*' The sales assistant greeted us, then bent over a collection of minuscule beads on the counter, her almond-shaped nails picking up this one, threading on that one. Her dress was standard-issue, sales-assistant black, but worn with authority. It inspired confidence. Made me ready to spend money.

I wandered for a few minutes, pausing too long in front of one display. The assistant snapped to attention. She whisked a necklace from its stand and held it not far from my nose. She draped it and twisted it and knotted it. She rearranged its half-dozen strands to lengthen and then shorten it. My resistance crumbled.

I turned to Mary. 'I could get a lot of use out of this.'

Oh yes, let's think practicality here. I let the assistant fasten it around my neck, always a mistake. *E presto.* From there it was but a short journey to the cash register.

Mary's turn followed. I watched the assistant slide one bangle after another onto her arm, deftly working them over her wrist and into position. Between thumb and elbow, Mary soon carried pretty much the shop's entire range. She rotated her arm to admire them, succumbing first to this and then to that *petit bijou*. A Lasbias on trainer-wheels.

Thirty minutes later, clutching our treasures and smiling our thanks, we backed out the door. The assistant returned to her beads on the counter. During the whole time we'd been in her shop, I realised, she hadn't spoken a single word of English. She hadn't needed to.

I gave a coming-to-my-senses laugh. 'Good grief. A major credit card blowout, that.'

'No fit of economy, please. If you don't plan to get wet, don't go to the beach.' Mary, ever-forthright, dipped into her stockpile of ready-made rationales and then, satisfied, lifted a hand to admire the red-berry cluster at her wrist.

We rejoined the crowds and turned into Fondamenta Manin. Shops lined the pavement and I pushed the credit card deeper into my purse. Secretly I hoped for more green and red menageries, places I could walk past without so much as a second glance. But no. Oh no.

There it was. *The* shop. Decorator goods proclaimed their authenticity in a spacious, gallery-like setting. Chandeliers dripped from the ceiling in elaborate icicles. Fragile wineglasses with the thinnest of stems stood to attention along a mirrored shelf, looking back at themselves with regal dignity. Here was glass with class.

'Let's go in,' Mary said.

Just when I was thinking it would be a good place to avoid. All that super-chic refinement: it made me feel hot and awkward and liable to knock stuff over. I wondered if I might break something merely by looking at it through the window. Mary's face took on a determined expression and she pushed the door open.

'It's not as though we have to buy anything,' she called back over her shoulder.

Arms fixed to my sides, I sidled in behind her. I leaned against the doorframe, preparing to stay there. Mary cruised the shop while I looked around. This was different from Retail Fendi: prices were up-front and obvious, placed like seating cards in front of important dinner guests. For safety reasons, I assumed, to avoid the need for customers to lift and look. *Oops. Oh dear. I had no idea it would be so heavy. Sorry.* I could almost hear the sound of smashing glass.

'What do you think of that?' Mary's voice reached my doorway station as she reappeared beneath a chandelier.

I looked at the prisms barely clearing her curls. But no, she didn't mean the chandelier. She nodded to a slender white vase, with contrasting black spirals winding from its base to overlap the rim. Delicate. Beautiful. The sign placed before it was adamant. NO PHOTOS ALLOWED.

'Protecting their designs from imitators,' Mary said. 'And over there; see the copyright insignia? Nothing Made in China here. This is a genuine Murano retailer.'

As if I'd been in any doubt.

By now object overload was setting in. It was time to recharge over lunch and a cold drink. At the end of our watery shopping mall a bridge led to a restaurant overlooking Murano's very own Grand Canal.

'Canal Grande di Murano,' I said. 'That's its actual name. I think someone got a bit carried away.' Nothing along the thin ribbon of water resembled the rows of palazzi, the 'chain of marble cliffs' as Proust described them, which lined Venice's Grand Canal. Here was the Lilliputian replica, the not-so-very Grand Canal.

We pulled out seats at a table on the restaurant's deck. A waiter arrived to take our orders, returning minutes later with a pitcher of iced tea. Mint peeked from between floating lemon slices and ice cubes clinked. He poured two glasses, then set the pitcher on the table between us. All at once, the Canal Grande di Murano looked a whole lot grander.

'And better prices than a restaurant on big-sister Grand Canal,' Mary said, replacing the drinks list on the table. The word price triggered an association and she frowned. Pulling her bag onto her lap, she rummaged for the hotel account and flicked through it, the occasional *tut-tut* sound of tongue against teeth reaching me across the table. She sipped her iced tea and frowned some more.

We settled into a comfortable silence. I brushed hair from my cheeks, tucking it behind my ears, then turned to gaze into the sunlight beyond the restaurant's deck. Mary settled into full, concerned-accountant mode, running her fingers through her hair and rubbing at her left temple, pushing aside her paperwork only when the waiter returned to slide plates onto the table.

Just a salad, we'd agreed, so we could enjoy a guilt-free evening meal. Between mouthfuls of rocket, Mary leaned her elbows on the table and sighed in a contemplative way. She glanced up to the cloudless sky. 'I'm well over crowds and shops. What I fancy is a l-o-n-g walk to the basilica. The heat doesn't worry me.'

A short time later we left the restaurant to walk to the Basilica Santi Maria e Donato. Sunshine beat down like a sheet of blazing metal and sweat glued my dress to my back as we tramped along deserted *fondamente*. It came as no surprise, then, to find just a scattering of people inside the basilica – a bonus, I thought. Fewer visitors meant we would have a better view of the floor mosaics for which the church was famous.

The church had a musty smell, but pleasant, like old apples and loam. We wandered, heads bent to the floor. Mary peered at the tiled image of an eagle carrying off a lamb, just to the right of her red-painted toenails.

'What's the meaning of this, d'you suppose?'

'That's not one I know,' I said. 'But I do know about this one.'

I crossed to the most famous mosaic, an image of two roosters carrying a pole between them. From the pole hung a fox.

'It's meant to represent the triumph of Christianity over paganism,' I said. 'Or, if you prefer, the fox may represent Cunning being defeated by Watchfulness. Which is a bit more interesting.' As with many things in Venetian history, numerous explanations were offered and there was no way of knowing which was correct. Or indeed if either were correct.

'I suppose they'd be something to look at if the sermon got boring,' Mary sniffed. 'As sermons so often do.'

One thing the congregation wouldn't be looking at were the bones of the dragon killed by San Donato. The dragon died, legend had it, when San Donato spat on him, and its relics were brought back to Venice from Catalonia, along with those of the saint. Unlikely stories about saints and their martyrdom abounded in Venice. Ditto holy relics. But this took the *torta*.

Displayed behind the high altar, but hidden by organ pipes from the congregation's view, were three bones, each a metre long. A nondescript lump, said to be part of the dragon's vertebrae, completed the exhibit.

'I wonder if the organ pipes were placed there deliberately, to hide the bones,' I said as we prepared to leave. 'Surely no one could take it seriously. The holy relics of a fantasy animal. I mean, really?'

We left the basilica and its improbable tenant and made our way back to the vaporetti platforms. No shade fell across our path. No breeze stirred. Curls encircled Mary's reddened face in solid, damp bubbles and pearls of sweat lined her upper lip. I trudged along beside her, wondering if I would ever feel cool again.

The heat of retail activity hadn't let up, either. Most people carried shopping bags, large or small, from grand or not-so-grand outlets. I carried several, too – little bags so delightful I knew I'd have trouble throwing them away. Nothing from the gallery on Fondamenta Manin, no. But nothing holding a Made in China impersonator, either.

✹

Hot. So hot. Back in Venice, we took refuge in the first restaurant we came across. The air-conditioning purred and I settled into my seat, letting cool air wash over me. Total bliss.

'*I Gesuiti* is just along there,' Mary said, referring to Chiesa di Santa Maria Assunta. She pointed to the *calle* we'd just walked down, leaning forwards to unstick her legs from the seat's upholstery. 'We could take a quick look. Seems silly not to, don't you think?'

Eight hours of sightseeing in blistering heat had not dented Mary's enthusiasm: if something was there, it needed to be seen. I'd always fancied myself an energetic sort of person, forever caught up with this or that activity, but I struggled to equal Mary's pace. It wasn't that I didn't want to see *I Gesuiti*, I just didn't want to see it right then. I'd settled on a rule during my time in Venice: no more than two church visits per day. Any more and my brain seized up.

'You've still got plenty of time in Venice,' Mary wheedled. 'My five days have gone just like that' – a snap of fingers – 'and I haven't seen half of what I meant to.'

She eyed me over her iced coffee, ready with the killer argument. 'I'd like to make it the last place I see in Venice' – heavy stress, meaningful pause – 'to round out a perfect day.'

Had I been a bloke, I swear I'd have felt the draught from fluttering eyelashes.

Crushed ice and chocolate gelato floated in my glass. I watched condensation trickle down the sides and onto a napkin folded beneath. Right then, and in all Venice, it was the thing I most wanted to look at. Closer to heaven than anything a church could offer up.

'Hmm. We've seen two churches already.' A gentle reproof. I felt as spent as a shrivelled balloon.

'You can't count that second one.' Mary's reply came in an instant. 'We barely put our heads inside the door.'

We'd made a brief excursion to see Murano's Chiesa di San Pietro Martire on our way back to the vaporetto. But that still counted, by my reckoning.

The waiter came by to check we hadn't melted into puddles of grease on the restaurant's upholstery. He overheard our conversation about *I Gesuiti*.

'Is very, very beautiful,' he assured us. 'Many people look. Is open now to six o'clock.'

Mary beamed at him. That settled things, apparently. The waiter smiled back, happy to have been of service.

I separated from the leather seat and followed Mary to the door, directing a black look at the smiling, in-house tour guide. *Unfair. Ve-ry unfair.*

Out of the divine cool and into the divine church. Once inside we stopped, gazing open-mouthed at the sea of white and grey-green that swirled around us. Columns proliferated on side altars and along the church's nave. The high altar was a gilded extravaganza, its dome supported by ten barley-twist columns. Hardly a square centimetre remained unadorned, covered entirely in damask-like fabric.

Except it wasn't fabric. An intricate mosaic pattern spread across the church – walls, columns, the lot. Even the decoration of the pulpit was mosaic work, crafted so the inlaid marble resembled heavy, draped folds. For unrelenting magnificence, this was the place to come. But not many had come. *I Gesuiti*'s distance from the city centre meant few visitors made the trip to eastern Cannaregio to see it. Few would be awed, as Mary and I were, by architect Domenico Rossi's use of Baroque excesses which somehow came together to form a cohesive whole.

'I'm thinking the word fabulous was coined for no reason other than to describe this church,' I said to Mary as we left, my arm slipping around her waist in a quick hug. 'I'm glad we saw it together.'

Truth to tell, I'd felt a connection to the church even before our visit. The link stretched back to my school days and our Year Eleven teacher, Sister Mary Loyola. On entering religious life she'd taken the name of Saint Ignatius Loyola who, in the sixteenth century, founded the Jesuit order. *I Gesuiti* was their church.

Sister Loyola and I had not always seen eye to eye and scoldings peppered my journey through Year Eleven. The

Jesuits were a touch quarrelsome, too. A spat with the governing council saw them expelled from Venice for fifty years, after siding with Rome in a dispute between Venice and the papacy. But the Jesuits had the last laugh when, some sixty year later, Pope Alexander VII negotiated their return to Venice. They built their church in a show of one-upmanship, a slap in the face to the city that had banished them. And it endured, long after Vatican–Venetian conflicts had passed into forgotten history.

I wondered what Sister Mary Loyola would make of the glorious church. As far as I knew, she had never ventured beyond Australia's shores. But Mary was speaking, and I brought my thoughts back to the present.

'I'm ready for a prosecco. We could sit on that deck over the lagoon.' She pointed to a restaurant at the end of the *calle* and set off towards it. *I Gesuiti*, tick; on to the next item. Unstoppable.

'Tomorrow I'll be in Aberdeen. It's raining there, Cathy said. I want to remember this warmth. This ... *snugness*.'

A north-of-the-border thing, I guessed. Queenslanders and heat.

We sat at a table near the platform's edge, looking back towards Murano. With a glass at my elbow and a meal ordered, I linked fingers above my head and stretched, contentment easing over me. Across the lagoon the setting sun threw shadows on Murano's buildings. Closer by, on the cemetery island of San Michele, the cypress trees took on a luminous green as the softer light of evening replaced the day's bright intensity. The changing light of Venice, the light that had captivated generations of painters.

'*Prego, signora.*' The waiter placed my meal on the table with the customary flourish. I'd settled on the classic

Venetian *baccala*, a simple dish of creamed codfish and polenta. I broke into it with my fork, releasing the pungent scent of sage. A melting flavour suggested the addition of a great deal of butter.

Across the table, Mary twisted tagliatelle onto her fork, stirring it through the roasted walnut sauce. A silence fell, punctuated by the clinking of cutlery against plates. Then: 'I think I'll go back to the hotel via San Marco.' Mary's tone was light, belying the fact that farewells were close. 'What about you? Fancy a detour?'

I drew a breath before answering. Mary's last view of Venice would be from a vaporetto moving across the Bacino and into the Giudecca Canal, with the sun casting the Salute into silhouette. It was Venice's premier sunset view and fitted with her wish to hold close everything she'd found wonderful about the city. But for me there would be other evenings, other sunsets. And you have to know when to say goodbye. A real goodbye, to someone you know you'll never see again.

'Hmm. No, I'm thinking Piazzale Roma and a walk to my apartment,' I said.

My gaze slid over Mary's shoulder. A flock of birds crossed the sky above San Michele, keeping a perfect triangular formation, as though connected by invisible wires. They swung around and caught the sun, turning silver.

I looked back to Mary. 'I've had a wonderful day. But bittersweet. Yesterday I met you, tonight I'm saying goodbye. It's something of a mixed blessing, don't you think, meeting people for a short time?' I thought of Raoul and Monika. Of Dixie.

Mary consulted the tablecloth, brushing out a crease. Those moments of silence – they said more than all her chatter. She looked up to answer. 'I've learned to accept things. As they are, and as they come along. I've had to. It's the way I've coped.'

From somewhere along the *fondamenta* an accordionist played to restaurant patrons; strung-out wisps of one song weaving into another. Mary tilted her head towards him. 'Right now is magic, whatever has gone before in my life. Or whatever may follow. And who's to say that because something lasts a short time it's of less value?'

We finished the main course. Like children resisting the dark that will cut short their games, we delayed our goodbyes. And now here was the waiter again, this time with the dessert menu. He placed it in the centre of the table, then gathered up empty plates and left Mary and I to our reflections. A moment's silence developed, and I guessed Mary was waiting for me to speak.

'This trip to Venice ...' I began, trying to gauge how much frankness to bring to the conversation. Yesterday's reluctance to set off along the path to intimate chitchat was at odds with the stories we'd shared since then. Along with the laughter and the talk, the shopping and the sightseeing, we'd talked of our away-from-Venice lives. Mary's openness had encouraged it, and it encouraged me now.

Another breath and I continued. 'Meeting people is easy enough, I've found. But forming some sort of connection, even a brief one, takes more of a ... what? ... *an outlay* than I'm used to.'

A gentle laugh flickered behind Mary's words. 'Then think of this as an oiling of the gears and do it again. You can never be certain what might follow. Chance doesn't initiate events, you know. It's how you respond to it that matters.'

Mary's greatest asset was her unwavering optimism, her belief that life would continue to offer up the unexpected and that the unexpected could be good. Her optimism was there in the hopeful tilt of her chin and her steady, bright gaze. It was there in her laughing interjections as she listened to me speak. *A middle-aged Dixie*, I thought, as a bubble of laughter rose in my throat.

'Oh yes, right. I could meet some bloke here in Venice and fall in love. An attack by aliens would be more likely.'

Mary smiled. 'You know the old saying: sometimes you can't see what's on the other side of the river until you're in the water and swimming towards it.'

I thought about that as we ate dessert. And it was true; I'd worn a groove for myself over the years and I couldn't help swinging back to it. *When I see a shell I feel it's my real home.* Sometimes I needed a nudge to move in a new direction. A young French couple stranded on my doorstep had managed it. So it could be done.

Colours changed. Golden glints on the lagoon dulled. Nearly sunset. Mary reached for her camera and took her last photos. Then it was time to go.

We hugged. Not the exuberant hug I'd shared with Dixie, but the embrace of two people who'd moved, if only for a short time, beyond the borders of casual acquaintance. A temporary friendship. I walked with Mary to her vaporetto platform, then watched her board and head to the back deck. A wave accompanied her farewell message.

'Safe travels, Mary,' I called over the water. 'Take care. Bye.' I turned back to my own platform, passing the patrolling musician. He dipped his head, acknowledging the coins I placed in the accordion case at his feet.

Be open to the accidental.

Mary's parting words lingered as I waited for my own vaporetto. I looked again at Murano, watching as evening shadows erased stretches of landscape. It would be late when I reached home, and sleep beckoned. But somehow I knew that when I woke tomorrow, I'd carry the thought with me. How could I forget this day of laughter and companionship, of images stitched piece by piece into a sparkling whole?

All from a chance conversation on a vaporetto.

CHAPTER 11

RAINING CATS …

Summer in Venice makes you believe that winter will
never come.

Venetians often said so. And I totally got it. I'd sweated so much and for so long that I thought I'd never again pull a sweater over my head. I thought back to my Murano day with Mary: an April-in-August morning that had become a sweat-dripping feat of endurance by lunchtime. Venetian trickery.

I couldn't imagine winter. Then from out of nowhere came a hint of Venetian winter, despite summer still having weeks to run.

I looked across Santa Croce's rooftops to a sky of thick, grey cloud. From her benchtop perch, Polly cast a bright eye over the gloomy outdoors. It was a day for staying close to home and under cover, which was fine by me. I had in mind a Guido Brunetti sort of morning, with a little investigative work of my own.

I'd read that before World War II, Venice had a population of 40 000 cats, one for every four of the city's human citizens.

That came as no surprise. During my trip to Venice thirty-five years earlier, I'd seen for myself the huge number of cats in the city. Wherever I wandered, there they were: stalking the *calli* with regal indifference, or sprawled across the wellheads of *campi*, raising a paw to lazily flick behind an ear.

Cats and gondolas: the twin icons of Venice.

So where had they gone? Dogs abounded, so to speak, but cats had vanished. I hadn't seen a single one. Not so much as a tail disappearing around a corner, or the telltale sprig of whiskers at the edge of an open door. *Il Comune's* tough public health regulations had waged war on *i ratti* and, with their nightly smorgasbord reduced, cat numbers declined. A few remaining felines could be found in Campo San Lorenzo, on the far side of the city, where they were fed by local citizens. But in Dorsoduro? Not a cat to be seen.

I had heard of one in my neighbourhood, though, and by the looks of things he might well be the only cat I saw during my stay. I planned to track him down. How many people could say they spent a cloudy day in Venice searching for a cat?

Even if he was long dead.

Thunder cracked a warning. I pushed the apartment door closed and headed off down the stairs, taking an umbrella from the rack on the landing. Those clouds meant business. And I meant to find that cat.

✵

In the nineteenth century, travellers visiting the Chiesa di Santa Maria Gloriosa dei Frari and the neighbouring Venetian Archives noticed one particular cat among the dozens roaming the area. An unremarkable tomcat, friendly and fluffy, but without feline attributes beyond that. His home was a cafe near the Frari church and every day he appeared, strutting the *campo* or lying on the bridge steps to sun himself, eyes slit in a self-satisfied smile. An ordinary cat doing ordinary cat things; an unlikely celebrity. But a certain star quality attached to this feline. Nini was his name, and so well known did he become that he developed a cult following. As his fame grew, people made pilgrimages to the district to see *him*, never mind the glorious Frari nearby.

Nini's superstar image was skilfully exploited by the cafe proprietor who, reaching new entrepreneurial heights, gave Nini his own visitors' book. Folk could pop by to see Nini and sign his book, then stay on for refreshments. Business boomed. A pope, a czar of Russia and an emperor of Ethiopia numbered among Nini's signatories. Composer Giuseppe Verdi scribbled a few notes of Act III of *La Traviata* in Nini's book.

Nini lived a long and pampered life. When he died at an unknown age, writers, artists and poets from around the world paid tribute. Their eulogies didn't pussyfoot around.

'A rare gem,' said one, 'most honest of creatures.'

'A gentleman,' said another, 'white of fur, affable with great and small.'

English scholar-historian Horatio Brown, tireless chronicler of all things Venetian, had passed many days in the Venetian Archives. From him came an obituary that ended:

> *What wit and learning died with you,*
> *What wisdom too!*
> *Take these poor verses feline cat,*
> *Indited by an Archive rat.*

It's a fair bet that no one mourned Nini's death more than the shrewd cafe owner. He commissioned a sculpture and memorial plaque to be placed on a wall of the cafe, assuring Nini's place in Venetian folklore.

❄

The rain had held off. I put my umbrella into my bag and looked at the cafes braceleting Campo dei Frari, then picked one at random and headed towards it. Frary's Cucina Mediterranea seemed about right as my starting point. Drawing closer, I peeked behind the potted rosemary bushes placed in the window and the unlikelihood of finding Nini in this cafe became clear. *Specialità Arabe e Greche,* a sign read, staking out the cafe's territorial claim in this pizza and pasta stronghold. Curious, I went inside.

The musky scent of spices greeted me, and trays of moussaka flowed along a workbench in a single, caloric wave. A woman stood behind them, head lowered over a slab of cheese and a grater. She looked up as I entered, a handful of cheese poised above the nearest tray.

'*Buon giorno.*' An underlay of gold glinted in her brown eyes, and a friendly voice matched her smile.

I felt encouraged. 'Er ... *buon giorno.*'

Now what? A tricky business, this; there are only so many ways of saying you're after a dead cat. I cleared my throat. 'I'm ... um. Well, yes. I'm looking for a statue. Of a cat. I think it's in one of the cafes around here.'

Nini found another admirer as I told the tale. The signorina's smile beamed on. I guessed she found this a change from taking cappuccino orders.

'A beautiful story.' She spoke in huskily accented English, as rich as the moussaka lining the counter. 'But Nini, I do not know him. Ask at Il Mercante, just along the canal. They are the oldest cafe in the area. They will know. And please, come back and tell me what you find.' She reached for the grater, still smiling. 'Or come back when you are tired of eating pizza.'

I walked the short distance to number 2564 and went inside. Behind the bar, a harried manager filled orders and barked instructions to waiters, all the while striving to convey a message of welcome. Lunchtime was approaching. The first drops of rain were falling and people had decided this might be the time to head indoors.

'*Buon giorno, signor,*' I said, risking a smile that wasn't returned.

His eyes flicked in my direction, then flicked back to the orders list. Black eyebrows pulled together in a frown. From the corners of his mouth, lines radiated like cat whiskers and I knew I'd found the place. With a deep breath I started the story again, my voice taking on the quality of someone repeating a fairytale.

The manager sighed and met my eyes for the first time. 'The plaque, the plaque. Everyone wants to see.'

His voice had a splintery edge, like something you wouldn't want to rub the wrong way. Far from being the first to ask about Nini, it seemed I was but one on a list. A long, bothersome list.

'Is gone last year,' he said, bending again to the order slips. 'New owner makes new plaque, with story of Nini. Was there.' A cursory head-tilt towards the far wall ended the conversation.

I followed the direction of his nod. A blackboard listing drinks had replaced Nini's sculpture and plaque. It told a different tale, and a good one. Cappuccino 2 euro. Prosecco 3.5 euro. Cat or no cat, I'd be coming here again.

But why rush off now? I could stay for a cappuccino – a prosecco, even, to celebrate. I'd found what I wanted. And it was lunchtime. Outside in the *campo*, umbrellas bloomed like multicoloured flowers and crowds clustered under awnings. The ambience inside Il Mercante became intimate as windows misted and the fragrance of toasted panini drifted from the kitchen. Bottles glowed from shelves behind the counter. Glasses tinkled, crockery clinked and voices murmured. An upright piano stood by the doorway, with a vacant table alongside. The last vacant table. I slipped behind it.

A waiter scurried over and took my order, then scurried away again. I looked around, noticing for the first time a narrow spiral staircase leading from the back of the cafe to a mezzanine level. Another waiter negotiated the climb, balancing two cappuccinos with casual expertise, and I remembered Sebastiano's effortless conversation as he carried my overweight suitcase up two levels to the apartment. Venetians did stairs well. Oh, yes.

'*Prego, signora.*' Panini and cappuccino clattered onto the table. The panini brimmed with mushrooms and prosciutto, barely contained within the crispy brown slices. I thought back to my first meal at Downstairs, the night I arrived in Venice, and the mushroom-risotto-with-no-mushrooms I'd ordered. A one-off misfortune, as it turned out. Most often, a Venetian dish promising mushrooms – or salmon or asparagus or squid – guaranteed a generous serve. Not for them a meagre few, artfully arranged to give the impression of plenty. No sprig of mint placed at a clever angle to make it all look pretty. The Venetian standard was simple food, unadorned, confident and delicious.

I finished my meal and sipped the last of my cappuccino. I hadn't entirely ruled out a prosecco. With the lunchtime rush over, the manager's amiability notched up a level, and waiters resumed their professional glide between tables. The cosiness of Il Mercante wrapped around me, warm and snug, pushing me deeper into my seat. Outside a grey drizzle persisted. Perhaps just one celebratory prosecco ... I'd put bad weather to good use: a search for a dead cat had turned up a hidden treasure. That's what I liked about Venice – surprises were part of the landscape; small pleasures that turned up as surely as waves on the beach.

Then the rain stopped, ending my excuse for staying.

'*Arrivederci, signora.*' The manager, now a smiling endorsement of Italian hospitality, nodded as I walked past him and outside to the *fondamenta*. A slot in the clouds let through narrow rays of sunlight, casting lean shadows at the heels of people crisscrossing the *campo*. Beyond the canal, splintered clouds outlined the stark grey walls of the Frari, still lingering on my to-visit list. Ahead stretched an afternoon without schedules or timetable, an uncharted ocean of time, and the church's main doors had reopened after the lunchtime break. The decision seemed already made.

I'd chosen the right time for my belated visit. Light beamed through the coloured-glass patterning of the windows as I walked through the church nave. Titian's painting *The Assumption of the Virgin* hung behind the main altar, imposing itself on the quiet vastness. I felt something like a cold trickle run down my spine. Nothing had prepared me for that moment, walking through light towards the brilliant reds and glowing sky of a painting I knew so well. Seeing it now, positioned where Titian had intended, I understood the faultless connection between it and the church. The painting owned its environment. It belonged nowhere but right here, in the Frari, behind the high altar.

Titian was buried fifty metres from his masterpiece. He died in 1576 as a result of the plague. Venice farewelled its greatest painter by permitting him a church burial – the only plague victim to receive that honour in the course of the outbreak.

Others of fame were also interred here. A plaque marked the burial place of composer Claudio Monteverdi who died in 1643. And who could miss sculptor Antonio Canova's mausoleum? His body was buried in 1822 at his birthplace, Possagno, but his heart was removed and placed in this giant, white-marble edifice. For the life of me I couldn't recall Canova's artistic achievements. All that cold whiteness made me think of ice cream.

So which gelateria today?

Outside again, I looked around the *campo*, my glance flicking back to Il Mercante. And there it was: the image of a cat emblazoned on the cafe awning – a large, red cat, tail curled neatly around its paws. I hadn't noticed before. It wasn't Nini's statue, it wasn't Nini's plaque, but it was close enough. As I see things, you have to hold on to any small triumph that comes your way.

A gelateria waited in a *calle* adjoining the *campo* – in Venice there was always one around. Unlike cats. I stood for a while in front of the metal tubs, wavering. As with the thirty-nine varieties of pizza, I was working my way through the possibilities. This time I settled on *fragola*; a modest, single scoop, so I could pretend to be doing the right thing.

By the time I'd crunched down to the last mouthful of cone, I was nearing the Scuola Grande di San Rocco. Unlike the Frari, I'd already visited the Scuola several times, unable to walk past. It was like my feet took over the decision-making and next thing I knew I'd be standing at the ticket office. Today was no different. An Englishwoman waited beside me in the queue, and we exchanged the customary pleasantries. Her hands clamped around a glossy, illustrated book that described the Scuola's collection of artwork.

'I saw Tintoretto's *Paradiso* yesterday,' she told me, referring to the immense work in the Palazzo Ducale. 'So of course this was the *scuola* I most wanted to see.'

'I admire your dedication,' I said, as she took her ticket and walked to the Scuola's ground floor. A few minutes later I followed her.

Nothing second rate, second fiddle here. So-o-o not Trades Hall. And yet *scuole* originated as something akin to medieval trade unions. The membership, or confraternity, might comprise a guild of craftsmen – jewellers, for example – or people whose forebears came from the same region. *Scuole* existed as charitable organisations, assisting members in times of hardship. Most confraternities were small, with modest administrative buildings, but a handful were prodigiously rich and powerful. These *scuole* used their headquarters to advertise their wealth, and they used their power to influence Venetian domestic and foreign policy. They attracted the title of Scuola Grande, and six still existed.

I wandered about the rooms of the Scuola, stopping in front of several favourite paintings. Twenty-five years – the better part of Tintoretto's artistic career – were spent decorating the Scuola with a total of sixty-one canvases. The woman I'd spoken to at the ticket office joined me from time to time and we exchanged remarks on this or that painting.

In front of *The Last Supper* I paused, moving to one side for a closer look.

'I've seen this painting several times,' I said to my semi-companion. 'So how could I have missed that?' I pointed to the lower edge of the painting, where a dog stretched up on hind legs, his front paws resting on a higher step as he inclined his head towards Christ.

'It's certainly different from the usual representation,' she agreed, before moving on, again immersed in her book.

I left the Scuola soon after, rejoining the *campo* to and fro. A busker sang from the steps of a church, working through a repertoire of songs about going home, staying home, being home and the errors of leaving home. *Do you know the way to San Jose?* he inquired now of his gelato-licking audience. Beside him lay his dog, a small, fluffy number. A nice touch, I thought, bound to encourage donations. The dog was plopped flat on his stomach, hind legs poking out behind him like pudgy chicken drumsticks. People walked past, looked down at the dog and smiled. The dog grinned back, placing one paw across the container of coins.

Other dogs led their owners on a late-afternoon *passeggiata*. Waiters flipped chalk-white cloths, crisp as cracker biscuits, over tabletops, and the homely smell of fresh ironing hung in the air. A woman tended her window garden, lowering a watering can's metal spout into the still-damp medley of pink and white flower faces. Friends chatted and exchanged greetings. The quiet, regular heartbeat of the city. The peace of my neighbourhood.

I ambled homewards, across a bridge and past Casa Torres, the twentieth-century 'artist's house' at the end of my *calle*. Heavy wooden studio doors and a high brick wall separated it from the street, and ivy hung like shreds of torn rigging through the courtyard railings. Most days I passed by without a second glance, but today I stopped. I stood on my toes, trying to glimpse the garden beyond the railings. But no luck. Leaves and vines formed a dense screen, ensuring privacy from passers-by on the *fondamenta*.

Okay, call me fanciful. Or say my imagination was working overtime. But as I struggled on tiptoe, my bag swinging from my shoulder, I swear I heard a faint meow.

CHAPTER 12

... AND DOGS

In Venice, it is the ambition of every dog to look as much like the Lion of St. Mark as the nature of the case will permit.

William Dean Howells, American novelist and Consul to Venice 1861–1866, in *Venetian Life*

I leaned against a doorway and looked across to Palazzo Contarini degli Scrigni. Could this be the palazzo that still used wax candles for its chandeliers, lighting them one by one from long, glowing tapers? One palazzo did that, I'd read, and it was somewhere in this neighbourhood. The atmosphere of flickering light and shadow was popular with cashed-up clients who wanted to mark their special occasion with something ... well, special.

Just imagine. Diamonds, pearls and a Versace gown ... drifting along the Grand Canal in a bridal gondola ... married by candlelight in a Venetian palazzo ... yes, it would be something to reflect on in the nursing home, alright. I stayed a while longer, thinking about weddings and the merit of sneakers over the heeled sandals I'd chosen for my day of walking. Then I headed off to the Gallerie dell'Accademia.

It was just after nine o'clock, but already crowds milled at the entrance. The Accademia was the most visited museum in Venice, chock-a-block with Venetian masterpieces from the fourteenth to the eighteenth centuries. Together with San Marco and the Palazzo Ducale, it rounded out the trifecta of must-see destinations in Venice.

I'd already done the tourist thing. This visit, my second, was to see just one painting. I wanted a closer look at art history's most controversial dog. It was upstairs in Room Six, I remembered, positioned away from the traffic flow in a sort of anteroom arrangement. The room itself might be overlooked, but once inside there was no chance of missing the painting. It covered an entire wall. So close inspection should be a straightforward business, you'd think. But not when it came to this particular painting.

Early start or not, the room was crowded with tour groups staking out their front-of-the-crowd territory. Solo visitors clutching well-thumbed guidebooks did the best they could, slotting into a vacant centimetre of space here and there. I stood behind a tour group and struggled to look over an undulating sea of heads as the guide mustered his charges into tight formation and called for attention, a slender finger indicating the painting. He spoke English overlaid with an accent of cultured Italian, a voice designed to instruct. I listened as he told the story of necessity being the mother of invention.

※

Paolo Caliari, called Veronese after his hometown of Verona, was a Venetian High Renaissance master, right up there with his contemporaries, Titian and Tintoretto. So it came as no surprise when Friar Andrea de' Buoni engaged Veronese to paint for the monastery refectory at the grandly Gothic Chiesa de Santi Giovanni e Paolo in Castello. Only the best would do. Across town at the Frari, Titian's *Assumption of the Virgin* had been installed to high acclaim. Was Venetian one-upmanship involved?

Quite possibly. In any event, Veronese set to work and in 1573 he delivered to the monks a large painting entitled *The Last Supper.* But blow me down, just three months later, Veronese was summoned by the Holy Office of the Inquisition to a please-explain. Oh dear, what could the matter be?

Simply this. The Inquisitors took exception to Veronese's depiction of the famous holy scene. Too little respect for the Gospel text, they said. Chief Inquisitor, Friar Aurelio Schellino, objected to the inclusion of 'buffoons, drunkards, Germans, dwarfs and similar indecencies'. He demanded that a dog, one of the indecencies, be replaced with the painted image of Mary Magdalene. *Pronto.*

Drunks and a dog, jesters with parrots – questionable taste, maybe. But Germans? What was the problem there?

It was this: Veronese's painting came at a time of uneasy religious reappraisal, with Protestantism spreading its unwelcome tentacles from Germany across Northern Europe, reaching even Catholic Italy. Venice, never a city known for its fervent Catholicism, might be vulnerable. So did the inclusion of soldiers in German armoury show Veronese's endorsement of Protestant Reformation ideals? The Inquisitors demanded an answer.

Veronese defended himself. 'We painters ... take the same licence that poets and jesters take ... If in a picture there is

215

some space to spare I adorn it with figures ... and that is why the odd figure too many has slipped in.' Veronese liked his painting and he didn't want to change it.

But the Inquisitors were adamant: change the painting or face the consequences. And the Holy Office of the Inquisition did not endorse lenient consequences. It favoured long-term imprisonment in damp dungeons with re-education sessions involving nasty metal gadgets. Or worse. There were dark hints about Veronese's possibly short future.

None of this appealed to the high-living Veronese. He liked his wife. He liked his mistress. He liked his painting, but ... rather than face a forced adjustment to his living arrangements, he came up with a compromise. It was so obvious, so easy after a little thought. And it cost him nothing, either financially or in terms of artistic endeavour. All parties were satisfied and could claim victory; a true win-win.

Veronese changed the name of the painting. *The Last Supper* became *Feast in the House of Levi*. The indecencies remained untouched and the dog retained its centrestage position. And when, five years later, Tintoretto's depiction of the same scene at the Scuola Grande di San Rocco included a dog, not a murmur of protest was heard.

So it must have been the Germans.

❋

The doors of the Accademia slid closed behind me. I retraced my steps, passing the palazzo and turning down a *fondamenta*. Walking was conducive to thinking. Candlelit chandeliers ... dogs ... so many Venetian paintings included dogs. They played and barked and grinned, sat on laps and lay across feet, or gazed up with interest at the humans overhead, as if following the conversation. Even Titian's venerated *Presentation of the Virgin* included a canine presence. Dogs were part of Venetian life.

One scampered past me now. A fluff-ball of activity, it ran onto the bridge and skidded to a halt, then looked back to its master, impatient for him to catch up. A lead joined the two, extended to its full length and taut as a clothesline. An elderly signor struggled to match the pace.

'*Buon giorno.*' The man dipped his head towards me, the words of a lengthier exchange forming on his lips. His steps slowed and he waggled a cautionary finger at the dog, then wheezed out a laugh as he turned back to me, all set for a chat.

The dog was having none of it. He flattened his ears against his head and gave a warning tug on the lead. A second tug. Then he turned forwards and kicked off with his sturdy hind legs.

'*Buon gio*—' I spoke to the man's back as he jerked onto the bridge and down the steps on its far side. A halo of sunlit canal framed his head as he disappeared into a *calle*.

Rather a shame, that. I wouldn't have minded a few words. Just a minute or two, perhaps; brief would be fine. Not since I'd farewelled Mary had I settled into a conversation of any length, and from time to time I wondered if I might have reached a turning point of some kind. I found I wanted people around me, people to talk to. Solo Venice was wonderful, yes, but it didn't tick all the boxes, not in the way I'd imagined it would during the holiday's planning phase.

I'd felt the same when Monika and Raoul left. Back in Perth, I'd taken a ringing telephone or a neighbourly, kerbside talk for granted, never realising the way these small things complemented my life. Sometimes, I admit, I resented their intrusion into my busy schedule. Now I acknowledged the value of these contacts and the lifeline they provided for many people.

So ... the morning was mild, the breeze cool. Church bells clanged and gulls circled in white puffs. There were worse things to be doing than wandering around Venice. My idea was to stroll through the area around San Trovaso, a residential neighbourhood of Dorsoduro, then walk across town to Madonna dell'Orto. The church I'd set out to visit the day I met Signor Natalino still waited on the to-do list.

Churches. And more churches. For a city always at arm's length from Rome and Catholicism, Venice sure had a lot of them. I thought Chiesa di San Trovaso might be worth a visit. Crossing a *campo*, I walked to the church and entered through one of its two main entrances.

So stark, and yet so full of the past. A sadness hung over the church, as though the enmity of past centuries lingered within its walls. I thought of its earliest congregations, the feuding Nicolotti and Castellani. The church's unfortunate geography placed it on the border of their designated territories. Rarely did they attend church together, and when circumstances demanded it – for a wedding, say – they entered and left through separate doors. The Nicolotti used the western door while the Castellani stuck with the southern door – two main entrances, and rivalry demanded they be of equal importance. Which left me wondering: which door did the bride and groom leave by? And what trust in wedded bliss would propel a couple down the aisle when such rivalry existed between their families?

Just one noteworthy painting adorned the church's sparse interior: a Tintoretto *Last Supper*. Sunlight played on the canvas and I had to look closely. But yes. There, to one side of a servant's foot and peeking out from behind a low table, crouched a dog. Tintoretto kept himself busy, alright, especially with this scene – his *Last Supper* canvases were scattered all over Venice.

The day warmed and my thoughts turned from painters and dogs to lunch and a sit-down, a chance to put some air back in the balloon. Lunch had become an almost-daily fixture on my Venice program. Eating alone at lunchtime felt more relaxed than a solo evening meal; daytime tables often held just a solitary diner or coffee drinker. I didn't feel, well, *obvious*, in the way a shy teenager might, if left standing alone at a party. Despite Mary's urging and the now-trendy belief that it's okay, even cool, to dine out alone at night – hinting, perhaps, of a career involving travel and a large expense account – I wasn't ready to stray that far from my comfort zone. Call me old-school. Imagine being solo in a candlelit restaurant full of whispering couples with romance on their minds. It hardly bore thinking about.

In Campo San Barnaba I took a seat at Ai Artisi, ready to order a spritz. I glanced across to the adjoining table where a waiter greeted an arriving customer. The man's face broke into a grin as he returned the greeting.

'*Ciao*, Angelo.' Even had he not addressed the waiter by name, there was something about the man's appearance that shouted Venetian. The casual, machismo bearing. The whiter-than-white shirt with designer logo, worn atop snug-fitting jeans faded to just the right shade. Sneakers that looked as if they were leaving a carpeted room for the first time. Bristly whiskers silvered his cheeks in a trendy day-old stubble, completing the fashion statement. What was it about Venetians that they always got the look just right?

The man glanced up and caught me watching him. His eyes twinkled a smile and he nodded. Embarrassed, I flicked my eyes to the table, pretending a sudden and deep interest in the pepper mill. A chat with an elderly signor walking his dog was one thing, a suave, younger man quite another. I wasn't ready to follow Mary's advice about jumping into rivers and swimming off towards distant banks. Sinking midstream concerned me.

'*Prego*.' With a plink of ice cubes the waiter placed a spritz on the table, followed a few minutes later with *buon appetito* to announce the arrival of my salad. Open-handed serves of smoked salmon and asparagus spread across rocket leaves and overlapped the plate's side. So-o-o unlike San Marco eateries which, I knew, were renowned for their skimpy serves and high prices.

I edged further beneath the umbrella as the shade moved. If I stayed for a cappuccino I'd be drinking it in full sun: it was a good time to leave and pick up on the day's program. From the next table, Signor Suave eyed me above a spritz and his mobile phone, rubbing two fingers across his forehead as if wondering about something. His eyes followed me as I gathered up my bag and walked inside to pay the bill. Passing him, I nodded: no *buon giorno* and just the faintest smile. In my mind's eye I saw Mary, throwing up her arms in a gesture of despair.

But it was a start, wasn't it?

I planned to cross the Grand Canal and then walk to Madonna dell'Orto. As ever, midday crowds jammed the vaporetto and I stood on the deck, wedged between bodies. The woman by my side lifted a gleaming black dachshund to her shoulder, out of the way of trampling feet and swaying suitcases. The dog quivered and snuggled into her neck.

Near the Palazzo Vendramin Calergi I left the vaporetto and looked over to a plaque on the palazzo's left wall, which honoured its most famous resident. His story went beyond a little mischief to one of turmoil and excess.

❋

German composer Richard Wagner first came to Venice in 1858. He returned many times over the next twenty-five years, claiming a love for the city's tranquillity. Tranquillity was a novel concept for Wagner. His domestic life in Zurich was in free-falling chaos. Wife Minna was crotchety. Some years older than Wagner, she was all too aware of her husband's appeal to women and doubted his fidelity. She craved a return to the independence of her former actress-lifestyle but alas, it could never be. Minna's youth and beauty had passed and the unfaithful Wagner was the best she could hope for.

Unhappy wife, unhappy life.

Other problems beset the Wagner household. Constant debt. The humiliation of relying on borrowed money. Times of desperate poverty when no benefactor could be found. Money and Wagner had never formed a happy duet. He'd fled Germany with an army of creditors hard on his heels, and now in Zurich things looked no brighter. Again and again he took risks to raise money, most ambitiously feigning a reciprocal homosexual attraction to Ludwig II, King of Bavaria. This, Wagner hoped, would secure the King's patronage and financial support.

Thank goodness there was Otto to fall back on. Wagner's mistress Mathilde was the much younger wife of a prosperous silk merchant, Otto Wesendonk. Quite remarkable, was Otto.

For years he remained Wagner's financial backstop, settling debts, funding three of Wagner's concerts and putting a roof over Minna and Wagner's heads. A cottage on his Zurich estate was placed at their lifetime disposal.

But having wife and mistress in close proximity proved bothersome. Life became 'a veritable hell', according to Wagner, and he decamped to Venice for a little tranquillity.

Poor he might be, but Wagner saw no need to reign in his extravagant tastes. Favouring a Grand Canal address, he rented the Palazzo Giustinian for a seven-month stay, then set about a few home improvements. He imported his own bed and grand piano from Zurich. He demanded that his landlord cover the palazzo's grey-washed walls with swathes of red velvet to accentuate the ceiling frescoes. 'My landlord, who is Austrian, was delighted to house such a famous name,' Wagner wrote to Minna. Restraint and modesty were never character traits associated with Wagner.

Wagner maintained his redecoration efforts put the outside world at a distance and fostered creativity. Perhaps they did. During his stay at Palazzo Giustinian, Wagner completed the first two acts of his opera, *Tristan und Isolde*. And it was during this time that he heard the haunting song of a late-night gondolier, the inspiration for the beginning of Act III.

But wouldn't you know it. Two years later Wagner was in Lucerne and broke. Otto shaped up as his best bet. Otto, however, made no promises; his business was in a financial tight-spot, he explained. Nonetheless, he and Mathilde were planning a pleasure trip to Venice a few months hence. Would Wagner care to join them?

Wagner tossed the dice and made his play. He borrowed the price of a fare to Venice, reasoning that Otto's business must surely recover in the intervening months, and that money would again flow. The gamble didn't come off. Otto was kindness itself, but his chequebook remained firmly closed. Otto's investment in Wagner had come to an end.

Fifteen years passed before Wagner saw Venice again. Now remarried, he and wife Cosima, the daughter of Franz Liszt, visited the city several times. Fortune had at last smiled on Wagner and money was no object. During his final Venetian stay, Wagner rented the entire *piano nobile* (the most spacious and best-appointed floor) of Palazzo Vendramin Calergi and installed his family with their large entourage of servants. But his health had been precarious for some time and five months later, ensconced in the palazzo, he died.

Some say Wagner made the conscious decision to die in Venice, believing the city would honour his passing more grandly than anywhere else in Europe. The Municipality of Venice obliged. A cortege, complete with full-sized symphony orchestra, floated along the Grand Canal and anchored in front of Palazzo Vendramin Calergi. As the orchestra played below, Europe's most famous singers stood on the palazzo's balcony and performed a tribute to the master. It was everything Wagner could have hoped for. Choosing to die in Venice – if that is indeed what he did – was one gamble that paid off.

An irony rounds out the tale of Wagner, the misbehaving risk-taker. The Palazzo Vendramin Calergi, where he died, is also linked to chance. It now houses the Municipal Casino of Venice.

❋

I walked towards Rio Tera' Farsetti, my getaway path from this crowded part of town. Madonna dell'Orto lay on the last of three *fondamente* in northern Cannaregio, making it one of the most distant of Venice's great churches. *Orto* means garden in Italian, and this area was once cultivated with vines and olive trees. Titian had lived here, and his extensive gardens reached down to the lagoon's edge.

Poor seafarers also inhabited the area and, at the time of its foundation, the church was named for Saint Christopher, the patron saint of voyagers. Then a statue of the Madonna in a nearby garden began working miracles and glowing at night: a gift fallen straight from heaven, believers vowed. Delighted church officials purchased the statue from its owner, one Giovanni de' Santi (who had in fact sculpted the statue), with a hefty sum of money and the promise of a daily mass to be said in his honour. Saint Chris' time was up. The church was renamed Madonna dell'Orto and the statue moved there in the late fourteenth century.

The fame of Madonna dell'Orto will forever be its link with Tintoretto. This was his parish church and his burial place. His *Presentation of the Virgin* hung near his tomb, to the right of the main altar, and I slipped into a pew to scrutinise it. While similar to Titian's representation, the signature colour and angular placement of the staircase marked it out as Tintoretto's work. I felt a pinprick of disappointment, though, looking at the painting I'd waited so long to see. Nowhere, *nowhere*, on the huge canvas was there any sign of a dog.

An hour later I left the church, stepping out into a mild afternoon. Rather than catch a vaporetto, I decided to retrace my steps through Cannaregio. Post-lunch shoppers crammed its *calli*, crisscrossing my path with noisy enthusiasm as they drew up to this or that window display to assess the merchandise on offer. Logo-emblazoned bags swung from most elbows.

I'd never been a fan of recreational retail: hard on the feet and a drain on the wallet, I'd always thought. No more than a tramp from one shop to the next, belonging in the same fun category as dusting off the dried flowers. Why some people enjoyed it was beyond me. I'd clean windows, unblock gutters or climb on the roof to fix ridge capping rather than spend a day at the shops.

Then I went to Italy.

An afternoon on Via Condotti, near Rome's Spanish Steps, changed my thinking. Brigades of Beautiful People, old and young, strolled the up-market street, dedicated to the project of choosing just the right pen or handbag or scarf. It wasn't about excess, about flaunting wealth with multiple purchases from the pricey boutiques. One item sufficed. Shopping became an event – an afternoon *passeggiata* thinly disguised with a sense of purpose. Shopping provided the reason to be out there, looking perfect on a perfect day and in a perfect setting.

I loved the *specialness* of it all. And when in Rome, as they say ... John and I had joined *la passeggiata*-shoppers to ponder and deliberate; we lifted, we looked, we compared. Sales assistants played along. Was this handbag the right match for a particular outfit? Did the stripe on my husband's tie sit at just the right angle? Chins were rubbed in contemplation and brows furrowed in concern, prompting return trips to the display cabinets. And later, as we sat in El Greco enjoying a gelato with our shopping treasures propped before us on the marble-topped table, I totally got it. Shopping could be fun.

I'd had hopes for a Via Condotti experience in Venice. The Mercerie had disappointed in a big way, failing to measure up to either Rome or to its own former charm. Tramping along those crowded streets I regretted my return visit. Better to just remember. *Com'era e dov'era.*

A visit to the fishing island of Burano, famous for its coloured houses and skilled lace-makers, proved no better. Legend held that each house was painted a different, bright colour to guide fishermen through the lagoon's heavy mists to their homes, where lace-making wives stitched away the hours awaiting their return.

The story belonged to a time when Burano flew below the visitor radar. The houses remained; cute as a button, prettied up for tourists' Instagram snaps. Lace-making, once carried out in front parlours and around kitchen tables, had turned big business, attracting shoppers in their thousands, and most often it was cheap, imported products that lined vendors' shelves. For me, the small artisan studios of Dorsoduro and San Polo offered the best chance of retail therapy: the kind of shopping when you leave the store feeling better than when you walked in.

No doubt about it, I was out of synch with 21st-century consumerism.

Despite the pleasant day, walking the shadeless *fondamente* from Madonna dell'Orto to Cannaregio had proved hot work. My face glowed and a blister rubbed. I ran a hand inside my collar, loosening it, and felt hair clumped into damp spikes at the back of my neck. A glass of lovely, icy prosecco would be just the ticket, I thought, and straight away I could taste its tight, sharp bubbles fizzing on my tongue. I'd said I wouldn't indulge but that was this morning. When I was cool.

My eyes lit on a *ristorante* where a waiter stood by the doorway and window boxes held geraniums in full flower. I felt an immediate connection – the scarlet blooms matched the colour of my face. *Air-conditioned*, announced a sign in the window, visible as I drew closer. That settled the matter, and the afternoon's program veered off in a new direction.

The waiter opened the door and led me to the coolest table. His dark eyes flashed with understanding as he pulled out a chair. 'I live now in Mestre,' he said. 'But I am from Pakistan. There it is very hot.'

I settled into the seat and jiggled my sandals loose, then began searching my bag for a bandaid. I found one, scrunched and damp but still fit for purpose. As I bent to paste it over today's new blister, my glance fell beneath an empty table. There sat a dog, holding a biscuit between his front paws as if he feared its escape. He looked up at me and yawned, then ambled over and sniffed my toes in an appreciative way. Biscuit forgotten, he slumped to the floor near my feet and dropped off to sleep, quite at home.

The waiter reappeared with my prosecco, moving aside cutlery to place it within easy reach. He knew a thirsty customer when he saw one. Then he nodded in the direction of the sleeping dog. 'Fritz is our house dog. He is a French bulldog.'

A French bulldog, named Fritz, watched over by a former Pakistani in a Venetian restaurant?

It spoke of Venice itself. For longer than a millennium, visitors from all corners of the globe had walked the city's *calli* and *fondamente*, and every language had reverberated from its walls. Different reasons brought people to Venice.

In its palazzi, operas had been composed, books written and life's big questions pondered. Travellers had arrived in Venice seeking inspiration or consolation, sometimes both. Now, as a glamour destination, the city had few rivals. Its appeal defied the twenty-first century. Gondolas carried brides along the Grand Canal and chandeliers were lit by candles.

The prosecco bubbled from glass to lips as Fritz and I settled in. The afternoon could take care of itself, pretty much. A thought reached me, as if on relay: was I being unjustly critical? So much was different from what I remembered. So much was not what I'd set out to find. The places I'd loved had changed and would change further. And not just in Venice. I thought of Darwin, the frontier outpost that once offered so many adventures, now a modern city, indistinguishable from many others. The islands of the Great Barrier Reef, where I'd swum and snorkelled in solitude, now sprouting busy resorts. And Perth, my hometown; sleepy hollow turned boom town. Of course nothing could remain the same, preserved forever in the aspic of the past. It's just that for me the past had been so very, very good.

I moved aside Fritz's tail and pulled the guidebook from my bag. Accademia. Done. Madonna dell'Orto. Done. Palazzo Vendramin Calergi ... my guidebook assured me the *piano nobile* had changed little since Wagner's day. The chair occupied by Wagner at the time of his death could still be seen. Sat in, even, should you wish.

But I'd made a mistake. The candlelit palazzo was not Palazzo Contarini degli Scrigni. No, it was in fact Palazzo Pisani Morosini, on the opposite side of the Grand Canal. I wondered: was it from this palazzo that Marina Morosini was sent to the convent of Santa Maria degli Angeli, on the island of Murano? As a nun, she later became the lover of Giacomo Casanova, identified in his memoirs only by the initials MM. Yet another tale from Venice's rich storybook ... I closed the guidebook and turned my attention to the prosecco.

Fritz's wet nose nuzzled against my toes. He started to snore.

CHAPTER 13

I MET HIM AT THE BUS STOP

Right from the water's edge rose long lines of stately palaces ... clad half in moonbeams and half in mysterious shadows ...

Mark Twain, American writer, in *The Innocents Abroad*

'So shall I give him your number or not?' Impatience looped through Trish's words, and the drum of her fingers on a tabletop travelled down the phone line. I imagined her holding a frown in check. Trish was not the sort of person to dither over such matters.

'I don't understand,' she said. 'Where's the problem?'

I rubbed a hand over my forehead and let the phone slip until I held it by the earpiece. Thinking, thinking. My eyes followed Karla Marx as she circled her empty food bowl, whiskers dotted with milk drops. She flicked her head in a dainty cat sneeze and looked up at me, also awaiting a response. It was Sunday morning and I'd just poured my first cup of tea. I sank into a chair and propped my elbows on the kitchen table.

'Who did you say he was again?'

'Gavin.' Trish spoke with the air of someone explaining everything in a single word. 'Pleasant chap. Wearing a pink shirt. You must remember him.'

I put the previous evening on mental rewind and came up blank. Frontal lobe shrinkage, no doubt; at a certain age it was inevitable. Blurred faces and snippets of conversation were the best I could manage. *Daffodil bulbs should always be planted before Anzac Day,* I'd instructed someone's teenage son, prompting an anxious smile and his hasty retreat to the far side of the room. I knew I'd talked a lot. I knew I'd enjoyed myself. But that was about it. And now here was this Gavin fellow it seemed I should remember.

'Hmm. I might be able to place him if I spoke to him again. I mean, I think I could. Possibly.'

I looked into space, assessing the chances of remembering Gavin. Karla Marx looked at me, assessing the chances of more food. The outlook didn't seem positive for either of us.

A moment longer, then I decided. 'Oh, go on, then. Give him my number. And thanks for last night. Great party. I'll let you know what happens with … uh, Gavin.'

I hung up and leaned back in the chair. Sunshine crept over the kitchen floor and Karla Marx took up her morning position, asleep on the warming tiles. I glanced to the other end of the table, where the last essay for the term, finished and ready to be handed in, sat under a pile of overdue books. Ahead lay an uninterrupted Sunday, with nothing planned until an evening walk through Kings Park.

'Aaah,' I said, in one long, all's-well-with-the-world sigh.

The phone rang again. Karla Marx woke and slitted her eyes towards it with a look of distrust. It was Gavin.

'Hello? Margaret?'

Nice voice, I thought, deep, finely grained. Encouraging. Off to a good start, at least.

Things seemed on the up-and-up as we worked our way through greetings and morning-after-the-party reflections. It had been fun, we agreed. How long had I known Trish, Gavin then wanted to know, and where did we meet? One thing led to another and before long we were chatting away like old mates. I poured a second cup of tea and spread Vegemite on a slice of toast. This Gavin was okay.

'I liked your joke about the nine-legged spider,' he chuckled.

I told that joke? I thought it was someone else. I took a bite of toast, surprised, but not to the point where alarm bells were called into pealing service. It wouldn't be the first time I'd said something then forgotten it in a storm of chatter. And the conversation was going so well, it seemed a shame to derail it with a small detail. Gavin's voice sounded better the longer I listened. I munched on as he continued.

'So. I've got tickets for a performance at the Subiaco Theatre Centre next Saturday. Would you care to join me?'

I liked his choice of venue for a first date. Much better than somewhere involving food and wine and good behaviour. Far preferable to an evening spent looking at someone across a narrow table, thinking up something witty or profound to say, all the time wondering if my lipstick had been reduced to a tired, jagged outline. And in unflattering light. Oh yes, I was beginning to have very positive vibes about forgotten Gavin.

'That's close to my home,' I said, after what I hoped was a gracious acceptance. 'We could even walk there if the weather's good. Parking can be tricky on weekends.'

'But I thought you lived in Nedlands.'

Still the alarm bells remained silent. I'd lived in Nedlands before moving to Subiaco, so perhaps I'd mentioned it in this conversation I didn't remember. Nine-legged spiders and suburban addresses were not my strong point on a Sunday morning. A return to sleep beckoned, right after this cup of tea.

'No. In Subiaco. Heytesbury Road.' I spelt it out, enunciating each letter, and then gave the street number. Twice. Not for want of a clear address would I miss my date with Gavin-in-the-pink-shirt.

'See you around seven, then.' I hung up and smiled into the sunshine. I believe I may have hummed a little. Karla Marx yawned.

Gavin presented himself next Saturday evening. With an intake of breath I answered the doorbell and opened the front door. There stood a man of about my age, with reddish hair cut close to his head. Wire-framed glasses gave him a professorial look, as though he spent a lot of time in the company of books and had notched up more degrees than a thermometer. A trimmed beard surrounded a mouthful of teeth that had not fared well. Remember him? I'd never seen him before in my life.

'Margaret?' he said, with barely disguised bafflement.

'Gavin?' I said, with barely disguised disappointment.

We made the best of things and went on our theatre date. And as I sat next to the man in the pink shirt – he'd worn it again that evening, or perhaps he had a whole wardrobe of them – I pieced together the scenes of our own drama.

I blamed my parents. Coming from a generation which revered the British monarchy, they had, like so many others, named their daughters Margaret or Anne or Elizabeth. I'd won the Quinella – Margaret for my first name, Anne as my second. The names emulated the beloved royals, if only in a small way. But years later, calling out the name Margaret at any gathering where there were women of my age present meant that several heads would swing in your direction.

So the confusion had a simple explanation. I was not the required Margaret. I had not caused the twinkle in Gavin's eye. He was after another named-for-a-princess partygoer. I sat through the performance, applauding in the right places and making polite remarks, smiling until the skin felt stretched across my bones and willing the dreary evening to an early close. A thought stayed with me as Gavin and I walked home along H-e-y-t-e-s-b-u-r-y Road. My parents and Princess Margaret had a lot to answer for.

Setting Gavin to one side, the dating landscape of my single years had been an unremarkable plateau; lacking soaring peaks, maybe, but equally devoid of deep troughs. I remembered the high season of my amorous life with a certain fondness, to tell the truth. One thing had always puzzled me, though, and it still did, all these years on. Mention a new male acquaintance and the response was always the same. *Where did you meet him?* No other information carried the same weight – even inquiries regarding the new suitor's name came as an afterthought. The mechanics of meeting remained the question uppermost in the minds of inquisitive friends.

Why this preoccupation with first meetings? I had no idea. Over the years I devised answers to cut short tiresome explanations. *I met him at my Tuesday night tap dancing class* had served me well. But after some reflection, I think I'm correct in saying it was Mum who responded to my dilemma by advising thus: *Just say you met him at the bus stop.*

I don't catch enough buses to estimate the likelihood of such a meeting, but I'm sure I'd get good odds on the fact it doesn't happen often. So I've had to wait until well into my middle years and make three trips to Venice to be able to say with hand on heart honesty that I met him at the bus stop.

❋

There I sat, in Castello, on a mild and muggy afternoon, the kind of day when it's hard to work up enthusiasm for anything. Certainly not for the no-holds-barred extravaganza that was the Venice Biennale. All that exhausting art, corralled into fifty-three national pavilions ... I yawned, weary just thinking about it. But the Biennale was a big deal and it was waiting on my list of goals still to be scored. I felt a responsibility to see it. Right after this coffee.

Venice delighted in promoting itself as a venue for art and performance. Sometimes it struck the right note and sometimes it didn't. Take the Pink Floyd concert of 1989, for instance.

City officials had been atwitter with excitement. What a coup! The British pop group had been engaged for a one-off performance and would wow their fans from a barge moored in front of the Piazza. A big-name event in a spectacular setting; guaranteed to put Venice on the international celebrity circuit.

Just one catch. The annual procession to Il Redentore Church would fall on the same night as the concert, the third Sunday in July. Il Redentore celebrations had taken place every year since the sixteenth century, with never a cancellation. Until now. Four hundred years of history and pageantry was pushed aside – nothing could be allowed to detract from the Pink Floyd concert.

It was a debacle. Come concert night, 200 000 patrons jammed the city centre, twenty times the area's population. And a small area at that. Of course it ended in tears.

Transportation away from the venue couldn't manage the huge numbers. Tens of thousands of concertgoers remained in and around the Piazza for hours after the performance. Others wandered off to all corners of the city, seeking an escape route. Toilet and litter disposal arrangements proved hopelessly inadequate, and the resulting mess was of such proportions that the army had to be mobilised for the clean-up. One Venetian journalist claimed at the time that the concert fiasco was more brutal than Napoleon's invasion of 1797.

Not the hoped-for success, then. City officials never sought to repeat the initiative. Better to stick with the Biennale and its sedate, art-loving patrons.

I picked up the coffee cup and studied what remained of my caffeine hit. Motivation eluded me. The Biennale was important. It was on my to-do list. But I just didn't want to go, simple as that. Hadn't I always said I preferred art in living spaces, close to people? Veronese's parish church or Titian's *Assumption* behind the Frari's high altar. Cottesloe's *Sculptures by the Sea*. Accessible art in bite-sized chunks.

So I changed my mind – you can do that on holidays. I walked off into eastern Castello's still-to-be-discovered *calli*; into the *sestiere* of the Castellani, the *sestiere* where Sebastiano, my Venetian-born landlord, still got lost. I slipped into the Venice of back alleys and back stories, the Venice I wanted to be part of.

The Venice that felt like home.

❋

Near-perfect images reflected in still water. A man helped his wife from the *fondamenta* and into a boat, tucking her walking stick into a space near the engine. Safely aboard, he picked up a cushion, swatted away the dust and arranged it on a bench at the prow. With a proprietary hand he took his wife's elbow and guided her to her seat. He started the engine and they puttered away, under a bridge and into another canal, disappearing from sight.

I wandered on, past the canal into which the boat had turned. All about me, buildings shed plaster in large chunks, revealing splotches of brickwork, and across the patchwork facades ran electric cabling encased in metal tubes, like ribbons holding everything together. Paint blistered and peeled in long strips from once-green shutters. Shredded wood lay beneath. A balcony garden flourished, defiant of its humble surroundings.

Over another bridge. I turned from the *fondamenta* and down a *calle*, then into a cobweb of alleyways huddling into each other, jumbled and knotted and tangled. Buildings leaned together, as if whispering secrets. Castello wrapped around me and I didn't want to move beyond its walls. There were moments of complete silence, when I might have been the only person out walking in Venice that day.

Laundry became part of the landscape. Washing hung from lines strung over canals, or stretched across narrow *calli* where sunlight reached for just a few hours each day. I rounded a corner and walked into a blizzard. Sheets hung like banners along the length of a wider canal, unfurling when the breeze reached them. On the *fondamenta*, fold-out laundry racks competed for their place in the sun.

I imagined the scene had changed little over the decades. As small traders abandoned the Mercerie to the likes of Prada and Dior and, on the other side of the world, five-star hotels sprung up on once-deserted islands, this little piece of the planet had remained untouched. But a thought troubled me.

What I found picturesque might be less endearing to the district's permanent residents. They could not walk away after a few hours, tucking into their memory the recollection of a stroll through a pleasantly shabby neighbourhood. As I was about to do.

Was it an indulgence? I'd photograph streetscapes where paint lifted from shutters and washing hung above tiny alleyways. I'd glimpsed the other Venice: a maze of *calli* and canals, where the only way of getting around was on foot or by private boat. Now I'd catch a vaporetto and head home to the comforts of a modern apartment. Perhaps Castello's residents would have welcomed that chance.

And perhaps an element of selfishness lay behind my wish to find things unchanged.

❀

Afternoon had given way to the powdery light of dusk when I walked to the vaporetto stop. Across the water, the Chiesa di San Giorgio Maggiore rose from its island mooring, solid and imposing, guarding the entrance to the Giudecca Canal. Familiar landmarks blurred in the distance, melting into a pearl-grey haze. The day loosened its hold on the city.

I took a seat on the vaporetto platform, lulled by its sway. This must be the world's most beautiful bus stop, I thought, putting a hand over my mouth to mask a yawn. Five hours had passed since I pushed aside my coffee cup and voted *no* to the Biennale. Sleep circled my head, growing closer with each revolution. My eyelids nudged downwards.

Two men and a woman walked onto the platform. They chatted in English, admiring the view and consulting the map on the platform's wall. Something here was familiar: the relaxed conversation, the accents. They were Australian. My eyelids snapped upwards and my brain reopened for business.

Australia could be proud of them. Scrubbed up and smiling, they were neatly arranged in the casual manner suited to an evening's sightseeing. The only grooming mishap was a baseball cap worn by one of the men. I'd never liked them, on men or women. And to wear one at night? I ask you. At least it was worn peak forwards and unadorned by sports logo or declaration of love for New York or Stockholm or Singapore.

The man beneath the cap took a seat not far from me. He leaned forwards, elbows resting on his knees, hands clasped in front of him. The others, husband and wife I guessed, discussed the merits of the number one vaporetto compared to its companion, the number two vaporetto. My thoughts slipped back to another vaporetto, another chance encounter. I remembered Mary's easy manner, and how pleased I'd been to hear that Aussie accent. Maybe now it was my turn; it wasn't pushing too far beyond the bounds of my comfort zone.

Here goes …

'Um, excuse my interrupting …' I began, aiming to avoid an I-know-the-answer-miss voice. 'But at this time it doesn't make a lot of difference. The number one is very crowded during the day because it makes every stop. But at night, if you just want a trip along the Grand Canal, I'd take whichever one gets here first.'

Baseball Cap looked up at me and smiled. 'We're from Australia. Just come over for the day.'

I'd never been good at witty rejoinders so I offered up the only response that came to mind.

'I'm Australian, too.'

Pretty lame, I admit, but Baseball Cap seemed prepared to overlook my less than engaging contribution. The conversational baton passed backwards and forwards between us and it all looked quite promising until the number one vaporetto thumped up alongside the platform. Why are buses always late except when you want them to be? The man in the baseball cap stretched and stood to join his friends. They boarded the vaporetto, taking seats in the almost empty cabin.

I made straight for the back deck; front-row seating for any trip along the Grand Canal. Shadowed palazzi lined the water, most of them state-owned or privately owned enterprises and in darkness when the interior lighting was switched off at the day's close of business. But what a sight it must have been when chandeliers lit the interiors and gilding sparkled. Now just a patina of faded elegance remained.

The cabin doors swung open. Baseball Cap joined me, taking a seat opposite. 'Brian,' he said, introducing himself before leaning back against the vaporetto's railing. We resumed our getting-to-know-you conversation.

'I live in Adelaide, out near the beach. A nice part of the world to call home. I retired a few years ago, so I have plenty of time to enjoy it.'

About my age, then. I was still considering this when Brian continued.

'And I'm restoring an old MG. Ten years it's taken me. Before that I was a high school teacher. Maths and physics.'

Impressive. Right up there in the smarts department. Perhaps I could overlook the baseball cap.

Low waves puckered against the vaporetto's sides. Ca' Dario slid by, its facade less than the length of a gondola. Blink and you'd miss it. Except that it was hard to miss, with jewelled discs and mosaics studding its walls.

'Will you look at that?' Brian interrupted his musings on the positioning of the MG's overheating oil cooler. He nodded towards Ca' Dario.

Allora. My chance to steer the conversation into familiar territory. I cast about for an arresting opening. 'It's something of a haunted house. A shiver looking for a spine to run down. Everyone who ever lived there has died a grisly death.'

Brian looked from the palazzo to me and then back to the palazzo. He seemed willing to listen all night. I took it as my cue.

It's not quite correct that all residents of Ca' Dario have met with a sticky end, but there have been enough to give the house a tragic notoriety in Venetian folklore. Giovanni Dario, a civil servant who distinguished himself on diplomatic missions to the Turkish court, built the palazzo with money received from a grateful Republic.

The curse started after his death. Daughter Marietta inherited the palazzo, part of an impressive dowry that enabled her marriage into the cream of Venetian nobility. But alas, it was not happy-ever-after for Marietta. Husband Vincenzo Barbaro was stabbed to death in the palazzo. Then Marietta plunged to her own death, jumping from a palazzo window into the Grand Canal. Romantic legend held that she died of a broken heart. Their son, Vincenzo Jnr, was later assassinated on the island of Crete, then a Venetian territory. One very unfortunate family.

All was calm for several centuries – the palazzo remained empty for much of that time – but then the murder and mayhem started again in earnest. The nineteenth-century English scholar and historian Rawdon Lubbock Brown sunk a fortune into the palazzo's renovation but lived there for just four years. He lost his money and later committed suicide following revelations of his homosexual liaisons, considered scandalous at the time.

From then on it was all pretty much downhill. In the 1960s, American billionaire Charles Briggs bought the house to share with his gay lover. But Venetian society proved no more accepting of homosexuality than in Brown's time, and Briggs abandoned Venice for Mexico, where his lover committed suicide a few months later. Then, in 1979, Count Filippo Giordano delle Lanze was murdered in the palazzo by his candlestick-wielding lover, who dealt a swift and decisive blow to Filippo's skull. The lover later died a violent death himself, in London, where he'd fled after the killing.

The derby of death rolled on. In 1981 Kit Lambert, musical director of the rock band *The Who*, died in questionable circumstances after relinquishing tenancy of the palazzo. At the time he was increasingly reliant on drugs and alcohol, and his fall down a flight of steps in his London home aroused suspicion. Did he fall or was he pushed? His drug dealer was implicated.

Death of a fiscal if not a physical nature befell Venetian businessman Fabrizio Ferrari, a later owner. Forced by debt to sell the palazzo, Ferrari offloaded it to the industrialist and yachtsman Raul Gardini in 1985. Eight years later, as a result of investigations into corruption, Gardini committed suicide in Milan by shooting himself in the head.

'So *ciao* Raul,' I said to Brian. 'A fairytale castle with one devil of a past. Woody Allen was said to be interested in buying it. He adores Venice. But he changed his mind when he heard its history.'

I looked again at the green porphyry and granite facade moving back into shadow. The jewelled discs winked.

Brian had been silent, impressed by this tale of woe. 'Ah yes,' he said, his face pensive.

I waited for further insights.

'So I decided to mount the new oil cooler under the apron. It seemed the most logical place. And the woodwork was in very poor condition. It had to be completely replaced. Rust, too—'

The obligatory thud as the vaporetto hit the Ca' Rezzonico platform and tied up alongside overtook Brian's commentary. How incongruous, I thought, to be talking about cars in the world's premier wheel-less city. Quite ridiculous. High time for another tour guide try-out.

I cleared my throat and pointed to the building looming from the darkness a few metres away. 'That palazzo has a story to tell. It was semi-derelict for almost seventy years, after the nobleman who commissioned it went broke.'

That nobleman was Filippo Bon, a prosperous Venetian merchant. Over many years he bought up adjoining properties, planning to build a mega-palazzo to showcase his wealth. Skiting was *so* Venetian. He engaged no less than Baldassare Longhena, designer of Santa Maria della Salute, to build his dream home. No half measures for the wealthy Signor Bon.

Then Longhena up and died, five years into the project. The building had only one storey and a few rooms completed. Filippo had sunk everything into the project and now his fortune was gone. But every man's home is his castle, and Filippo lived with his family in those semi-intact rooms. Flooring in most rooms was wooden planking crisscrossing rubble and debris. Windows remained unglazed and open to the elements. Then the temporary roof gave way and rainwater rotted the ceiling beams. For the next thirty-two years, until his death in 1750, Filippo toughed it out in his collapsing, meant-to-be mansion.

Ah, but then.

Along came the Rezzonicos: in-your-face wealthy and looking for a perch on that precious branch of Venetian real estate, the Grand Canal. Now things moved apace. Six years after being purchased by the Rezzonicos, and almost one hundred years since its commissioning, the building was completed. The Grand Canal had a new and spectacular landmark.

'But it's not with Filippo Bon or the Rezzonicos that most people associate the palazzo,' I said, working on the loosely founded notion that Brian might be interested. 'The poet Robert Browning lived here. He died in one of the palazzo's upstairs rooms.'

By the time of Browning's death in 1889, Ca' Rezzonico had been purchased by his son, Pen, and undergone a superb refurbishment thanks to the deep, deep pockets of Pen's American wife, the heiress Fanny Coddington. Browning stayed there for lengthy periods, penning his sonnets, happier than at any time since his wife's death.

'There's a plaque on the side of the building,' I said. 'You can't see it at night, but it commemorates the fact that Robert Browning lived here. It's a mark of respect, I guess.'

I gave Brian time to chime in with a suitable response, but it seemed he didn't want to. A short pause developed. Then:

'I used an additive called TPRDA, which allowed the resin to soak into the wood.'

My history attempt ricocheted into the night.

Brian resumed his car restoration highlights, approaching a final summation. 'I'd describe the process as a love–hate relationship, I suppose. And more hate than love sometimes. But now it's finished, well, it's all love. A beautiful little car.'

Architecture and history weren't for everyone. I took off my tour guide cap and listened to Brian as he moved on to talk about his trip to the Ghetto that day. He'd met up with a business contact – something to do with Murano glass.

'I walked from our hotel on the waterfront through every street in Venice,' Brian said. 'I didn't realise how much of the place there is. From the water it doesn't seem that big.'

'So you've seen a lot of Venice then, one way or another.'

'I've seen more of Venice than I meant to. All those unmarked streets, all those bridges … they look exactly the same.' He gave a rueful chuckle. 'It took me all morning to get there, and then I got lost on the way back.'

I decided to spare Brian my own lost-in-Venice story. I'd done enough talking.

Water seesawed and Venice slipped past. Words flowed without effort, light and spontaneous. I smiled. Here I was, on a water bus, on the Grand Canal, chatting with a man who felt like a mate. A sense of ease percolated our disjointed conversation, and where impatience might have flourished there was instead good humour. I smiled some more, right up to the moment when the vaporetto thumped into its next stop.

If Brian had kept talking, I would have kept quiet, I swear I would. Instead he lapsed into a comfortable silence, perhaps exhausted all over again by recounting his adventure with

Venetian *calli*. I couldn't help myself. My mouth just went ahead without consulting me.

'See that building?' Brian followed my pointing finger. 'That's Palazzo Balbi. The owner was Nicolo Balbi, and he was dead keen to see his palazzo finished. He moored a boat alongside the building to watch as work progressed. He even slept on the boat, all through winter. That's how he caught pneumonia and died. Dead keen, like I said.'

Of course, as with everything in Venice, there was a counter-story. It held that Signor Balbi squabbled with his about-to-be Grand Canal neighbour over their financial dealings. Things got heated. Signor Balbi sought revenge by dropping anchor in a position which obscured the other's water view. The whole Balbi family then came aboard and lived in the floating home for more than a year. For whatever reason the boat came to be there, Signor Balbi *did* die aboard, and never lived to see his palazzo finished.

'A Venetian saying once maintained there was nothing harder to find than a rich Balbi,' I said. 'But they must have had money once, to build that.'

'Hmm,' said Brian, assuming an expression of courteous attention.

We passed under the Rialto. By now my knowledge of car fix-ups, makeovers and general restoration exceeded my requirements. Brian possibly felt the same way about Venetian palazzi. We listened as voices from the *fondamente* restaurants rose and fell, spreading across the moonlit water to reach us on the back deck. With few passengers boarding and alighting at each stop, the trip was moving along at a rapid clip. Now the Ponte degli Scalzi lay ahead, and then the train station, where Brian and his friends were ending their journey.

'We'll wander around for a while, take a look at things, perhaps have a nightcap.' Brian stood to leave, his arm reaching towards the cabin doors. He hesitated a moment. 'Would you like to catch up for dinner tomorrow night?'

Be open to the accidental.

Those had been Mary's exact words, called across the lagoon as she waved goodbye. I thought about her take-a-chance optimism. I thought about Signor Suave with his silvery cheeks and snug-fitting jeans. Then I said yes.

I pointed to the Santa Croce side of the bridge. 'I'll meet you on *this* side of *this* bridge at eight tomorrow night.'

The pleasant man in the baseball cap nodded and said goodnight. He strolled through the vaporetto's cabin, hands in his pockets, to rejoin his companions.

※

I looked at Brian over the antipasto. The fork wavered for a moment, then halted in its journey between the plate and my mouth. I blinked, blinked again. Just when everything had been going so well.

'What do you mean, you don't like footie?' I said.

Over the years I'd met no more than a handful of men who didn't warm to the subject of sport. It was a conversation stalwart, guaranteed to ignite the spark of interest when chatter stalled. Not that I was casting about for something to say; far from it. Our talk had followed the same relaxed pattern as the previous night.

But I wanted to talk football. It was August, approaching AFL finals time, and I was gearing up for my annual lament. It varied little from one year to the next. A couple of narrow losses in games we'd expected to win. Unfavourable umpiring decisions at critical times in the game. Too many players sidelined with injuries. The curse of Ca' Dario was as nothing compared to the curse on the Western Bulldogs. It was sixty-one years since we'd won our last premiership. Our only premiership.

I finished blinking and stared at Brian. He was serious, I could tell from the twist of his mouth. And it had nothing to do with the anchovy he was eating.

I couldn't quite believe it. 'But South Australia is a traditional AFL state. You've got two half-decent teams to pick from. And Port Adelaide has the same underdog fighting spirit as we do.'

Brian rubbed his hand over his chin and spoke to the glassware. 'Football doesn't interest me. Never has. If I'm going to watch television at all, it's more likely to be one of the current affairs programs.'

Cracking stuff. Another favourite topic. I was happy to leave the problems at Whitten Oval and cast a wider net. I reached for my prosecco, brought it within easy reach and settled back to consider things.

'I'm a bit of a news junkie myself,' I said. 'I did politics and economics at uni. Loved it. But I was interested long before that, even. I remember staying up all night to watch the American hostages being freed from Iran. That seems like forever ago. What year was it, do you remember?'

'Hmm. Somewhere in the early eighties, I think. It happened at the same time as Ronald Reagan was sworn into office.' Brian leaned back against the wall. He traced a half circle around his glass before speaking again.

'Not many people are that interested in politics.' He looked at me with a quizzical expression, surprised to find someone who was, sitting just a metre away.

Oh, yes. If I couldn't talk footie, then politics ran a close second. We switched from American hostages and American presidents to matters Australian. In furious agreement, we discussed and rectified the parlous state of the nation's economy, detailing and bemoaning the foolishness of our political masters. The antipasto was finished down to the last olive before we stopped chewing over political issues and turned our attention from the ridiculous to the sublime.

I lifted my glass of prosecco and watched a ribbon of bubbles bead to the surface. I took a sip, long and appreciative, feeling the bubbles fizz under my nose.

'*Bellissimo*. This one's the real deal, from the Conegliano Hills. Venice's best kept secret.'

Another sip followed, to confirm my assessment. Each mouthful got better.

'The name should be copyrighted, I reckon. Like champagne. And it's best really, really cold. *Achingly* cold. A waste, letting it get warm.'

Little chance of that happening. My immediate future included a second glass, possibly more. This was great fun, talking about things that mattered to me with someone who shared my interest. Our conversation moved along with the speed of an in-form midfielder. Tackles were made and points scored. So absorbed did I become that I didn't realise the waiter had cleared the table until he arrived with our main course. Minutes later he reappeared with a second bottle of Venice's best kept secret.

Perhaps it was the second bottle of prosecco that did it. One glass into the new bottle and we were decanting our life stories.

'I've only recently separated from my wife,' Brian said. 'We'd been married over thirty years, and I would have said it was a happy marriage.'

He looked down at his hand resting on the placemat, then spread his fingers in a contemplative way, lifting them a few centimetres before bringing them back to the table with an air of finality. Marriage over.

'It wasn't as though she'd met someone else. There was no third party involved. She said she just didn't want to be married anymore. All those years, and then she changes her mind. Inconvenient, to say the least.' A smile flickered but didn't make it beyond his lips.

I nodded my understanding. Not the usual first date conversation perhaps, but travelling friendships were different from other friendships. Goodbyes came too soon after hellos. I looked at my plate and said nothing, twisting pasta against the spoon and onto the fork.

Brian sifted a more sombre note into his voice. 'This trip to Venice only came about because of the two friends I was with last night. They'd already planned three weeks in France and Italy. They said I should come along. Part of my recovery therapy, I suppose ...' A wry smile completed the sentence.

I couldn't think of anything useful to offer so I stayed silent.

'Why?' he asked me, sitting forwards to rest his arms on the table. 'Why does this happen, totally out of the blue? For no reason? My life's been turned upside down and I don't even know where things went wrong.'

I moved my plate to one side. What should I say? I turned to the waiter to give myself a moment to think.

'Could we have some more ice, please?'

The waiter picked up the ice bucket and walked off. I took a deep breath, uncertain of my words even as I began to speak. Once started, I'd found, these conversations could take on a life of their own and become difficult to pull back from. I wasn't sure I was up for that.

'Everyone has their reasons, I guess ...' My words were hesitant, punctuated with gaps. They seemed to be coming from somewhere else. 'And those reasons make sense to them. At least at the time. Even if the future is unclear, it's more appealing than the present. Sounds harsh, I know.'

Brian straightened as if a string had been pulled. A puzzled expression clouded his face.

I took some time to pick at a stray thread on the placemat, then looked up. 'And for the recipient of the news, it *is* harsh. I can only guess at the cold sense of loss that must accompany the ultimatum.'

Just as I'd thought might happen, there was no way back. And so, sitting in a restaurant beside a canal, in a city on the other side of the world, I balanced the conversation with my own story. I matched Brian's honesty. The story I told was not rouged and lipsticked, not done up and made to look pretty. The story I told could have been his wife's story.

'I've done the same thing. It seems a lifetime ago, as though the events were lived by somebody else. My husband encouraged me to go to uni and look what he got for his troubles. A wife who changed her mind about being a wife.'

Memories flooded back – an *acqua alta* deluge. 'University showed me another world. It was – what do they say – a small space through which to see vastness. The promise, the expectations ... I'd never imagined ...'

Brian listened in a sort of clenched silence.

'And the fun. Oh, we had fun. Not just the parties and the pub, but the talk. Hours and hours, talking about anything ... politics, literature ... whatever. Marriage seemed staid by comparison. Even to the very best of husbands. All the women I met had plans for careers, and I thought, "Well yes, I could do that, couldn't I?" Home and husband would be in the way.'

What was Brian thinking? He gazed back at me from behind a neutral mask that offered no clues. Then he pulled further away and folded his arms across his chest.

I ploughed on. 'The exact nature of the future I couldn't have said. No one ever can, really, can they? I just knew I wanted to buy in to whatever presented itself. Nothing is as powerful as an idea whose time has come – all of that. This was the early 1980s, remember, and the feminist movement was strong. Especially on campus. Germaine Greer had replaced God.'

I paused and looked at the table. Like tiny islands, grease stains speckled the placemat where a raised fork had punctuated my commentary. Time to lighten up.

'Anyway, Germaine now reckons that shopping is the new sex for women over fifty.'

Brian's lips twitched. Then he laughed. Not a robust, echoing laugh, but enough to carry the mood back to the evening's beginning. He glanced around the restaurant. Close to our table, too close to allow for any misinterpretation, the waiter polished silverware. He lifted a knife for inspection, then busy fingers set about rebuffing. Message received. Time to go.

'How about a coffee somewhere?' Brian said.

Where else on a summer's night but Campo Santa Margherita? I led the way. The *campo* had become my trusted recipe: like a never-fail cake, it always delivered. And that night it had risen to perfection. Crowds gathered in bars or sat on benches under trees, their voices climbing over each other in animated chatter. We took our coffees to an outside table and settled down to watch *la dolce vita*, Venetian-style.

Brian twisted in his seat and looked around the *campo*, nodding approval. 'Great choice. It's nothing like the area around my hotel. This could be a different city.'

'To me it *is* a different city. I prefer these neighbourhoods, lesser known, away from the tourist circuit. It reminds me of the Trastevere neighbourhood in Rome. I guess that's what drew me to Dorsoduro, the idea of finding somewhere like that.'

I sipped my coffee and wondered about a Disaronno, then turned to follow Brian's gaze around the *campo*. Another corner of my Venetian backyard. We lapsed into silence for a few minutes before Brian spoke, returning to our earlier conversation.

'So tell me, then. Are you happy with the way things turned out? Any knots you wish you could go back and untie?'

I shrugged; an easy, relaxed gesture. 'Events happened. I chose one path and not the other. Forks in the road and all that. The other path will always be unknown. I just got on with things. And yes, I've been happy. Contented. That's probably a better word.'

And probably not quite the truth. Does anyone walk away from a marriage without a backward glance, a thought that perhaps they've made a mistake? Along with the laughs and the new friends came lost friendships; people I'd known as part of my married life and the world of couples. With the best will in the world, theirs and mine, adapting to my new single status proved unwieldy. And it wasn't just people who went missing. Small pleasures – walking our dog by the river, following the cricket in summer – these things slipped away unnoticed until some small incident reminded me they had once been part of my life. More than anything, I remembered a feeling of guilt, of regret for the hurt and disruption I'd caused. And sometimes, just sometimes, when exams loomed or I set off for a ten-hour nursing shift, the thought would come to me: *I needn't be doing any of this.*

I got on with things. A funny little expression that, and I found myself wondering about its French equivalent. *C'est la vie? Comme ci, comme ça?* It was how I'd approached post-marriage life and, over time, it delivered contentment. As I told Brian. I turned to him now.

'And how about you?'

Brian pinched his lower lip between thumb and forefinger and looked at some point out there in the night. 'Well, I know if you dwell on regrets they just flourish under your attention. I imagine I'll work my way through it. I've got good friends, a comfortable life. I'm lucky.'

Our silences were easy. So was our talk, and fringed with the humour that comes from a shared culture. I pointed across the *campo* to Margaret du Champs. 'They named that bar after me, you know. They did it to honour my steady patronage.'

A companionable chuckle passed between us. We'd moved a long way from our initial blending of car restoration and Venetian palazzi. I remembered another night of easy camaraderie, sitting here with Raoul and Monika. It had been wonderful, but without the final element – the cherry on the cake – of a shared language. It made all the difference.

At 3 am we left the *campo* and walked to my apartment, to wait until the vaporetti resumed full service at six. Up those two flights of steps we clomped, pausing on the landing while I changed keys. Brian looked back down the stairwell.

'Indentations in stone steps? How many feet must have walked up and down to cause that?' He reached for his phone and took a photo. That had been my reaction, too, I remembered, setting out for Downstairs on that first Sunday night.

I pulled the apartment door open. Lamps glowed and windows swung out to an inky sky just beginning to change to pre-dawn grey. Polly Parrot sat alongside a fruit bowl on the kitchen benchtop. Across the dining table lay books and papers, stacked into tottering heaps. My home.

'Orange juice? Disaronno? A cup of tea, perhaps?' I filled the kettle and switched it on. What was the correct drink for this time of night anyway?

Brian crossed the room to the table and began leafing through books. An oh-my-gosh whistle followed. 'Just get a load of this.'

A book with full-page illustrations of Venetian palazzi lay open on the table. I walked across to Brian and sat down. From the book's glossy pages leapt an interior of jaw-dropping opulence. Curling, swirling stucco. Somersaulting cherubs. The full Rococo deal, and home-sweet-home to the mega-rich Albrizzi family who, like their mates the Lasbias and the Rezzonicos, had made the grand palazzo statement when they purchased a place in Venetian nobility.

No, I didn't start a history lesson. I was tired. It was late. And in any case I didn't get the chance.

Brian had his phone out again, poised over the book. 'I'll just get a few shots of this. I can tell Colin and Pauline it was your apartment. That'll get them thinking.'

A smirk of delight worked across his face as he angled in for a better view. *Click, click.* Chortle, chortle. A huge joke.

I thought about it. Then I reached over to the hand that held the phone. Smiled back at the smiling face. I said to Brian, 'It's the way people deal with hardship rather than success that sets them apart. And you're special.'

✺

The sun rose behind Castello, pointing fingers of red and gold across the city. We walked from the vaporetto to Brian's hotel, then joined Colin and Pauline for breakfast. They would all be leaving Venice later that morning, taking a water taxi from the hotel to Marco Polo Airport.

'The cost is outrageous,' Brian said, breaking open a croissant; buttery and warm and flaky, just as you would expect from the breakfast buffet of a five-star hotel.

I've never stayed in a Venetian five-star, I thought. Or caught a water taxi. I'm happy with Alilaguna or a vaporetto. And happy, too, that I'm the one staying behind in Venice. Heading back to Perth would come as the full stop at the end of a book. It would mark the finish of something I didn't want to end.

Brian and I said goodbye as we'd said hello – on a vaporetto platform. He turned away with a wave of his arm, not looking back. The man I'd met at the bus stop. I watched him walk to his hotel, then looked down to unfasten the present he'd given me. Fumbling a little, I clipped a Murano glass locket around my neck.

I sat in morning sunshine and waited for the vaporetto – a number one or a number two. *At this time it doesn't make a lot of difference.* Those were just about the first words I'd spoken to Brian and his friends two nights ago. I leaned back against the wall, deep in thought. The friendship of strangers met while travelling was most often temporary – a need for connection in unfamiliar surroundings and lost as quickly as it was formed. But length wasn't always the yardstick by which to measure worth. As Mary had told me.

I reached up to touch the locket, turning it between my fingers. My meeting with Brian had come with another gift. Finally, *finally*, I could tell anyone who asked that I met him at the bus stop. I never thought it would happen.

But then, I never thought the Western Bulldogs would be AFL premiers, either.

Life had its rewards.

CHAPTER 14

DIMITRI'S VENICE

*What is worst of all is that these tourists wield a
terrible power: they bear an image of Venice back out
into the rest of the world as a city too-seen, too-visited,
too-crowded, too-known to bother with. Venice: been
there, done that.*

Paolo Barbaro, Italian author, in *Venice Revealed*

I never did get to the Biennale.

In the days after Brian left I settled down to exploring
off-grid Venice. The stifling heat had passed, and I wandered
wherever chance or fancy happened to take me. I followed
what turned up, falling into step with it for the length of
time it held my interest, then moving on to something else.
It was just me and Venice and whatever came along.

Most often it was San Polo that beckoned, and I ventured
further into its tangle of dead-end *calli* and canals. San Polo
was coming to rival Dorsoduro as my favourite *sestiere*, the
place in Venice I would most like to call home. I was on my
way there this morning, with just a sketchy outline of where
the day might lead me.

It led me to Calle Rio Terà dei Nomboli. A shop caught my eye the minute I rounded the corner. Stationery flowed across tables and over shelves; books bound with leather of Venetian red showed edges of thick, fraying paper, and gold embossing, as delicate as a spider's web, stamped the sheets of writing paper stacked beside them. Notebooks, photo albums and diaries pressed against music manuscripts, everything positioned with artistic flair.

Unable to resist, I pushed the door open. Vivaldi's *The Four Seasons* and the smell of old paper greeted me. The proprietor looked up from his counter.

'*Buon giorno*,' I said. 'What a beautiful shop.'

He smiled a greeting, then turned his attention to the customer standing with him at the counter. 'The gift is for a man, signor? Or a lady?'

'It's for my wife. She couldn't join me on this trip, and she loves coming to Venice.' The customer looked down at the counter, admiring his selection. 'She must be one of the last people on earth who still writes and receives letters. A tradition of correct manners, she says ...'

I peeked at the gift for a wife who shunned texting and email. A slim letter opener rested in its presentation case. The shop owner dipped beneath the counter and whisked out sheets of different coloured paper, placing them on the countertop and angling them over each other before edging corners into position. With deft movements he wrapped the gift, and now multicoloured stripes ran across the outside of the package. Ribbon secured the arrangement, and a thumbnail scraped along it produced a springy curliness. Then it was into a carry bag – a tiny affair, matching one sheet of the wrapping paper. A sticker between gold handles announced its Venetian provenance.

All ready for the journey home to the letter-writing, letter-receiving spouse.

'*Grazie mille. Arrivederci, signor.* Your wife is happy with this, I think.'

I looked around the shop, my eyes halting at a display of bookmarks fanning the corner of one table. Handpainted bookmarks; perfect little gifts. My holiday had reached the time-to-think-about-presents phase, and this could be just the place. I twisted the price tag upwards. A sharp intake of breath returned to the atmosphere as a dumbfounded *pouf.* Not a store for bargains, this.

But price had not deterred everyone. Near the window, a couple stood beside bouquets of finely nibbed pens. Furrows creased the man's brow as he examined each item, remarking on its particular merits. Beside him stood his wife, nodding from time to time as she listened to his commentary.

'*Je pense* ...' The man lifted a pen and touched the nib with a forefinger, then gathered up several more, assessing them in the same manner. '*Ah oui. Formidable.*'

The woman turned from her husband to a row of boxes, each containing a single, coloured quill and a bottle of ink. She moved in my direction, stopping close by. Her eyes glinted with humour as she tilted her head back to the window.

'My husband is a retired architect. He has firm ideas about a good drawing pen.' She spoke in English, overlaid with a French accent.

I put down the silver ink pot I'd been admiring. Why was I even looking at it? No way could I afford it. 'You're visiting from France? But your English is perfect. I'd love to be able to speak a second language so well.'

'Oh no, not France. We're from Canada. Quebec. So we speak French as often as we speak English. But it's been mostly English for the past week, while we've been here.'

She sighed, and her gaze moved across the room and out to the *calle*. 'I don't think I can bear to leave Venice.'

She turned back to me, a question forming. 'But your accent ...?'

'I'm Australian. And I'm thinking the same thing. I'm here for longer – a month. But it's still not long enough.'

I looked over the woman's shoulder to her husband. He could be here for a month, too, and it still wouldn't be long enough. With the matter of pens sorted, there was now the question of ink. Handmade ink, to use with the handmade pens, to take home to Quebec. Supplies could be ordered online, I heard the proprietor tell him, as they moved off to the counter. No need for gift wrapping this time.

The woman continued our conversation, in no hurry to join her husband. She rested her shopping bag on the floor and picked up my ink pot, twisting it to the light. It wouldn't be outside her price range, I thought, noting the jewellery. A diamond the size of a quail's egg slipped around her finger.

Again she looked out to the *calle*. Again she sighed. 'What I love most about Venice is that it offers the best of the greatest – the Piazza, the Basilica, you know – and the most enticing of the smallest.'

What a stunning insight. I waited for more. But any identification of the small and enticing was cut short by her husband's return, bubble-wrapped packages bristling in each hand. He bent down to his wife's shopping bag and placed his treasures into its already bulging shape.

'Just put them on top.' She lifted the bag and rearranged parcels, then reverted to her theme. 'We've tried to get away from the usual tourist places. Why do people only visit San Marco when there's so much else to see in Venice?'

I wasn't sure who the question was meant for – her husband, or me, or the shop's proprietor who stood nearby, rearranging a shelf of Murano magnifying glasses.

'But you are good tourists, I think.' The proprietor turned from his work to the couple. 'You want to know Venice. Most people, they don't. Our churches, our history … this does not interest them. You have seen the church of San Giacomo di Rialto? It is the oldest church in Venice. People sit on the steps and eat their lunch. Don't bother to go inside. They are interested only to buy from the markets next door. Souvenirs of Venice, made in China.'

Not your usual local-to-visitor wisdom. I waited for the response, again toying with those bookmarks.

The husband spoke. 'We've been here for a week, and yes, we've seen that church. And the Frari, of course – we're on our way there now for another visit. There's a cafe across from the Frari that once owned a cat named Nini. The cat became famous, you know.'

A chuckle filtered through his beard. He pushed his hands deeper into his trouser pockets and rocked a little on his feet, in the manner of someone ready to say more.

I drew a breath to speak and then changed my mind. There was no need. And no time either.

His wife propped her tortoiseshell glasses above her forehead and took charge of the conversation. 'I agree with you about those tourists,' she said to the proprietor. 'They are more bother than pigeons, and every bit as messy.'

Plus mauvais que les pigeons. I looked at her tailored pants and crisp top and imagined her talking to friends in Quebec. A thought crossed my mind; something to do with pigeons. Or possibly tourists. Whatever the nature of my observation it amounted to little, pre-empted even as the words formed on my lips.

A torrent exploded through the door. Five young gelato-licking customers splattered across the shop, chatting and chortling and touching stuff. Aghast, the proprietor dashed off.

The woman laughed in a good-natured way then turned to me. 'Enjoy your time in Venice. It was nice meeting you. I have friends living in Australia, and I always look forward to visiting them. Australians are such welcoming people.'

I watched the woman and her husband weave a path towards the door. A courteous and pleasant couple: good tourists, wasn't that what the store owner had called then? Not the tag of approval he would award to his latest customers.

The gelato brigade roamed free-range. Scandalised little gasps erupted as they flicked over price tags. They left in the same tumble of noise that had announced their arrival, slamming the door behind them. The shop owner breathed an audible sigh and walked over to me.

'I am busy since you arrive. Can I assist you?'

I chose six handpainted bookmarks. Possibly I shouldn't have, but there you are. 'Some little gifts for friends at home,' I said, handing them to him and following as he walked to the counter. One final, wistful glance in the direction of the silver ink pot.

A thought struck me. *How do you gift wrap a bookmark?* I watched as red tissue paper was cut to size before encircling each one, then secured with a 'Hand Crafted in Venice' sticker. Into a carrier they went, before being passed to me with a smile.

The Four Seasons played on. The shop remained empty. I hesitated, not wanting to seem pushy. We'd been smiling at each other for a while now, and I sensed an *arrivederci* hovering. I wanted to postpone its arrival.

'You mentioned San Giacomo di Rialto,' I said. 'I went there a couple of days ago, to buy concert tickets. It was just like you said – people sprawled all over the portico, eating burgers and drinking Cokes.'

'We Venetians have a name for people who eat in the street. *Turistico morde e fugge*. Snack-and-run tourists.' He shook his head in a what-can-you-do gesture.

I shook my head along with him and threw in a few *tsk-tsks* for good measure.

What a total fraud I can be. I'd done the same thing – last year, with Jenny. We'd munched away on sandwiches as we sat with our legs dangling over the Grand Canal, never giving it a second thought. Now I made a mental note. *Morde e fugge*. Never again.

My etiquette director continued. 'Often they bring their own food, these tourist. They do not eat in restaurants. They leave no money in Venice. All they leave is their litter.'

Jenny and I had purchased our food. And we took away our leftovers. Just saying.

The shop door remained closed. No new customers. I ran a finger around the bag, wondering if I should continue. *Yes*, I decided, *why not*.

'I remember Venice from thirty-five years ago,' I said. 'There wasn't a single waterfront restaurant in San Polo. I couldn't believe the changes when I came back last year. Just so many people ...'

'Tourists are a problem for Venice. Most see nothing except San Marco. And they feed the pigeons, which is illegal.'

Venetian tourism concerns were not new to me. More than eighty per cent of visitors, by most estimates, stayed in Venice for less than thirty-six hours and remained araldited to San Marco, its most famous site. As for pigeons ... they were synonymous with Venice, loved by visitors but a headache for city officials. For years, *Il Comune* had plotted their demise. Operation Pigeon had employed sonic scaring devices and oral contraceptives, it had trapped and it had poisoned, all to no avail. *Il Comune*'s only success happened as a by-product of Il Redentore celebrations: the fireworks caused dozens of pigeons to drop to earth, dead from apparent heart failure.

People and pigeons and too many of both: a reality of today's Venice. I took a deep breath, then spoke before I could change my mind.

'Venice is so different now, with tourists. I'd love to come back and talk for a bit.' I looked up at him, assessing his reaction. 'Is that possible? Do you have a time that isn't too busy? Oh, and my name's Margaret.'

'Dimitri.' He extended his hand. 'In the morning, early. I open at ten, but tomorrow I am here at nine o'clock. Work ...' He raised a hand, indicating the shop. 'We can talk then.'

Who would have thought? San Polo, the *sestiere* that once intimidated me, had become my home turf. Not quite like Dorsoduro, not yet, but familiar enough that I could leave the map behind when I set out the next day. An easy ten-minute stroll led me back to Dimitri's world of paper, pens and Vivaldi. Just after nine I pushed open the door.

Dimitri greeted me, looking up from the carton he was unpacking. 'These are from our warehouse on La Giudecca. The manufacturing side of our business has existed as a family concern since 1848. And this shop, it has been in my family for thirty-two years.'

He removed photo frames from their wrapping, dusted off specks of lint and laid them to one side. His hands delved back into the carton. 'But please, you must tell me why you are interested in Venice.'

'Because I love the city.' The simple accuracy of the statement hit me with a jolt: I really did love Venice, every bit as much as Perth. Venice felt like *my* city. I could find my way around. Sometimes I showed other people *their* way around. And I had a shopping buggy. I fitted right in.

I paused, assembling my thoughts. 'Last year I was here for a week and there was so much I didn't see. I only came to this side of the Grand Canal once, but I felt a connection somehow. Now I'm wondering if I could live here.'

Dimitri raised his head from the packages, a tactful smile dimpling his cheeks. I guessed he'd heard a hundred visitors say the same thing. Venice had never suffered a shortage of admirers. American writer Donna Leon, for instance, had come to Venice on a visit and stayed for thirty-two years, writing about the adventures of Commissario Guido Brunetti in her adopted city.

'And San Polo is such a vibrant neighbourhood,' I said, completing my explanation.

'It is, yes. With my family I live here, near the Rialto. I am born here, and for fifty years I have lived nowhere else. My wife Elizabeth also. She helps in the business now that our children are older. We have two sons, and one, Nicola, he, too, works in the business.'

Dimitri reached into a drawer for scissors, then slit open another carton. 'Each afternoon, Nicola manages the shop. One day he will have complete responsibility.'

I looked around the shop, at the large amount of stock and the intricacy of the displays. 'I imagine it takes up a lot of your time.'

'Ten hours each day I am here or in our factory. There is no time for anything else. I would like to paint. It was to be my career – I spent four years at art college. But I had my family to think of …' He shrugged. 'So I took over the shop.'

'And your other son,' I asked, 'is he involved in the business, too?'

'No, no. Tomas is a musician, but he lives with the family.' Dimitri pushed back his sleeves. He gripped the carton's edges and tugged them apart with a ripping sound.

'My sons, they are lucky. They have a secure future. A home, here in Venice. Most young people do not have this. They cannot afford to live in the city. Many, many young Venetians work in tourism and earn low wages. They must live in Mestre and travel to Venice each day.'

Dimitri worked on as he spoke, moving across the shop to place the unwrapped items on shelves. 'Overseas migrants, they also earn low wages. They work in kitchens. Seventy per cent – more, even – have no visa. They just arrive, and they stay.'

I followed him, moving between the tables. 'So are they paid at a lower rate than they should be, these migrants? Do they pay tax?'

'Who knows? The problem of illegal migrants is now too big to handle. There is nothing that can be done.'

Dimitri's observations disturbed me, but I was forced to admit he might just be right. As I became familiar with my neighbourhood, I learned where to expect each request for money. From the young man standing outside the local supermarket with his cap outstretched. From the pair who moved in a constant circuit around the cafes near Campo San Giacomo dell'Orio. And from the man stationed on the bridge below my apartment, clutching his bouquet of red roses, hoping for a sale. They spoke of bleak lives, of day-to-day survival, no more.

Dimitri spoke again, moving the conversation to my time in Venice. 'You stay much longer than most tourists. You take time to learn about our city, to know it from the heart.'

So did I qualify as one of his good tourists? I mentally reviewed my credentials. They were less than compelling. Brash and insensitive mistakes blotted my copybook, too numerous, too embarrassing to retell. *Morde e fugge* was just the smallest smudge by comparison.

Dimitri walked back to the counter, returning with leather-bound notebooks. He arranged them one atop the other, the uppermost lying open to display its thick, cream-coloured pages. Across it he balanced a nibbed, wooden pen. Head tilted, he stepped back, appraising his work like the artist he was.

'When I travel,' he continued, 'I learn about my destination. I am like you, I stay for a longer time. Most people stay only a day in Venice.' Dimitri dusted off his hands. 'Italian tourists, you see. They are part of the problem.'

That's right. Most visitors to Venice are, in fact, other Italians. They travel from nearby towns, streaming from Ferrovia Santa Lucia to the Piazza and making few detours. By late afternoon they are back on the departure platforms. Others head straight for the docks of western Dorsoduro to join a cruise ship. To this influx can be added thousands of students on school excursions, each toting a backpack of drinks and lunch along with their notebooks. *Il pendolaro* – the single-day tourist – is considered the particular enemy of Venice. Having only time to see the central sites, they flood the Piazza, not visiting museums and historical sites.

A thought came to me. Listening to Dimitri, I recalled the insights of Venetian entrepreneur Piero Pazzi on the matter of tourist empathy. 'Venice,' Pazzi maintained, 'must be visited with sensibility and intelligence.' Then he added: 'If you don't believe me, buy a video and stay home. It's the best thing you can do. We already have too many tourists and we don't need one like you!'

Strong words. And perhaps they have been heeded.

'Tourist numbers are down,' Dimitri said, repositioning the pen by a fraction of a millimetre. 'And the tourists who do come to Venice buy cheap imitations, produced overseas in large factories.'

I thought back to my day on Murano and the menageries of Made-in-China glass animals. At the other end of the spectrum were the Fendi–Dior–Versace stores of San Marco, selling internationally known and manufactured brands. Both threatened the survival of local craftspeople.

'How can Venetian artisans compete?' Dimitri lifted his shoulders in a questioning shrug. 'And it is not just artisans who suffer. Tourism affects us all. Residents are more and more concerned. The people we need, they are gone. Today Venice has six plumbers. A city built on water. Six plumbers.'

The muffled sound of feet outside in the *calle* reached inside the shop.

Dimitri turned to me. 'Everything is about tourists, always tourists. Only tourists.'

❀

Perhaps the writing was always on the wall.

As the cities of Western Europe moved towards industrial modernisation in the early twentieth century, Venice stuck fast to its tourism legacy. Had it not served the city well for centuries? Decision-makers saw no reason to rock the gondola.

'Tourism will be the bread of Venice,' declared Giovanni Ponti, then mayor of Venice. And why not? A mysterious, floating city, undamaged by the wars that had ravaged much of Europe, ready to welcome visitors to its brand-spanking-new hotels. A sure-fire model for success. But what tourists would not want, *Il Comune* decided, was to see a Venice sullied by industry: that could happen in the mainland centres of Mestre and Porto Marghera. One by one, small-scale enterprises that had operated for decades closed down as the push to become a tourist city gathered momentum.

Privately owned palazzi were sold to accommodation chains and the number of hotels burgeoned. Big hotels. Hotels designed to get more bodies into more beds. The 'bread of Venice' was to be baked with 'modernity', declared Ponti, never mind conservation and restoration. Architecturally brazen additions to the Danieli and the Bauer hotels disregarded aesthetics, jarring with their surroundings and destroying ancient vistas. But who cared? So long as tourists flocked to Venice, nothing else mattered.

At least for the time being. By the late 1970s, however, the paradox of tourism was becoming apparent. On the one hand, it had replaced all other economic alternatives to become the dominant industry and essential to the city's financial survival. On the other hand, its expansion was now an obstacle to the daily life of Venetian citizens.

Tourists consumed Venice. They crowded the *calli* and clogged the vaporetti. Stores selling everyday necessities closed down, replaced by retailers focused on the tourist trade. Basic service industries declined or disappeared. Housing became scarce, with accommodation given over to visitors. Residents were left with little choice but to relocate, forced from their city by the tourism push. Town planners postulated that Venice would in time cease to be a city of Venetians. The city, they warned, risked becoming a Disneyland for grown-ups; a watery theme park, existing for no reason other than to entertain tourists.

❈

Dimitri turned back to his work, leaning against a table as he coaxed notebooks into a spiral column, balancing the arrangement just so. I watched him, my thoughts racing.

For two weeks I had wandered through every *sestiere* of Venice. I'd seen gift shops, craft shops, leather shops and clothing shops, from Prada posh to strictly souvenir. Designer to detritus, kitsch to cool. But nowhere had I seen anything like a Target or a Bunnings or a Marks and Spencer. Nothing at all; not even a scaled-down version of these purveyors of everyday essentials.

So I put the question to Dimitri. He had finished the spiral construction and moved to the boxes of quills and ink, persuading them into alignment. The writing implements of a bygone era served as my jumping-off point to the subject of 21st-century shopping.

'Where do Venetians go to buy their day-to-day items? Things like household goods? Work gear?'

'For most shopping we must go to Mestre. It is inconvenient, yes.' Dimitri shrugged again. 'But it is the way of things.'

My mind went back to a comment I'd come across not so long ago. It carried the same sense of resignation that I heard in Dimitri's voice.

'It's not beautiful. It's not ugly. It's just necessary.' So said former Venetian mayor Giorgio Orsoni. He was responding to criticism of the enormous advertising hoardings placed on maintenance scaffolding to generate income for the cash-strapped city.

It's just necessary. The words might equally apply to tourism, I thought, listening to Dimitri. And change won't happen overnight. It can't. *Il Comune* is not about to meddle too much with the city's financial lifeline. Tourism is a net cost to Venice, but fully seventy per cent of its present income is derived from this source.

Dimitri looked up from the quills and ink, dusting off his hands. 'More and more residents ask for restrictions on the number of visitors. Smaller groups. Perhaps staying for a longer time.'

As the idea of limiting visitor numbers continues to gain traction, accommodation in all its forms is under review. The hundreds of listings on holiday accommodation websites – housing that could be used by locals – remains contentious, and there are no new hotels planned for Venice.

Dimitri paused. I knew what was coming next. The elephant in the room.

'But especially residents ask that cruise ships are stopped. You have seen the banners, yes? When you walk around San Polo?'

I'd seen them. *No Grande Navi*. The banners hung from apartment windows in San Polo's *calli*; images of a ship with a red or black cross drawn over. Little chance for misinterpretation.

'I often see cruise ships when I'm out walking, especially on the Zattere,' I said. 'From the pavement they look like floating office blocks. Very ugly office blocks.'

I waited for Dimitri's comment.

'Hmph,' he said, as if that were response enough.

And really, ugliness is the least concern; the real damage happens below the water's surface. Water displacement – as much as eighty thousand tons – creates a turbulence that erodes building foundations. The turbulence lasts up to twenty-four hours after the ship has passed, long after passengers have dined, danced and retired to restful sleep. As their ship carries them across the Adriatic Sea, Venice is still feeling the effect. With almost daily arrivals and departures, there's no time when building foundations are not under stress. For as long as a millennium, these foundations have been carrying the weight of a city on their shoulders. They deserve a rest.

It's little wonder cruise ships are so disliked by locals. They are a constant, in-your-face reminder of the damage being done to Venice by the mass tourism on which the city's financial survival depends. And then salt is rubbed into the wound.

'Venetians call cruise ship passengers gelato tourists,' Dimitri said. 'They eat a snack in a cafe. Buy a few souvenirs. Often return to the ship for their evening meal. They crowd our city, but leave us nothing.'

Dimitri made his way back to the counter, talking over his shoulder. 'Venetians have voted in a referendum. Ninety-eight per cent, they say no to cruise ships in the Giudecca Canal.'[3]

'That's a pretty clear endorsement.' I fought to keep a sceptical twist from my voice, but I wasn't overwhelmed by

3   See Author's Note on p356.

an outbreak of optimism. I rubbed my forehead to mask a frown, recalling the MoSE saga.

The final word goes to Piero Pazzi. Of the damage caused by group tourism, including cruise ships, he says '... you are actually breaking the balls and compromising the fragile equilibrium of a little city that was built on a human scale and not for oceanic crowds.'

It's something to think about as you walk up the gangplank.

Dimitri lifted a final package and placed the empty cartons behind the counter. He sent a quick glance around the shop and nodded, satisfied. Everything was in order for another business day. Any moment now Vivaldi would start up. I delved into my bag for sunglasses, preparing to leave.

'Thank you so much for spending time with me,' I said. 'I shouldn't hold you up any longer.'

We shook hands and Dimitri walked with me to the door. He turned over the *Chiuso* sign.

'I have enjoyed talking to you,' he said. 'It is good to meet someone who wants to know Venice. Please, you will visit again before you leave?'

'Oh, I'd like that. And I almost forgot ... I wanted to ask what you like most about living in Venice?'

I stood in the *calle*, blinking away purple spangles that swarmed across my vision in the sudden brightness. A comment about the city's cultural riches waiting to be discovered, if only tourists would take the time, was bound to follow. But no.

Dimitri spoke without hesitation. 'I like the small streets and the small spaces of Venice. They bring people together. When I walk around Venice, I am walking around my home.'

Dimitri's comment stayed with me. Could I ever feel as he did, so at home in Venice that wandering about it was like moving from one room to another? Out there in San Polo's *calli* was one place, I knew, that *did* feel like home. My only doubt was whether I could find it without a map.

I surprised myself. Ten minutes later I crossed a bridge and walked into Campo Santa Maria Mater Domini. A ragtag little *campo*, with nothing of note to attract the attention of visitors, it embodied Venice as it used to be. My sort of place.

A wellhead stood at the *campo*'s centre and a hodgepodge of buildings encircled it. Off to the right was a cafe. Sunshine slanted under the awning above its three tables, all of them occupied. At the table nearest the cafe's door, a man sat behind an espresso cup, walking cane by his side. The sun's glare crumpled the skin around his eyes, and freckles stood out in bands across his cheeks. I guessed he passed a lot of sunny mornings in that chair.

A dog circled in the chair's shade, a bit-of-this-bit-of-that dog, collared and clipped, fur still moist from recent grooming. Finding the right position it settled, chin on paws and paws on a rubber ball. The man sipped his coffee, gazing ahead.

I leaned against the wellhead and folded my arms over its rim – idling, really, in the hope that one of the cafe's patrons would leave. I rubbed at the ache behind my forehead. It had been nagging me for some time, overlaying a bothersome thought I couldn't quite get hold of. It ran like this: in the whole of history there had been only three million Venetians. Now, in the twenty-first century, twenty million tourists descended on the city every year. They jostled through Dimitri's small streets and small spaces. They crowded through his home.

Plat. Plat. Plat. A ball bounced along the pavement beside me, followed a second later by the metallic smell of damp dog. Wet gums encircled the ball and I watched as the dog, a-quiver with excitement, carried it to his master. He dropped the ball onto a sandalled foot and looked up, head cocked and eyes expectant. The man clucked and reached down to pat the dog.

I had no wish to rain on the tourism parade. However much I liked to believe otherwise, I was a tourist myself. My feet pounded across Venice, adding to the millions that weighed on the wooden piles supporting the city. I used accommodation that could have housed locals. Wake from the vaporetti I caught compromised the underpinnings of the palazzi I visited. Even if I qualified as one of Dimitri's good tourists, I wasn't without blame.

My eyes closed for a moment as I stood there in the sunshine. Everything seemed out of focus – a photo not printed the right way, the colour not quite within the lines. Venice relied on tourism as its main revenue stream. At the same time, Venice was being destroyed by tourism.

A soggy splat. A fast-moving blur of dog tore past, skidded to a halt and pounced. He flicked the ball once, twice, wiping it to and fro across the paving to show who was boss, then strutted off to return his conquest. I spluttered into a laugh before turning to walk towards Campo San Polo. A gelato beckoned, double-scoop chocolate this time. It felt like a chocolate sort of day.

How less vexing the whole question of tourism used to be. Lord Byron could swim across a pollution-free lagoon, or along the Grand Canal, unobstructed by anything more than a gondola or two. And travellers could walk across town to sign their names in a cat's visitors' book.

CHAPTER 15

THIS CHANGES EVERYTHING

Love makes your stockings floppy.

Venetian proverb

The evening started well, blossomed into something bright and shiny and alight with promise and then came unstuck.

An umbrella swung from its strap around my wrist as I tripped along the *fondamenta*. Clouds had been gathering for several hours, scudding across the sky in a soup of blacks and greys, but so far they remained an empty threat. Venetian late-summer evenings could be like that, I'd found: an afternoon cloud squiggle crawling over the sky might grow to cover the city in a gloomy dome without the guarantee of rain. Autumn approached with a jerk, failed to deliver, then backed off a bit.

But rain or no rain, I was out to enjoy myself. My post-Brian nights had been sedate affairs, with an early evening prosecco at a nearby cafe or a nightcap in Campo Santa Margherita marking the limits of my after-dark adventures. So tonight was big.

I stretched my fingers from the umbrella to my handbag, feeling the stiff cardboard square inside. It was an invitation to a concert by Interpreti Veneziani at the Scuola Grande di San Rocco, and I'd received it yesterday as I left the Scuola after my sixth visit. *Please join us for a special event*, the young, black-suited man had said, leaving his station to hand me the gilt-edged card. All those visits, I guess. He probably thought I was a staff member.

Clip clip. My steps rang on the pavement. The Scuola Grande di San Rocco was my patch; just a comfortable stroll and three of Venice's four hundred bridges stood between it and my apartment. Not much walking then, I'd figured, when I reached to the back of the wardrobe and, flush with confidence, pulled out the Statement Shoes. Tight and bright shoes. Shoes with tapering, four-inch heels. Shoes that presented a challenge after my daily-duty sandals. I'd sat on the bed, looking at the fish-white markings left by sandal straps on my sunburnt feet, then wedged The Shoes into place and levered myself upright and ambulatory. So not Cinderella.

But very Venetian, I reminded myself. *Clip. Clip. Clip.* The city's noblewomen once donned *chopines* – clogs up to sixty centimetres in height – to put distance between themselves and the grubby pavements they walked over. A maid or two was needed to prop up la signora when she made her *passeggiata*.

If they could do it, I could do it.

Clip, clip. Clip, clip. My feet chopped out a rhythm as I walked on, passing the shop where I'd bought tonight's outfit. I glanced towards it, catching my reflection in the darkened window. The dress skimmed my hips, just as it had done yesterday in the fitting room. *Sophia Loren*, the saleswoman had assured me, fluttering and fussing and patting the dress into place with little sighs of approval. *Ah si, si, Sophia Loren.*

How could I put it back on the hanger? A cunning little number, as deceptive as a magician's silk scarf, it hid bumps, lumps and sundry bulges. A burst of tenacious dieting had kept things that way and now a virtuous, empty feeling sat around my middle, keeping me company as I clipped on to the Scuola.

A minute or so later I was there. Guests crowded through the entrance, skirting around gossiping clusters and picking their way between chairs. I found my seat, right behind the area reserved for confraternity members. The straight-backed wooden chair would be enough to keep even a non-music-lover awake during the performance, and I felt a twist of envy as I looked at the upholstered seats in the roped-off confraternity section.

A dozen or so women had gathered there. Absorbed in chatter, their voices spangled the air in high-pitched trills, not unlike the brightly coloured birds they resembled. My eyes slid along the rows and then halted, stopped as if by a traffic light. There sat a woman in a red, red dress. Gaudy, almost, and saved only by the supreme confidence of its wearer. She chirped away to her friends, the loudest of the flock, her demeanour suggesting she herself could be the performance. The confidence statement continued to her hair, coiffed into stiff, waterfall loops and secured at the back of her head, 1960s style. I caught whiffs of a scorched, chemical smell.

Sprinkled among the women sat their husbands; sleek and glossy men with smooth, tight-fitting skin, men who probably looked better with age and prosperity than they ever had when young. They talked with noisy enthusiasm, rising now and then to exchange greetings with arriving friends. *Ciao Mario, ciao Roberto,* they shouted, as if calling out from the window of a passing train.

A woman slid into the seat beside me and I turned to smile my acknowledgement. Her severe, grey-black outfit offered a drab contrast to the coloured-bird festival happening in the confraternity section. Just by looking at her I could tell she thought prettiness was a waste of time. Muttering through pursed lips, and with displeasure written all over her face, she watched the show of conviviality taking place in the rows ahead. A tumble of curls bobbed as she shook her head, and from time to time she reached up to pat the locket at her throat with little spanking sounds. Irritation radiated from her slight, brooding presence.

She looked at me, then spoke from the side of her mouth; a tossed-off handful of Italian words. I guessed her meaning even before she tilted her head in the direction of the chattering women. Being addressed in Italian no longer surprised me and I rather enjoyed being taken for a local, delaying my admission of *non parli Italiano* for as long as I could.

I did that now. Still nodding, still smiling, I turned from her to the painting on the wall beside me. *The Annunciation.* Each time I saw it, I found something I hadn't noticed before: wicker trim unravelling from a rickety-looking chair, or Joseph's tools scattered in disarray as he worked in the background. I looked again at Mary's physical reaction to the news of her imminent divine maternity. Sewing fell from her hands and, open-mouthed, she raised an arm in surprise, a hint of alarm, even. *You're telling me what?* Mary's reaction held none of the serene wonder that characterised this scene in every other representation I'd looked at over the years.

It was Tintoretto's power to shock that drew me to his work. He delivered what I wanted: a different point of view. Giandomenico Tiepolo's *Stations of the Cross* in the Chiesa di San Polo did the same thing. And ...

My thoughts stalled as the rustling and chair-scraping lessened. The musicians walked to the stage, taking their places in a thicket of music stands before starting the pre-performance ritual of testing chords and flipping through music sheets. Ahead, the happy exchanges continued.

My neighbour leaned towards me, so close I could feel her breath on my ear. '*Non sanno stare zitti,*' she grumbled from a centimetre away. '*Come trovano ...*'

Her sentences rippled over me. I smiled and nodded some more – it seemed to work. Expecting no more by way of reply, la signora swung forwards again, arms clamped over her chest.

Music of the eighteenth century billowed through the sixteenth-century Scuola. Chattering voices gusted from the confraternity section. In the pause between *allegro* and *largo*, three of the women drew their heads together for a more in-depth review of affairs. Red Dress Lady spoke as her companions listened, their fingers pressed across open mouths. Forget Bach, this really mattered.

My neighbour had had enough. She scowled, then edged forwards in her chair. Her arm reached over the rope barricade and into the hallowed confraternity section. There it hovered, the axe about to fall. I smoothed my skirt and sat back to watch the next development.

She tapped Red Dress Lady on the shoulder. '*Silenzio, per favore ... ascoltate la musica ... la moda del vestito rosso ...*'

My understanding of Italian was rudimentary at best. But had my neighbour made some reference to a new red dress? And showing off in that new red dress?

No, it wasn't possible. Of course she didn't say that.

I watched as a flank of astonished faces turned towards us, eyes and mouths rounded in surprise. But not one woman. Stiff with outrage, her face tightened into three straight lines as she glared at my neighbour. Then she lifted a hand to brush it ever so slowly, backwards and forwards, backwards and forwards, over her scarlet dress.

Yes, it was possible. She did say that.

I released the breath I hadn't realised I'd been holding. In front of us, faces pivoted forwards and a dumbstruck silence hung over the confraternity section. My neighbour settled back to a deeper appreciation of Bach's second violin concerto, fanning herself with the program. Behind it, an expression of triumph lit her face.

Interpreti Veneziani played on. Since its debut in 1987, the ensemble had gained worldwide acclaim; its performances, reviewers agreed, displaying '... exuberance and all-Italian brio ...' Tonight's audience clapped the skin off their hands, stomping and bravo-ing five encores.

All too soon it was over. A stunning evening, in more ways than one. My neighbour bade me farewell.

'*Arrivederci, signora. E bon salute. Spero ti sia ...*'

That last comment. Did she say she had enjoyed our chat? That might be stretching credibility a little far.

Light rain was falling when I left the Scuola, dimpling puddles on the *campo*'s paving. Over by the Frari garden, a cone of illuminated drops spilled beneath a street lamp. The feel of the city was quiet and intimate, with cafe tables tucked indoors and few people out walking.

It was just 11 pm, early by Venetian standards. I'd always been a late-night sort of person, so adjusting to a Venetian timetable had been the easiest thing in the world. And whenever I stepped out to explore after-dark Venice, I remembered Sebastiano's guarantee.

'Venice is safe, anywhere, any time,' he had assured me during my orientation brief on that first Sunday. I'd taken him at his word and wandered through Dorsoduro and San Polo at all hours, sometimes with others and sometimes alone. I'd ventured down small *calli* to discover tucked-away, midnight-to-dawn places, the haunts of locals. Or I'd overestimated my skills and trekked off into the night, winding up in alleyways about as navigable as a South American rainforest. Never had the slightest rub of anxiety caused me to reassess my safety options. Late-night Venice and me. A duck to water. Soda to Campari.

Thinking of which … A nightcap might be just the thing; a fitting wrap-up to the evening. Yes, I decided; way to go. With a new sense of purpose, I straightened under my umbrella and quickened my steps. But not Campo Santa Margherita, not tonight. The rain suggested somewhere cosy, to match the mood of the city.

I had an idea. On my walks around Santa Croce I often passed a small bar-restaurant. Straight from a tourist brochure it was, with a red awning and umbrella-shaded tables at the canal's edge. White lettering on the awning announced it was Ca' Leon. I'd taken a peek inside and seen the bar area. Very chic. But like so much else in Venice, Ca' Leon had slipped further and further down the to-do list, consigned to the status of somewhere I'd like to get to, sometime in the future. Tonight it ticked all the boxes.

And it was just a short distance from home. My debut visit beckoned, ten minutes away at most.

I came to a bridge and stopped to look back along the canal. Noise was sparse and distant, and shadows fell over a *fondamenta* where two figures stood, their heads bent together in murmured conversation. The Venice of intrigue and mystery ran before my eyes, a tapestry of the past, evoking images of dark deeds and treacherous whisperings. I might have stepped back through the centuries.

So little time remained. Next week I would be back at the *ferrovia*, pulling my suitcase along the platform to a Milan-bound train. Then so much time to follow, back in Perth, reunited with the daily tasks of running a life. I pulled the umbrella closer and leaned over the railings. Never mind the rain and what it might do to my hair or my dress or my shoes. Nothing in the world mattered as much, just then, as standing for a while on that little wooden bridge.

A rustling sound came from behind me. A tap on the shoulder followed.

Venice is safe, anywhere, any time.

I looked over my shoulder and saw the silhouette of a Christmas tree in a large planter box. My eyes refocused in the dimness. No. No, this was a bloke. He stood behind a suitcase, wearing a plastic, hooded poncho that spread over his body in a perfect triangle. Across it, raindrops glinted like so many stars.

Close by stood his wife, wearing a similar costume. She waited, feet planted in a rigid, hostile stance, glowering at her husband and the damp wad of map he was clutching. Her look summed up the situation. They were lost. It was his fault. Men were supposed to know about these things, weren't they?

The man passed the wad from one hand to the other and gathered up his words. He fixed his eyes on my face with a hopeful expression.

'*Ferrovia?*' he tried. 'Station?'

I raised the umbrella a touch and looked from one to the other. We were no more than five hundred metres from Ferrovia Santa Lucia, and the path there was straightforward. *Sempre diretto*, near enough. I could explain it easily, so long as ...

'Do you speak English?' I asked.

'Japan,' he replied.

I remembered my early days in Venice; the times when wandering turned to lost and lost was not what I wanted. I remembered the frustration that followed, chasing up one unsigned *calle* to a dead end, then retreating to try the next, often with the same result. I felt for this man with the sodden map. My eyes moved to his wife, an authoritative, no-nonsense little package, her feet still anchored to the wooden bridge as though nailed there. With her right hand she smacked a furled umbrella into the open palm of her left hand. Ready to clamp down on the world, if need be, to keep it in order.

The poor fellow. I smiled my understanding, ready to help. In any case, Ca' Leon lay in the direction they needed to go. We'd pass it on the way. Altruism and convenience coincided in one neat arrangement. I didn't need to think twice.

'I'll take you there. Really, no trouble at all.'

I signalled for them to follow me. They looked at each other before the wife's glance flicked to my shoes. She spoke to her husband. Perhaps she said she didn't trust the judgement of a person who would wear such shoes to walk over slippery pavements. Her husband made a brief reply. Perhaps he said they were running out of options.

I started down the bridge. Those shoes. Sitting at the concert had been okay – not comfortable, but tolerable. Walking was another matter. My feet had been plugged into their casings for some hours now, and swollen skin puffed above shoe-edges like rising dough overlapping its container. The grip had notched up from snug to pinching-tight. Bone realignment couldn't be ruled out. I walked in the careful, picky manner of someone navigating a freshly mopped floor as the wife watched me, her worst fears confirmed.

Clomp. Clomp. Clomp. I led our little tribe, threading my way between puddles. The suitcase-toting husband followed with hurried, rocking steps, his raincoat settling around him in a swaying triangle. The smaller triangle followed. We walked past a restaurant where lights glowed yellow behind a rain-speckled window and geraniums flowered in terracotta pots at the doorway. A pretty sight. But the couple trundled on, looking neither this way nor that, eyes glued to the pavement. Their faces reflected their thoughts with the clarity of the first line on an optometist's chart: *How much further?*

We approached the turn into Fondamenta dei Tolentino. I looked up from the puddle I'd just splashed through and saw my apartment. The curtains were drawn back, and before setting out for the Scuola I'd switched on lamps. Now they marked out the unlit building – three oblongs of light punched into the darkness. The dining room's chandelier spotted prisms onto the walls and ceiling. Here was another pretty sight, and this one I wasn't about to ignore. I stopped and pointed across the water.

'Look,' I said. 'That's where I live.'

I knew the comment wouldn't be understood, so I suppose I said it for myself. *There. That's my little toehold in Venice. I'm part of this amazing place.*

The couple pulled up alongside and followed the line of my finger. A burst of rapid conversation followed. They looked at me. They looked at each other. Baffled frowns spread across their foreheads. New to Venice they might be, but they knew for certain that was no railway station they were looking at.

I flashed my brightest, most encouraging smile, a believe-me-I-know-what-I'm-doing kind of smile. More conversation passed between the pair while I stood there grinning. At last they smiled back – hopeful little smiles, I felt, although I could have been wrong. Perhaps the meagre lip-stretching had more to do with resignation. The soaked map had been jettisoned a while back. I was their only way out of Dorsoduro.

Not far now.

To the right lay Campo dei Tolentino and I paused for a moment. Nothing of its summertime vibrancy was on show tonight. No white-clothed tables ruffled its edges, and no accordion-squeezing musician wandered between them, dodging waiters as he entertained patrons for a euro here, two euro there. At the rear of the *campo*, the facade of Chiesa da San Nicola da Tolentino looked austere in the rainy greyness.

So different from last Sunday night, when couples had waltzed and foxtrotted on the church's portico. Over the stone surface they'd skimmed, the women's flamboyant costumes matching the church's extravagant interior. Dark-suited men, standing as straight as the Corinthian columns they flashed between, held their partners' waists or spun them into coloured circles. A seventeenth-century church became the setting for a 21st-century dance competition and the connection was perfect.

I'd joined others, that night, to sit on the church steps and watch. A memory caught up with me, and I pictured myself back at the dancing classes of my long-ago school days. There we were: ponytailed girls wearing lipstick secretly applied after school, lined up against a wall. Reluctant teenage boys pressed against the opposite wall, each unwilling to be the first to Make a Move across the empty expanse of dance floor and choose a partner.

The memory brought a smile before I turned away from the deserted *campo*. The two triangles pressed hard on my heels, almost bumping into me before I walked on. I wondered how they would have responded to that scene of a week ago. Perhaps they would have been as enchanted as I was. Perhaps they would have paused for a moment. Smiled, even.

Or perhaps not. Their eyes remained fixed on the pavement, and distraction of any sort seemed unlikely. *Chin up*, I thought, *we're almost there*. And just as well. By now my feet were sending out a clear message. *No more walking*, per favore. *That's it for the night. Let's think about a spell in a basin of warm water. Radox salts, if you can manage it.*

Our pace picked up; I felt like someone leading a horse that has sensed the home paddock. As we zipped past Ca' Leon, first triangle sent a comment over his shoulder to second triangle and chuckled for the first time since our meeting. Then he laughed. His wife smiled.

Allora. He'd spotted the Grand Canal. On its far side a white glow bathed the *ferrovia*'s forecourt, unmistakable in the surrounding gloom. Passengers edged suitcases up steps or pulled them along the ramp, heading for the platforms. The husband clamped one hand on his wife's shoulder and pointed with the other. He laughed again. *No doubt about it*, his beaming face said, *that's the railway station alright. The other building, the one she pointed out earlier, that must have been a ticket office.*

His wife turned downright jolly. Her smile widened, threatening to become a laugh, as she grasped my hand and bobbed her head up and down in thanks. Her husband put down the suitcase and did the same. With much hand waving they started off towards the Scalzi Bridge and destination *ferrovia*.

I waved back like a host farewelling guests, then watched them melt into the darkness. The rain seemed to have stopped. I closed my umbrella and tilted my face upwards to check. Far away in the inky sky, a star winked down at me.

❁

By now my shoes were seriously reminding me they had four-inch heels attached to them, and the nightcap that half an hour ago had seemed like a good idea had become emergency first aid. I retraced my steps to Ca' Leon.

And how good was this? From the damp pavement I walked into a warm glow of light reflected from crimson walls. Subdued voices mingled with music drifting from the adjoining restaurant, making for a cosy, tucked-up feel. A cushioned banquette extended around two sides of the room, and behind the service counter liqueurs and aperitifs lined shelving that rose almost to the ceiling. First aid never looked so good.

I was alone in the bar area. Two waiters idled at the counter, stacking glasses onto trays before carrying them through swinging doors to the kitchen. An end-of-the-evening atmosphere settled over the room and I dropped into a seat.

The younger waiter greeted me in Italian, then spoke a little English as he placed my drink on the table. 'Tonight is very quiet. The rain keeps people at home, I think.'

Soft lighting. A Disaronno. The Eagles singing on the restaurant's stereo about peaceful, easy feelings. I lifted my glass, twirling ice cubes through the amber liquid. How had sixty-four years come and gone before I discovered this almond-scented magic? Then another thought came crashing in. How had sixty-four years come and gone, period? Sixty-four sounded like some other person's age.

I sat a little straighter, patted my hair into place and brushed a hand over my dress. *Ah si, si, Sophia Loren.* My guidebook sat on the table and I pulled it towards me. Another look around, then I settled down to read.

Tomorrow I planned to tackle the Palazzo Ducale, a drawcard attraction I'd so far avoided, not wanting to be caught up in the tourist crush. It might be less daunting, I thought, if I picked out just the things I most wanted to see, like Tintoretto's depiction of the welcome extended to King Henri III of France. Or his immense *Paradiso,* begun when he was seventy-seven years old. Just looking at it would make sixty-four seem young.

I leafed through the book's pages, then reached for my drink.

And that was when I saw the shoes. There they were, shiny and smart and nudged up beside me, despite the empty couches encircling the room. I lost track of the sentence

I was reading as my eyes darted from the book to the shoes and back to the text. I peeped sideways, then up. The man attached to the shoes sat looking straight ahead, making no attempt at conversation.

What on earth should I do? Anything? Nothing?

This wasn't something I'd learned about at school. The convent curriculum stopped well short of the response demanded by such a situation. I thought back to all the years of algebra and trigonometry I'd endured, for no apparent benefit. Now I wondered if some form of instruction regarding social protocols would have served me better.

I turned back to the book. Few words in modern literature have received the attention I gave to that guidebook over the next few minutes. I flipped a page, then risked another peek. Still there. Still looking straight ahead.

So how does this work, exactly? What's meant to happen next?

I hung back from starting a conversation. In a bar? With a stranger? But it was impossible to avoid some form of acknowledgement – he sat right there, alongside me. Should I take the initiative? Or had he already done that?

And then, somewhere in the deep recesses of my brain, the memory screen clicked to refresh. I saw Mary, still on about distant banks and crossing rivers to reach them. Monika and Raoul, stranded on my doorstep. Brian's companionship after a chance meeting. Then up popped Dixie's pretty face. And the kindly woman on the train from Milan, visiting Brescia with her dog. All of them were waves that had rolled me forwards, one after the other, and this wasn't going to beach me.

On your mark. Get set. Ready for anything.

'*Buona sera, signor.*'

I turned to face a man of about my age, with longish, silver hair swept back from a wide forehead to curl over the collar of a white shirt. He was slim, with a precisely chiselled profile and his shoulder, mere inches away, sat above mine, suggesting height. Not too shabby, I thought, crossing my legs so the dress sat a little higher above my knees.

'*Buona sera,*' he replied. '*Tu non di Venezia, le noto ...*'

His sentences spilled out in a rush. I couldn't identify where one word ended and the next began. After a minute or so he paused, as if to check he was off to a good start. He smiled and extended his hand.

'Rossano.'

I looked at him with a blank stare. How many times had I been embarrassed by my language shortcomings? How often had I promised myself I'd learn more Italian? But of course I hadn't, and he may as well have been speaking into a dead telephone. Smiling and nodding wouldn't cut it here, not like they had with my concert neighbour. There was just no way around it.

'*Non parli Italiano.*'

There. Done. The admission, along with my three words of greeting, made up a goodly percentage of my vocabulary. I didn't even know the word for sorry.

'*Scusi,*' I added as a hopeful afterthought.

'Ah,' Rossano said. Nothing more.

But there had to be more, surely. He'd sat next to me in an empty room. His conversation had been enthusiastic, more than mere courtesy. And then there was that smile. Lips moving upwards, then parting with exaggerated slowness over white teeth. Totally sexy. I shifted in my seat.

'Do you speak English?' I asked.

But it hadn't been my night for English speakers and that wasn't about to change now. Rossano's eyebrows rose above the metal rim of his glasses and continued upwards to merge with his hairline.

'No,' he said. *Like, why would I?*

Well why don't you? I wanted to say. *Why, when I've met so many Italians who do speak English? And with those divine accents. Why aren't you one of them?*

A possible friendship was about to end after a dozen or so words. My seize-every-opportunity bravura had amounted to nothing. I picked up my drink and contemplated the alternatives. Long periods of silence. A pantomime of hand gesturing. Or a fast-approaching farewell. The latter seemed the most likely, so I nodded and went back to my book. Rossano went back to gazing straight ahead.

I leafed through pages, waiting to see what would happen. Minutes passed before I felt a tap on my shoulder. Putting on my best smile, I turned to Rossano.

'Er ... *vous parlez français, peut-être?*' he asked.

Some nights you just get lucky. My language workout with Raoul and Monika was about to pay dividends. I smiled on, as though my photograph was being taken for a toothpaste commercial. Rossano finished his drink and stood, ready for a return trip to the bar. He picked up my glass, empty but for half-melted ice cubes sloshing around the bottom.

'Would you care for another?'

A second round of almond indulgence seemed a marvellous idea. *Oui* was such a dear little word and it rested on my tongue, all set to go, awaiting instructions. But I needed to be on my toes for whatever followed. Although probably it was better not to think about toes.

'I shall have now a coffee, thank you.'

A phrase straight out of French for Beginners. Too easy. I could do this. Oh yes I could.

With excessive generosity, I fancied myself an adequate French speaker. My conversations with Raoul and Monika had been a happy fusion of French and English, and we'd managed well. Raoul's English had been at least as good as my French and Monika was always game to toss a few words into the mix. All this had left me with an inflated notion of my abilities. And now here was Rossano, who spoke no English at all. Not a word. A one-on-one conversation proved much harder than a conversation split three ways, I discovered; no one else shared the burden of understanding and responding. Everything was down to me. So on I went, mumbling and stumbling, grasping at words. We established that I was Australian, holidaying in Venice for a month.

'Which hotel are you staying at?' Rossano asked, a predictable enough question. I wondered if he was trying to make things easier for me.

'No hotel. No, no. I rent apartment. Is close. Is good.'

Rossano persevered. 'Did you find it on the internet?'

Things were slipping into a Q and A format here. I felt I should spread my linguistic wings and flutter off to broader horizons. After a moment to gather my words and arrange them with some sort of grammatical accuracy, I offered up a response.

'Yes, I find apartment on internet. Last year I come to Venice with friend. Then we stay in Cannaregio. That apartment also we find on internet. Was good.'

Better, I felt. Lacking pronouns and conjunctives – such capricious little words – but an advance on my previous efforts. Rossano leaned back and sipped his drink, smiling encouragement. I forged ahead.

'Cannaregio, too many tourists are there. This year I wish for apartment away from tourists. I come to other side of Grand Canal, here. I like very much here. I like restaurants and churches and very much I like Campo Santa Margherita. All days I go to Campo Santa Margherita.'

I drew a breath and reached for my coffee. What an exhausting business language was. I took a sip while my mind worked behind the scenes, plotting an expanded contribution.

'Yes. Ah, yes. Campo Santa Margherita. Is good.'

Rossano examined the toe of his left shoe and his lips twitched as if he were trying not to chuckle. A thought raced through my mind: had he even understood me? *Okay mate*, I decided, *it's your turn. Over to you and give it your best.*

'You live and work also in Venice, *oui?*'

A broad, open-ended question of the type favoured at interpersonal communication workshops. I sat back and waited.

'I have lived in Venice all my life, apart from holidays. I love the cultural aspect of the city and I can't imagine living anywhere else. My apartment is also close by, and like you I avoid tourist areas.'

So he had understood. My hopes soared. As I watched him speak, a certain *je ne sais quoi* zinged through me like an electric current. From our first exchange, a heady sense of possibility had circled my thinking and now it established a stronghold. Perhaps we might see each other again? I tried out the notion, testing it.

Was good.

Rossano twisted his glass, swirling the ice cubes in a contemplative way. 'For many years I taught Italian literature. I'm retired now, but I still work part time as a music critic. I write a column for *Il Gazzettino*.'

Opportunity knocked and I rushed to the door, throwing it open to a new world of conversation. I tucked my reading glasses into my handbag; with any luck I wouldn't be needing them again. At least not tonight.

How lucky can one girl be? Meeting a music critic on the very night ...

'I did go this evening to concert at Scuola Grande di San Rocco. Was very good.'

What I lacked in imagination I made up for in enthusiasm. I clasped my hands and leaned so far towards Rosanno that I occupied only the front two inches of the seat. My eyes scanned his face, gauging his reaction. I did not find the endorsement I'd hoped for. Was he missing something? Was *I* missing something?

'*Interpreti Veneziani*,' I enlarged. 'Vivaldi. Bach.'

There I sat, perched forwards and wondering if I'd just failed a test of some sort. Perhaps my choices were *trop ordinaire* for a Venetian music critic. Perhaps I'd have to do better.

'And next week I see opera at La Fenice. Yes.'

I so wanted the approval of this man with the stylish shoes and the flirty smile and the curling silver hair. But Rossano's interest was less with the music than with the venue.

'And did you like the Scuola?' he asked.

I was out to impress. If my musical taste had come in below par, then I'd switch to art. And if I couldn't find the correct words, at least I could supply plenty of them.

'*Très, très beau. Et j'adore Tintoretto, et ...*'

I paused a beat, recalling Monika's particular language insight. Relevant to the circumstances, I thought. *Think French*, she'd said, *speak French. Accept that you'll make mistakes, just get the words out there.* So on I charged.

'The way he uses colour and movement in his work. Two of his paintings at the Scuola fascinate me. *The Annunciation* in the Lower Hall, where we sat tonight – *stupéfiant*. And *The Crucifixion* in the Sala del'Abergo.'

Three verbs and a few nouns, the same in English as in French, almost. But something must have gone wrong. Rossano looked at me. He opened his mouth to speak and then changed his mind, instead raising his glass to his lips.

'And Chiesa della Madonna dell'Orto has Tintoretto's painting of *The Presentation at the Temple*. I believe it rivals Titian's more famous work at the Accademia.'

Rossano's glass jerked upwards in a sudden, startled movement, sending ice blocks crashing against his nose. I guessed he was asking himself where-to-next – the door perhaps, and a fast getaway. An unfinished drink was all that kept him in his seat.

'Pardon?' He managed at last, replacing the glass and dabbing at his nose. I re-evaluated my skill level and tried again.

'I like Scuola. I like Tintoretto. I like Titian, but less. I go to Madonna dell'Orto. Tintoretto stays there dead.'

Throughout my art discourse, Rossano's eyes had been growing steadily wider. Now they threatened to depart their sockets.

I beamed on at high voltage, feeling I had something to contribute. 'Yes. And Titian stays dead at the Frari. Veronese stays dead at San Sebastiano. I have many photos. You would like to see?'

'*Ah non, merci.*'

Behind the words lay the flicker of a laugh; a kindly sound, making me feel a bridge had been crossed and the path forwards eased. Monika had been right. We journeyed on to new conversational territory, my confidence rising with every word. Particles and pronouns made a welcome return. I remembered verb conjugations and threw them about like so much confetti. The use of different tenses emerged as a clear possibility.

Rossano's chuckle became a smile and then a broader smile. Perhaps encouraged by my spurt of fluency, he started off on a new train of thought.

'I live in San Polo, near the Grand Canal. The apartment is quite small, but sufficient for one person.' He paused, as if to allow time for the information to be received and processed, then moved on. 'It is on the *piano nobile* of an old palazzo.'

I wondered if the ceiling might have frescos of plump-bottomed cherubs peeping through clouds. Or if sunshine reached the apartment's interior through mullioned windows, lighting the computer screen as Rossano worked on his column. Most of all I wondered if this might be Rossano's way of declaring his unattached circumstances. He'd spoken in a way that seemed to invite reciprocal information and that suited me: I'd been puzzling over a subtle means of getting across my own single status. In case he was interested. Or might become interested. If this conversation were to continue.

'I have a big home in Perth. Too big. So much work to do and no one to help me. I am by myself. I live alone. Always I live alone.'

I was pretty sure that nailed it. Always best to be certain.

'Ah,' said Rosanno.

He finished his drink and I reached for my camera to show him a photo of Margaret du Champs in Campo Santa Margherita.

'My name,' I said, tapping the screen. 'They have named it after me because I go there so often.'

I remembered making that comment to Brian. But it doesn't count as the same old joke if you say it in a different language, does it? Rossano took the camera for a closer look and out came that smile again. I'd had more brio in one night than in a preceding lifetime.

Rossano twisted the camera to catch the light. He chuckled, and in all the bonhomie quite forgot my novice language skills. A clutter of words hit me. I tried for a sip of coffee while I weighed up a response, tipping the cup upwards, then further upwards. It was empty and now a chocolate rim circled my cheeks and nose. Still no response came to mind. My heart chose that moment to change position, lurching upwards in my chest. I had an inkling, you see, that nestled among all those words was an invitation.

'Er ... Pardon?' My voice sounded odd. A minute ago it had been fine.

Rossano tried again. And I'd been right. Mixed in that jumble of words was a reference to Cafe Biafora, a late-night bar in Campo Santa Margherita. He was on his way there now, it seemed. But did he mean I might like to go with him? And go there now, or at some other time? Or was he indeed going there to meet someone else? I still wasn't certain. A minefield of misunderstanding lay ahead.

I replaced the coffee cup on the table and folded my arms beside it, then refolded them the other way. Language was such a tricky beast. Had we been speaking in English, it would all have been so easy. I would have said *I'd love to go to Campo Santa Margherita with you, Rossano, but here's the thing. My feet are killing me. If I take another step in these shoes I'll scream – I will, yes – scream in a way that gives a whole new meaning to the term pierced ears. But what we could do is call by my apartment – it's on the way – and I'll change shoes. Or we could stay put in my apartment, if you like. I've got a whole bottle of this lovely Disaronno stuff. And if breakfast time rolls around and you're still there, don't feel you have to rush off. In fact, if you would care to stay for the rest of your life, that would be okay.*

That's what I would have said.

But it didn't solve the problem of what to say right now. In French, not English. Maybe I should try another open-ended comment and leave it up to Rossano to say something. Something I could understand.

I rubbed at my right temple and waited for inspiration to strike.

Late night walks under a Venice moon. I could say I liked late nights. Then Rossano could say *allons-y!* Or not. At least I'd have a clue to point me in the right direction. I looked at my watch, then twisted it towards Rossano. He looked too. Ten past midnight, the watch informed its audience.

'*J'aime se coucher tôt,*' I said.

Rossano's gaze slid from my watch to my face, eyes as dark as last night's storm clouds. His mouth formed a compressed circle, as though self-control alone held back the words he wanted to speak. Faster than you could say Giuseppe's your uncle, he was on his feet.

'In that case, I shall wish you good evening and good health.'

Standing very straight, very correct, and with just the right inclination of his head, he spun on his heel and walked out. Just like that. Gone. *Arrivederci. Il est allé.* There was no time to smooth things over or pat them back into place.

My last sight was the heels of those shoes as they disappeared out the door and onto the *fondamenta*.

What had I done? What could possibly have caused such offence? I'd said I kept late nights, that was all. That *was* what I'd said, wasn't it? *Tard* meant late, anyone knew that. Tardy was its English first cousin for goodness' sake.

A prickle of anxiety scratched at my memory. *Tard*, I'd said. Surely I'd said that. But then again, there'd been a lot of thinking happening at the time. Maybe confusion had got the better of me. Maybe ...

I looked from the empty doorway to the bottles lining the shelves. They glinted back, row after row, mocking me. Sophia Loren, sitting alone in a bar at midnight.

Oh, dear. There was nothing maybe about it. Everything had got tangled up in my mind, all jumbled and muddled. I had said *tôt* instead of *tard*. I'd told Rossano I preferred early nights. And it wasn't as if it were a straightforward vocabulary mistake, something I could fix with a little revision of French for Beginners. No. But it might be useful to go back and look up the French verb meaning fob off.

Empty tables watched on like witnesses as I gathered up my handbag and uncurled myself from the banquette. My feet throbbed in protest. With the awkward steps of a wind-up toy, I set off across the room.

To think how pleased I'd been with myself! I'd trotted off to the Scuola, all tricked up and clutching a concert invitation. The neighbourhood I walked through was my home turf, as welcoming and reassuring as my own backyard. I'd done it! I'd become a local, spoken to in Italian and asked for directions by lost strangers. Venice was mine!

How dumb. As if fitting in could ever be that easy. And so much for taking a chance. I'd tossed the dice, only to have it knocked clean off the table by a French-speaking music critic with delicate sensibilities. Now the evening's finale shaped up as a solo trip back to my apartment. Although not quite solo. Disillusionment kept me company. Foolishness tagged along. Just when you think you're getting the hang of things, your knees get knocked out from under you.

It seemed that way at times. At times, it really did.

CHAPTER 16

ROSSANO'S VENICE

I like the way my heart beats in Venice.

Alice Steinbach, American journalist and author, in *Without Reservations*

The waiter peered out from his station behind the orchestra and spotted me. With a jutting, chicken-like movement of his chin he perfected his bow-tie arrangement and started down the steps, heading in my direction. I watched him move through Florian's clientele; middle-aged couples, by and large, cradling their drinks and taking occasional, token sips. At Florian prices you had to make a drink last.

What was I doing here, sitting in the Piazza di San Marco? So not my sort of place. No locals gathered in chatting clusters to review the day's events. No dog uncurled over sandalled feet, sniffing with happiness, knowing a pat was on the way. This was strictly tourist-and-pigeon territory.

I'd been to the opera – *La Traviata*, performed at La Fenice – and I put my change of heart down to that. Watching Verdi's famous opera presented in the city where he introduced it to the world had lit some dormant tourist spark. I'd seen next to nothing of the Piazza, and with my holiday running down to its conclusion I wondered if that had been a mistake. The Piazza lay an easy stroll from La Fenice. It was now or never, I'd decided, time to make the dutiful visitor-to-Venice pilgrimage.

So there I sat, about to pay too much for a drink. The waiter advanced. I thought of the damage I was about to inflict on my credit card, all for three mouthfuls of warm prosecco and a frosty greeting.

Total madness. I stood, pushed the chair beneath its white-clothed table and made for the vaporetti platforms, watching from the corner of my eye as the waiter raised his shoulders in a nonchalant shrug. He straightened his jacket, fiddled some more with his bow tie, then retreated to his post behind the orchestra. *New York, New York*, they played, from the terrace of an iconic Venetian landmark.

Twenty minutes later I left the vaporetto and walked along Fondamenta dei Tolentino, glancing inside Ca' Leon as I passed. And who should be sitting there, right where he'd been a few nights ago. From the doorway I watched Rossano fossick through sections of *Il Gazzettino*, lifting one clump of paper and then another, bending his head closer as a smile lifted the corners of his mouth. It seemed he'd found what he wanted.

So had I. A second chance stood ready and waiting. But annoyance spiked my optimism and I wavered. Should I bother? He'd walked out on me, after all – *abandoned* me – and in my new glam dress. Still … I could cross my fingers and try again; maybe I'd fare better second time around. Not that my language skills had improved, rather I'd seen the reach of Venetian prickly pride. Would it be all too hard? Or an opportunity missed, something I'd regret if I turned and walked on? Could have, would have … No, I decided, *should* have. I went indoors.

'*Bonsoir, Rossano. Ça va?*'

He looked up. Round-eyed, dropped-jaw surprise crossed his face, heralding the approach of recognition. *Oh Lord, no, it's her again. The one who likes early nights.* I planted myself near the doorway; a sturdy eucalypt, blocking his only escape route. He managed a watery smile and flapped the paper towards the empty seat beside him.

'*Ça va bien*, Margaret. Another concert?'

Rossano's face held the braced, defiant expression of someone not about to make the same mistake twice: I would remain suspect until proven otherwise. Like the half-empty cartons of milk I sometimes found at the back of the refrigerator.

I answered with a hint of smugness, taking a seat beside him. 'Not a concert, the opera this time. *La Traviata.*'

Rossano's face relaxed a touch, and I knew my choice met his approval in a way the Vivaldi concert had not.

'Ah. And you enjoyed Violetta's performance? *Supérieure*, I thought. I went last night.'

He returned the paper to its place on the table and smiled again; still half-hearted and lacking commitment to full engagement, but a start. The remnants of my irritation floundered and sank. I wondered if we could just hit the erase button – go back to the beginning and set aside the ruffled feathers that had followed. I considered an explanation, but that might be tricky. And it was too much thinking that had landed me in trouble last time. Best to just let it go. I decided instead on light chatter with plenty of meaningful eye contact. Fixing Rossano with a gaze that bordered on vision impairment, I began.

'*Ah oui*. Violetta was wonderful.'

I went on to explain that I'd had a first-class box all to myself. The young couple sharing with me lost interest and left twenty minutes after the opening curtain.

'*Les jeunes*.' Rossano shook his head, ruing the musical appreciation of young people. His face loosened from its fixed-jaw expression as we took up the thread of our first conversation. Words – often inaccurate, sometimes misunderstood – tumbled over each other and I had the sense he no longer wanted to run away. I knew I didn't. Midnight came and went without any reference to early nights.

We saw each other again the next night. And the next. And every night that remained of my time in Venice. We strolled along *fondamente* and lingered on bridges, or followed small alleyways as they unfolded into larger spaces where bougainvillea tumbled over the walls of a hidden garden, moving from sunshine to shadow and back into light. The magical light of Venice, said to have influenced a generation of artists and changed the course of painting. I thought my three-week discovery mission had shown me authentic Venice. No-o-o. I'd barely scratched the surface. With Rossano, I found the Venice of the Venetians.

I found places like Campo San Cassiano, the first place in the world where opera was performed for a public audience. It was an out-of-the-way place of locals and residents, a small *campo* in Rossano's Venice.

'Every Italian town once had its own opera house,' Rossano said, as we completed a circuit of the *campo*. The tone of his voice suggested this remained a goal to be aimed for. 'They were well patronised, always.'

Toujours. Always. My thoughts wandered. I watched evening worshippers leave the church, fanning across the

306

campo before scattering into adjoining *calli*. Next week I'd be gone, and the world would go about its business without so much as a long face. Life in Campo San Cassiano, in Venice, would continue without me.

As though I had never been there. As though I had never sat with Rossano beside a canal to watch sunrise glint on water. Or been surrounded by a blur of Italian voices under the low-beamed ceiling of neighbourhood *ristorante*. Never tasted their simple fare. Food from the heart, served in restaurants with soul, according to *mon professeur. Keep your trendy, minimalist eateries*, he declared. About as cosy and inviting as the windswept Russian steppes.

Rossano was a complex knot of information and opinion. His conversations were often taxing, and because I lacked the ability to communicate beyond the superficial, listening became my default position. When I did speak, it was without the reserves of knowledge and insight that come from a language learned as part of culture. The thoughts directing my words puttered along for a few seconds, then collapsed and vanished.

'*La petite Australienne,*' Rossano would chuckle from behind a glass of pinot grigio. A kiss would arrive on my forehead, an arm encircle my shoulders. And so I listened some more, soaking up his words like panini absorbing *jus. Toujours, toujours.*

Then came the last Friday in August.

I watered the geraniums and pulled the windows closed, clicking down the latches. Across the canal, a shopkeeper cleaned windows and rearranged the displays of his souvenir kingdom – his pride, his established realm. One last look back. My neighbour's petunias, tumbling pink and white.

Evening dog walkers on the *fondamente*. Canal barges. My two bridges. I closed the curtains and turned away.

My month in Venice was over. Rossano came with me to the *ferrovia* and we said goodbye in *carrozza* seven of the Milan train. Then he walked back along the platform and into Venice.

The word beating in my brain was *remember*. I gazed out the window, tears spiking my lashes. The lagoon slipped past, flushed with the red and gold of sunset, just as it had been the night Mary and I sat on a restaurant deck and talked about the chances life can offer. Then a clunk, a jolt, and we were on the mainland. The drab, grey outskirts of Mestre filled the windows and I thought of Dixie. *I so can't believe we're only ten minutes from Venice.* My thoughts moved to Monika and Raoul, home from Croatia by now, back in their flash Lyon pad. Mary, a new grandmother, in Aberdeen. Brian, driving his red sports car around Adelaide.

And Rossano. Still in Venice. Always in Venice.

❀

He was the first thing I thought of when I woke in the morning and the last thing I thought of as I closed my eyes at night. He took up the better part of my waking moments as well.

Holiday romances were nothing new, of course. Some people even considered them an essential part of the summertime vacation package, like an arrangement you could make through Flight Centre. I'd been a bit that way myself, once upon a time. But the years had rolled on, and I'd come to believe that serious romance lay in the past. Now I discovered it might not.

Rossano. Was he a frill, an unforeseen luxury, the final something that reshaped my holiday from good to perfect? I'd been smitten by Venice and all things Venetian; perhaps I had transferred that feeling to him. We'd spent only a week together, an impossibly short time to get to know someone. And yet …

At the very least he represented a jolt in the established order of things. I was left with an almost physical memory of those last days in Venice. It didn't lessen as I went about the tasks and pleasures of my home-again life in Perth. Tax return time. Petunias to be planted, ready for summer. Bridge on Mondays and Fridays. But always there seemed to be a Rossano-shaped hole in my life.

Like today. I tucked a cushion under my knees and bent over the azaleas. The back garden was a mess. Winter weeds proliferated; some sprouting upwards, others spreading sideways, all of them thriving. Beside the pathway thistles nodded their yellow heads. I reached to uproot a handful then stopped, my attention hijacked by a familiar voice.

Why not go back to Venice? You could, you know. There's nothing keeping you in Perth. Go back and see what happens.

Are you kidding? I don't do stuff like that. It's too silly.

It might be fun, being silly for a change. You don't have to be the same person from cradle to grave, you know.

No. No, it's not an option. Think of the money, for one thing. I need to save for next year's holiday. Mountain trekking to see those gorillas doesn't come cheap.

The gorillas can wait. Don't be so organised. You always want the edges matched and the corners squared. Why this instinctive hostility to anything that pops up outside your plans?

That's not fair. That's not fair at all. I did heaps of unplanned things in Venice, remember? Things I wouldn't normally do.

And it turned out well, right? So try it again.

Hmm, I don't know … Holiday romances … Memories often shine brighter than the reality … And I'd miss the footie finals. No, I'll just stay here and pull weeds.

Queen Careful. Ms Look Both Ways. Life isn't a sort of practice run, something you can afford to play around with. They don't offer second and third chances to get it right. Use it better. Live it fuller.

But Rossano and I are very different people. We don't even speak the same language, for heaven's sake. We're not some neat pairing, like the figures on a wedding cake.

Okay, it may not work out. So what? Make a mistake. Make every mistake you can think of. Have a stab at adventure.

The phone rang and I shuffled to my feet. *That could be Rossano,* I thought, ducking beneath windows and pulling the back door open. And yes, it was Rossano; his third phone call since I'd arrived home. I wedged the phone under my chin and pulled off gardening gloves – a reprieve for the thistles. Damp earth sprinkled the kitchen bench as I listened to him tell me of the perfect Venetian morning he'd woken to. *Mais vous n'étiez pas là.* My fingers traced through the sand and my mind slipped back to the city of *calli* and canals. As if it had ever really left.

A goosebump moment. Should I go back to Venice? Rossano thought so.

I knew it. Waiting to be rescued from your own indecision.

I pressed the heels of my palms against my eyes until I saw dancing dots of light. The clock on the kitchen wall ticked as loudly as footsteps.

❁

So, then. Five weeks after leaving Venice I was back.

I pulled the suitcase along Calle Lunga San Barnaba, towards my apartment. Summer had left Venice, slamming the door closed on the way out, the shudder sending leaves falling to pavements and cafe patrons heading indoors. Autumn had moved in, bleak and hard-edged. A leaden sky nudged towards twilight and a raw, damp wind tunnelled along the *calle*, whipping hair across my face. I blew at a strand to free it from my lipstick.

Not only the weather had changed since my last visit. Sebastiano's apartment, my treasured little piece of Venice, had not been available at short notice. But I'd still be living in Dorsoduro, in a *corte* near Campo San Barnaba. An excellent neighbourhood, Rossano had assured me during our last conversation.

I didn't think so, to be honest. A covered alleyway led to the *corte*; drab and narrow, with all the natural light of a prison cell. Buildings leaned together, and the *corte* itself had a meek, deflated look. I pushed open the street door and stepped into a vestibule cluttered with umbrellas and rubber boots. Junk mail lay in a drift across the floor. My soon-to-be home nestled under the building's eaves, a climb of two floor levels. I peered up the stairwell and grasped the suitcase handle. Then, like a child squaring up to a plate of spinach, I sighed and made a start.

I unlocked the door to a tiny apartment. No chance of feeling like a lone pea in an oversized pod here. My eyes moved across the living room – it didn't take long – and stopped at the study alcove with its antique desk. Across the leather surface, stationery lapped at precise, mathematical intervals and a lamp had been switched on. *How charming,* I thought, *even though I'll need to bend double to reach it.*

Beyond lay the bathroom. I drew in a whistle of breath. Full marks to the builder who figured out these ablutions. The shower was over the bath and the bath was wedged into a sloping corner. Ceiling met wall at the level of the soap holder. A Pilates squat in the tub was the only way to take a shower. And just to be sure I didn't miss the comedy of the event, an oversized mirror hung on the opposite wall.

But what the heck? Within a day or so I'd grown to love my cubbyhole under the rafters. Snug and cosy, it matched this different, wintery Venice. Heating murmured, with an occasional hiss to prove its good intentions. The desk lamp cast butterscotch ribbons across uneven walls, the first thing I saw each time I opened the front door. In the light by the kitchen window, potted cyclamens stood to attention. I walked from room to room, humming as I ducked beneath low beams.

The apartment's main attraction was its proximity to Rossano. Close enough without being too close, it allowed both of us to get used to the idea of having the other around. As I saw things, incremental change, slowly paced, was the most hopeful path forwards, although I had little idea of how that path forwards might progress, or even what I'd expected from my impromptu return. It just seemed the right starting point for whatever might play out between Rossano and me. One thing I did know: staying with Rossano in his apartment was not an option. I'd lived alone and suited myself for years, way too long to make the transition to live-in companion overnight. Two people in a small space; two people who'd spent slightly longer than a week together and sometimes struggled to communicate – I didn't need a crystal ball to foresee disaster.

Above all I didn't want Rossano to feel responsible for me. In my mind, the success of this visit – whatever loose definition I held of success – depended on my ability to fit in, to make an independent adjustment to Venetian life. I needed to show, and to believe, that Venice could become my home.

And so far so good. I waited for Rossano now, sitting in Osteria Biafora, ready for *cicchetti* – a glass of prosecco and canapes, Venetian-style. *Cicchetti* was a tradition Rossano enjoyed, and one I could happily adapt to.

There he was. He walked towards me and I felt the flood of warmth that comes when someone familiar steps out from a crowd of strangers.

'*Ça va*. Sorry I'm late.' Rossano slipped into the seat beside me. He shrugged off his jacket, then reached over to deliver a long, warm kiss.

I liked the way Italians never hesitated to show affection. Children, babies, animals and lovers were all the happy recipients of bountiful kisses and hugs. Here was another tradition I could adapt to, no problem at all.

Rossano signalled the waiter. I felt like one half of a regular couple, chatting about the day's events. Two separate lives, linking up together. How amazing. By the time the waiter returned with our prosecco, Rossano had moved on to an explanation of his lateness.

'I've been caught up with research. Did you know more than one thousand operas have premiered in Venice?' He paused to manoeuvre an artichoke heart to the edge of the platter, then twisted the arrangement towards me. 'Ah *oui*. Venice is at the heart of opera.'

He smiled, all knowledge and certainty. The teensiest spasm of one-upmanship darted behind my temples, a wish to challenge his Venice-centric view of the world. I seemed to remember there were operas that had premiered in Australia, and to critical acclaim. But getting them front of mind and passing on the information proved troublesome.

'In Australia, too, there is much opera. It is very popular. I think ... um. Yes, I think ...'

I'd upgraded from French for Beginners to French Language and Conversation and spent the last five weeks lost between the book's pages. But the small improvements I'd made were *so* small, the effort so far in excess of the achievement. My conversations were either too brief or, more often, long-winded and shapeless, full of repetitions, self-corrections and pauses to search for an elusive word.

I masked a pause now, picking up a plump egg and celery sandwich. Then I laid my head on Rossano's shoulder and traced the stitching of his shirt pocket with one finger. Something was puzzling me.

I adored Venice. Venice was where my heart sang. I remembered that first evening, just after my return, when I'd pulled my suitcase along Calle Lunga San Barnaba. Back in Venice! Like a child on Christmas Eve, alive with expectation – *with joy* – I'd rested my suitcase against the wall of the Grom gelateria and set off across the *campo*; walking at first, then breaking into a run. Before I realised it, I'd been skipping. Had Commissario Guido Brunetti been watching from his fifth floor sitting room, he would have been downstairs in a flash to arrest me.

Why, then, did I feel so protective towards Australia, the country I was willing to leave? Mention something wonderful about Venice and my need to speak up on Australia's behalf clicked on like a pilot light being lit; a defensive mindset I couldn't explain. I wondered if it had to do with Rossano's self-assurance and my need to show that I, too, knew of special things. Different things.

I looked at the tin-coloured Venetian evening outside and thought of October in Perth. The early signs of spring, with summer to follow. My mind turned to beaches: I'd rather be talking about them than opera. And my vocabulary around the subject was sound. A final munch of sandwich and in I plunged.

'*Oui, oui, Rossano, l'opéra. C'est formidable.* But Australia has wonderful things, too. I love the beaches.' *Oh yes*, I thought, picturing them waiting for me on the far side of the globe. Tropical beaches. Rocky beaches. Remote or suburban beaches, millpond expanses for infants with bucket and spade, or beaches with waves for serious surfers. And with a little time, a little thought, I could tell Rossano all about it.

But Rossano's reply came in an instant, delivered with some relish. 'Venice, too, has a beach. Le Lido. *Célèbre. Splendide.* Did you know ...'

Oh, I knew about the Lido alright. The early twentieth-century stomping ground of the rich and famous. Outshining even the French Riviera on the European social circuit. *The* place to be seen. Once ritzy and glitzy, today it spoke of faded grandeur, the remaining shadow of something wonderful, now gone.

For it had been wonderful. In 1907, entrepreneur Guiseppe Volpi acquired the Hotel Excelsior, a Moorish-Gothic statement piece right on the Lido beachfront. He set about a serious revamp, aiming to create the most fabulous destination on earth. When the hotel reopened its doors a year later, wealth, fame and beauty walked through them.

As it began, so it continued. Hollywood royalty joined European royalty to sign in at reception. Wannabes tagged along, hoping to rub shoulders with individuals of truly legendary wealth. When the Aga Khan endorsed the Excelsior with frequent visits, the name Lido became a byword for seaside luxury.

I'd seen the Hotel Excelsior. I'd walked along a tree-lined boulevard to the once equally sumptuous Grand Hotel des Bains, looking over manicured hedges to glimpse that celebrated strip of sand. Chains of deckchairs and changing cabanas stretched on and on, lining the beach in four parallel rows. Scantily clad bodies preened and frolicked; a new generation of beautiful people. Italian pizzazz abounded.

And I'd walked onto the beach itself. Gritty, grey sand scrunched between my toes. Ahead lay the Adriatic Sea, as grey as the sand it lapped against; a boring, placid sheet of water. Flat all the way to Croatia, probably.

From my position against Rossano's shoulder, I listened to his recitation of the Lido's merits. He bent down, smiling in the expectation of agreement. Wilfulness crept up on me. I remembered the soft, warm touch of sand against my feet and heard the tumbling surf of City Beach. Behind my eyes spun the coloured dots of beach umbrellas, scattered across the sand with a lack of order that suggested they might have washed up with the last wave. I saw Jake beside me, his paw prints a sandy echo of my footsteps along the wave line of a pristine coast.

I tipped my head back and laughed. 'Beach? You call the Lido a beach? I've seen bigger waves in a fish tank.'

At least that's what I wanted to say. But I hadn't come across the word for fish tank in French Language and Conversation. Perhaps there wasn't much call for it. And anyway, it then raised the problem of a good-natured, no-harm-meant delivery, which a long-considered reply would miss. That was the thing of it, really, this whole second-language business. Wit and spontaneity disappeared faster than a plate of *cicchetti.*

'*Non, non,* Rossano. Not as good as my beach in Perth.'

Rossano shook his head and chuckled. 'My little cabbage. How can you not admire that boulevard of trees? I walk there when I need to think.'

He took a final sip of prosecco. Rossano enjoyed an aperitif. Singular. For me, moderation was a lesser concern and settling back into the cosy comfort of Osteria Biafora seemed like heaven. Not a chance. Hardly had my glass touched the tabletop before Rossano straightened, ready to leave.

We walked through the chilly evening. On the Ponte dei Pugni we stopped and leaned on the railings, watching the moon struggle through clouds. The Nicolotti and the Castellani once fought their ritual battles here, and back then the bridge had no railings. For most combatants, a damp trip home rounded out the hostilities.

I held the railings in a firm grip and clutched the collar of my coat more tightly. Rossano led the way from the bridge and we strolled through Campo San Barnaba. The rhythms and texture of the city had altered over the last month. Pedestrians hurried past, shoulders hunched and heads lowered. No chatting groups sat around outdoor tables, or enjoyed *la passeggiata* with their dogs. How easy, in the hushed *campo,* to picture the Barnabotti flitting between shadows, dressed in their ragged silks. Calle Lombardo had been part of their territory and I glanced along it as we passed. A wedge of light showed around the partly opened door of Casin dei Nobili. Their food was the best in Venice, Rossano maintained. In the seventeenth century, this *ristorante* had been a brothel, and the original charts detailing prices and services still hung on the walls. Discounts were offered to seafarers.

A breeze sprang up from nowhere, ruffling Rossano's hair, and I reached up to smooth it.

'It's like strolling through a history book,' I said, turning to look back at the *campo*. 'You were right. This is an excellent neighbourhood.'

❋

Rossano swung the gate closed and we crossed the courtyard. Leafless autumn branches shone silver, lightening frozen against dark sky. Close by water tinkled. A moss-covered cherub cavorted in a fountain.

'*Alors. C'est beau, n'est-ce pas?*'

Rossano's eyes moved around the garden and I followed his gaze. Yes, it was beautiful; a hidden treasure, walled off from the grey pavements. I'd walked past several times, assuming a private residence of some note lay behind the ivy-topped wall. But no. This was Palazzetto Bru Zane, the Venetian Centre for French Romantic Music and tonight I was attending a performance with Rossano. My music-critic mate had a column to write for *Il Gazzettino*.

'*Bon*. We're early,' Rossano said, checking his watch.

Early or not, most of the seats were taken. Pre-concert chatter filled the room and French accents pinpricked the familiar buzz of Italian-speaking voices. Against the far wall I spied two vacant seats, only three rows back from the stage.

'*Ici*, Rossano.' I set off towards the seats before someone else claimed them. Rossano followed, patting his jacket pockets to check for program and pen, then pausing to greet a couple in the front row. We sat down and smiled at one another, as though just getting a seat represented a small victory.

Could Venice throw up any more surprises? Each night offered some new adventure, and now a concert in the former ballroom of a palazzetto. I felt as delighted as the cherubs overhead, romping through the cotton-wool clouds of their ceiling fresco. Any number of musical performances were available in palazzi and churches around the city, catering for the I-heard-Vivaldi-in-Venice tourist market. But this was the real deal: a Venetian event for Venetians.

Voices blurred, winding down. Baritone Eduardo and his pianist walked to the stage, bowed deeply, then took their places. The audience rustled to attention and a sepulchral hush descended. *So* not the confraternity wives.

The pianist gave a throat-clearing murmur, then plunged his fingers to the keyboard. Eduardo paced to the right of the stage and back to the centre. A forlorn expression washed his features. He lowered his eyes to a spot on the floor then raised them to the cherubs. A few chords later, his honeyed voice rolled across the audience.

Eduardo had lost his true love, he told us, by the banks of a gently flowing stream. Sometime last spring. *Perdu. Au printemps dernier.* I listened, attempting to follow his words without reference to the lyrics written in the program. It all sounded so much more impressive without translation. Not unlike the opera, really. How often had I listened to a soprano's voice tremble with emotion as she delivered her signature aria? Watched her bosom heave behind fluttering hands? Then looked at the screen to discover she'd been on about falling snow. Little more than a weather report when you came right down to it.

I folded my program and glanced across to Rossano, interested to see how a music critic went about the business of critiquing music. Not with the flurry of note-taking I'd imagined, it seemed. Rossano leaned back in his chair, listening. From time to time he tapped a pen to his cheek, then picked up the program to place an arrow – up or down – above a particular word. Nothing more. All too easy. I considered the chances of my future employment at *Il Gazzettino*.

Another arrow appeared, down this time. Rossano sat on my right and I noticed his wedding ring. I'd never seen it before, supposing it consigned to a bottom drawer after his wife's death six years ago. I looked at the delicate filigree pattern encircling the third finger of his left hand and a thought came to me, warm and melting. People might think Rossano was my husband.

Imagine that. Imagine a lifetime sprinkled with nights like tonight. With Rossano. In a palazzo. In Venice.

It never occurred to me that a future which included Rossano would be anywhere but in Venice. The two were linked in my mind as inseparable. Venice was the centre of Rossano's world, the epicentre of civilisation. *If Venice had no bridge, Europe would be an island*. I smiled, recalling writer Mario Stefani's assertion, and knowing that Rossano would agree. As a holiday arrangement or on a permanent basis, I would be the one packing the suitcases.

A heart-pounding thought registered. I could be part of this. I could be part of this for as long as I wished. I could begin the next era of my life; another way of being, shaped by a different purpose and changed priorities. I could – no, I *would* – move to Venice and make a life in this city of art and music and discovery. Church bells and the hum of chatter from the *calli* would become the background sounds of my life. The thought deepened, taking hold. I looked from Rossano to Eduardo, to the ceiling frescos and then to the stylish audience around me.

Venice, my new hometown.

My plans halted as Eduardo, resigned to his lost love, completed his tale of woe. With a fulsome sigh he turned to the pianist, arms spread and palms upturned in a manner of acquiescence. *There is nothing I can do.* With several fortissimo chords the pianist agreed. *That's right, mate.*

I started to clap. Two sharp explosions flew from my hands before a woman in the row ahead turned around. She raised both chins and her eyes flicked over me with the disdain appropriate to a cultural outlier. The tips of her fingers engaged in dainty applause as she acknowledged Eduardo's efforts. Having registered her displeasure, she swung forwards again. Rossano coughed into his fist.

Oh dear, oh dear. A serious faux pas, when I'd hoped to become one of the gang. The Australian interloper, as out of place as a splash of colour in a sepia photograph. I drew myself upright, sitting straight-backed like an Egyptian queen, hands folded in my lap. Rossano forgot the arrows long enough to place a reassuring hand over mine. Eduardo got back to business.

The performance concluded with the same taps of approval that had marked the end of each *chanson*. But Eduardo knew the ropes. The delicate *pat-patting* represented sufficient praise to warrant three encores. At last, with a hand pressed to his heart, he bowed to the audience, acknowledged the pianist with a flourish, then took his leave.

I turned to Rossano, glancing down at his program with its slim tally of markings. Was that a good or a bad thing?

Rossano folded the program around his pen and slipped the package into his jacket pocket.

'That was wonderful,' I said.

'*Pas mal*,' the music critic replied.

Not bad? Hardly a thundering endorsement. Surely Eduardo deserved more than a two-word summation. I persevered. 'And the arrows? I don't understand the arrows.'

Rossano reached into his pocket and pulled out the program, unfolding it across his knees. He leaned forwards, ready with an explanation.

'*Alors*. I know the music well. The songs are eighteenth-century French standards, performed often. The arrows show the precision with which certain notes were delivered. *Ça suffit*.'

I took the program from Rossano and studied it. Downward arrows exceeded their up-tick companions. Things weren't looking good for Eduardo. I wondered if Rossano would commit his less than glowing opinion to the printed pages of *Il Gazzettino,* three days hence. Would Eduardo turn to the music section and splutter into his morning espresso? Would tonight's concert goers re-evaluate their three encores? Perhaps there were more skills required of a music critic than I had first believed. Diplomacy might be one of them.

The arrow tutorial meant we were the last to leave the ballroom. Rossano stood and I clasped his arm as we headed downstairs. *This is all so civilised*, I thought from my perch on his sleeve. *A palazzetto concert followed by a champagne supper. What could be finer?* Expectations for my Venetian future grew rosier with each escorted step. Then I saw the supper table.

Five minutes, that was all it had taken.

In the time Rossano and I had spent talking, those finger-tapping Francophiles had descended on the supper table and stripped it bare. Empty white plates sat atop the starched white cloth, and on the blinding snowfield sat a lone chicken sandwich. Rossano made a few *tsk-tsk* noises and set off to find two glasses of champagne. I chalked up another lesson to remember in my new Venetian life: always get to the supper table early.

The rising notes of leave-taking sounded around Palazzetto Bru Zane. Rossano brushed a sandwich crumb from his jacket – we'd shared, going halves – and returned the farewells of several concert-goers. We left the palazzetto and walked through the courtyard into the silent *calle*. I thought back to our first meeting at Ca' Leon, remembering Rossano's abrupt departure. My lips shaped a private smile and I nuzzled my face against his shoulder. Rossano leaned down and planted a little brush-stroke of a kiss below my ear.

Talk about buying into a fairytale.

❄

Rain was falling by the time we reached my apartment. Its *plunk-plunk-plunk* sounded comforting, reassuring, just as it had in my childhood when I lay in bed listening to its beat on the roof. I woke during the night and heard water splashing onto the terrace. Close to my ear, Rossano whispered. He should be home, he said, in case the rain continued. I moved to the warm hollow left beside me, then burrowed back into sleep.

The bells of San Barnaba woke me at eight o'clock. Thin morning light fell across the bedroom, grey and dreary.

I walked to the windows and looked out. Pellets of rain bounced off railings and pinged their way over the terrace. Across the *corte*, a woman stood by her kitchen window, concern lining her face as she held back a panel of lace curtain. She looked around the rim of buildings and, seeing me, waved a hand towards the leaden sky. Her mouth formed a message, but the words were lost between two sets of glass and the constant drum of rain.

In the kitchen I flicked on the kettle and thought about the day ahead. Rain or no rain, some things couldn't wait. Grocery shopping topped the list. The kettle boiled and I reached up to the overhead cupboard, searching for a tea bag. An unsettling resemblance to last night's plundered supper table greeted me. Supermarket, I decided, ASAP.

At ten o'clock I set off. Outside in the *corte*, I splashed through puddles, my toes squelching, then turned into the alleyway. I stopped, aghast.

Was this what my neighbour had been on about? Why Rossano had said he should go home?

Water lay across the alleyway, above door height, and boards had been slotted into position to seal the entrances. Now I understood why so many street doors around Venice had metal frames at their lower edges. The boards fitted into these frames, preventing water from reaching the ground floor. Beyond the doorways I could see Calle Lunga San Barnaba, also underwater. Pulling a shopping buggy through the watery expanse was out of the question; even walking through it would mean the end of my shoes. I was marooned, as surely as Robinson Crusoe.

Midday came and went. Drizzle replaced the hammering deluge and I headed downstairs to reassess the water situation. Far from receding, the pond had deepened. Water was trapped along the length of the alleyway, where stone walls met stone paving, leaving nowhere for it to drain away. I stood at the shoreline and made a decision. There was only one way out.

I rolled up my jeans. I removed my shoes. I took my first tentative steps into Lake San Barnaba. Water reached my ankles, then my calves, then edged up to my knees. Scratching noises made me look up. A rat, made homeless by the rising water, scuttled across a ledge, searching out new accommodation. I closed my eyes and tried not to think what my bare feet might be walking over. I prayed I wouldn't step on anything soft or furry. On I waded, holding my shoes at chest level, stepping in a cautious, swaying motion, as if practising some exotic dance move. From the safety of his dry ledge, *il ratto* watched.

One thing was working in my favour, at least. I knew the location of an inexpensive shoe shop not far away. And I knew the astute Venetian owner would be sure to have a supply of the footwear most demanded in the city that day.

Knee-high rubber boots. The only way to deal with *acqua alta*.

❁

This weather. October should be mild, autumnal, conducive to long walks and relaxed cappuccinos in Campo San Barnaba. But in just a few weeks the climate had done a complete about-face, moving from steamy tropical to pseudo-Arctic.

I switched on the heating, listening as it clanged to life. The purring sound that announced the arrival of warm air remained stubbornly absent. Today of all days, when Rossano was coming to dinner. I'd based my menu on hearty serves of cosiness and comfort – a homey atmosphere, suggesting future possibilities. Now it looked as though I'd be dishing up the ambience of a Nordic ice float.

Another clank. I crossed to the window and looked at the bleak offering outside. Puddles lay splashed across the *corte* and the sky held the colour of old pewter. A day indoors with French Language and Conversation made sense. I picked up the book, flipping to a section I'd been working on: Chapter Forty-Five *Un pique-nique dans le park*. Where were the chapters about snuggling up on a winter's day?

I put the book down and reached instead for *The Peggy Guggenheim Collection* lying next to it on the table. Peggy was the larger-than-life American art collector who called Venice home for thirty-three years before her death in 1978. Her palazzo-home on the Grand Canal showcased a collection of modern art considered among the world's most significant. She had bequeathed the entire collection – and her palazzo – to Venice, the city she adored. The collection's monetary value was beyond quantifiable estimation, but certainly exceeded one billion dollars.

A woman who loved Venice and changed her life to live there. It resonated. And I knew the heating would be good.

An hour later I left the vaporetto to walk to the gallery. A sudden tug of wind pulled at my hair and the first drops of rain wet my face. How much harder things became in winter, when going anywhere most often involved a soaking. But the rain had its advantages, as things turned out.

I stopped for my usual pre-cultural fortifier at a cafe on Piscina del Forner. Four euro fifty for a cappuccino, without so much as a wafer biscuit resting in the saucer. Outrageous. I'd paid the same amount at a cafe near Campo San Fantin and sat on the pavement in an honest-to-goodness armchair.

And been served cucumber sandwiches so thin I hardly needed to open my mouth to eat them. But this was handy and it was open.

Al fresco seating had been moved indoors, out of the rain. Patrons crammed the cafe's interior, leaving bare centimetres between tables. Raised voices struggled to be heard above the clatter of crockery and neighbouring conversations. An empty seat beckoned near the front of the cafe and I worked my way towards it, settling alongside two men. The waiter, still clearing the table after departing customers, took my order and disappeared into the crowd.

I nodded to the men. Opposite me sat a man of older vintage, good-looking in a weathered, sea-captainy sort of way. He returned my nod and went back to the paper he was reading, shaking out its pages over his coffee cup. I took out my book, ready to research the afternoon's visit.

The closeness of our tables made conversation inevitable.

'Ah. Peggy Guggenheim. The museum is around here some place, isn't it?'

The younger man beside me pointed to the book, all glossy and self-important and announcing itself. I was pleased he'd been the one to speak first. Not wanting to seem pushy, I still hesitated at times, reluctant to strike up a conversation with strangers.

The man's eyes turned from Peggy to me. I'd registered the American accent.

'Just up the road a ways,' I replied, for some reason falling in with the American manner of speaking. 'You've not been there?'

'No. No, we haven't. What do you think, Dad?' He looked to the man sitting across the table, still immersed in his newspaper. 'Should I use it?'

I wondered how a person might use the Guggenheim and was still pondering the matter when the waiter reappeared. He stretched across two tables with my cappuccino and set it by my elbow. The smell of fried onions followed him from the kitchen and all at once lunch seemed like a good idea. I surrendered and ordered a hamburger. It was shaping up like an American kinda day.

The young man continued, nodding towards Sea Captain. 'Dad here is lucky. He can take things easy. But for me, this trip is all about work. We only have four days in Venice and I need to see a lot of places.'

The older man lowered his newspaper, ready now to join the conversation. Perhaps a sense of propriety had held him back. I listened to his modulated, Southern-gentleman voice. 'Yes. Just four days. And for Evan, why, it's all shoulder to the wheel. He works as a location scout, you see.'

My lips parted in surprise. 'I didn't know there were such things. I mean, I've heard the term, but I thought it was just kidding around. A bit fanciful.'

Evan took over from Dad. He leaned forwards, his voice alive and eager, making this unlikely job seem not only credible but a career to be aspired to.

'Oh no. It's big business. My agency back in Atlanta employs a dozen or so scouts. Mostly it's work within the States and Canada. I've been to Venice before, so I scored this gig.'

Dad folded his newspaper. I could see the waxy white of his knuckles beneath the skin as he pressed it to a compact oblong. He'd heard all this before, no doubt, and good Southern manners demanded that he move the conversation along. He looked at me with a questioning smile. 'Say, you're Australian, if I'm not mistaken.'

I dabbed cappuccino froth from my mouth and smiled a response.

'It's quite a country,' he continued. 'I chatted with a young couple yesterday, outside the Basilica. From Philadelphia, I believe they were. They'd travelled to Central Australia, they told me. To be married as the sun rose. Went to a place called Uluru.' He paused. Wistfulness travelled across his face and he sounded the name out again, as if testing it. 'Uluru.'

How times change. This was not the first conversation I'd had about Australia during my visits to Italy. Many Italians had family members living in Australia, so Melbourne might arise as often in their conversations as Milan. My friends in Perth included many of Italian descent: I knew more Domenicos than Peters, come to think of it. Americans in particular spoke in glowing terms of everything from Australia's healthcare system to our climate. Everyone knew about Australia, it seemed – and no one held the image of kangaroos hopping down the main street, either. Australia was spoken of with knowledge and respect. I felt quite proud, to be honest.

But rather than talk about Australia, I turned the conversation to their hometown. 'I remember reading *Gone with the Wind*, years ago. Is there really a Peachtree Street in Atlanta?'

'Why, sure there is,' they both rushed to assure me.

Further talk was cut short as the waiter arrived with our meals and slid them onto the table. Mozzarella bubbled beneath scatterings of pepperoni, olives and mushrooms on two large discs of pizza. My hamburger lodged between toasted panini, sliced tomato and wedges of bean sprouts, as plentiful as I'd come to expect in Dorsoduro eateries.

Dad was determined to talk about Australia. He knew a thing or two, well beyond the usual traveller's repertoire. He talked at some length about Sydney, his favourite. Humour underscored his words and beneath white tufts his eyes twinkled.

'The big cities on the east coast are very different from each other,' he said. 'In Sydney, people ask you where you live. In Melbourne they ask you where you went to school.' He paused a moment, then gave a rich chuckle. 'But in Brisbane they ask you which pub you drink at.'

So he knew the old joke, told and retold by generations of Australians. I laughed along with him, then decided to expand his knowledge.

'That's right, yes. And in Adelaide they ask you which church you go to.'

'Well now, I hadn't heard that one.'

He fell silent, pinching his lower lip. A story was being assembled for the retelling, I knew.

'So that leaves Perth,' he said. 'What do they ask you in Perth?'

Stumped. What *do* they ask you in Perth? For the life of me I couldn't think of any characterisation attaching to the city where I'd lived most of my life. Dad rested his arms on the table, expecting an answer. I had to say something. I couldn't let my hometown disappoint.

'In Perth they ask you which beach you swim at.'

Not bad at short notice. Dad gave a satisfied chortle. I guessed it would prove a handy addition to his Australiana stockpile.

Evan laughed, too, then picked up a slice of pizza and launched the conversation on a new path. 'So what brings you to Venice?' He bit into the pizza, trailing a thread of mozzarella over his chin.

Nice trick, Evan, I thought. *Keep me talking so you can eat.* I pushed the knife and fork to one side of my plate. 'Well ...'

Five weeks ago I met a fellow. Here in Venice. I believe I fell in love. Crazy, I know. Nothing more than a holiday romance. But I felt a connection that's been missing from my life for a long time. I had to come back. Unfinished business, I guess. I like things sorted and where they belong. So here I am.

I didn't say that, of course – it mattered to no one but me. Instead I took a breath and sent the air back to the room in what I hoped was a chirpy laugh. 'I have a friend living in Venice. And October seemed a good time to visit, after the tourist season. Although I had hoped the weather would be better.'

All true, as far as it went.

Evan flicked a glance to the *calle*, then shrugged. 'Still better than the heat of summer. I've been here in August and you wouldn't believe ...'

The pizzas and hamburger disappeared as our chatter continued. Evan was adept at flying several conversational kites at the same time, talking with me, his father and a group of new arrivals – also American – at another table. A second round of coffees followed before my companions stood to leave.

'It was wonderful meeting you,' I said. And I meant it. I couldn't have wished for better company. Or imagined people less like Earl and Mrs Earl, their pizza-eating compatriots.

'Oh, likewise, likewise.' Dad shook my hand and walked off to settle the bill. Evan bent to gather up notes and his phone.

A thought came to me. 'I know more about location scouts than I did an hour ago. But you never did say just what you're hoping to find in Venice.'

Evan brushed back the hair that had fallen across his forehead. I could tell he was pleased I'd asked.

'I'm working for a fashion house,' he said. 'Their idea is to show evening wear in strong, primary colours – red, say – against black and white backdrops. A couple of famous sites, like the Rialto, so people get that it's Venice. Then out-of-the-way backstreets. Very important. A dichotomy.'

The contrast of grit and glam. I got it. But whatever would Dimitri say?

Or Rossano. A crowded cafe near the Guggenheim would not be to his liking. *All the charm of a bowl of spilled spaghetti,* I could hear him muttering. Rossano's Venice was the city of Palazzetto Bru Zane and Eduardo, of neighbourhood *ristorante* in one-time brothels. Hidden places, as locked away as the prisoners in a Doge's dungeon. This cafe spoke of a different, on-full-display city. But on a gloomy afternoon, and if only for that afternoon, I wouldn't have missed it for the world.

Evan and his Dad walked into the *calle*, turning up their collars against the chill. I hoisted myself upwards and left the table, sidestepping the waiter in a no-please-after-you dance. Outside, cold air fell around me and my breath formed wet, coffee-scented clouds. Afternoon sun parted the clouds, casting lavender shadows onto building walls. Rubber boots squished on pavements.

I set off homewards, taking a shortcut to my apartment. No vaporetto this time, and no visit to the Peggy Guggenheim Collection either. My heart just wasn't in it. The day seemed full enough already.

❀

Rossano arrived at seven o'clock. I heard the slap of his knuckles against the door and the slide of his key in the lock. Seconds later he stood beside me. The distance between the front door and the kitchen was just three paces, but at least it could be traversed in the upright position. Now Rossano bent, his hair tickling my cheek as he kissed me. I stood poised over the stove like some housewifely advertisement, lifting lids from pots and fiddling with gas dials.

'*Voilà la chef.*' Rossano smiled, then reached into the refrigerator for last night's unfinished bottle of pinot grigio. He poured a small glassful and placed it beside me. This moderation thing again. Honestly. The concept itself should be applied with moderation, if you asked me.

'*Ça va?* You've had a good day?' A final stir of the pasta sauce and I sat down beside him, pushing the cyclamen pots to one side, away from their daytime spot near the window. I reached for my wineglass, allowing myself a birdlike sip.

Rossano slouched in his chair and crossed his arms over his chest, gazing at the ceiling from beneath a corrugated brow. What was this about, then? And what about the cheery, relaxed evening I had planned? I sent him a questioning look.

'I ran into a former student this afternoon.' Rossano's frown deepened. 'An outstanding student, always at the top of her class. I met her by chance, in Cannaregio. You remember I had a meeting there?'

Yes, I remembered. And I remembered how Rossano disliked touristy Cannaregio, avoiding it whenever possible. Goodness, I felt the same way. But crossing the Grand Canal had never given me such a long face.

Rossano went on. 'She had high hopes for a career which drew on her language skills. Journalism perhaps, or a career in the public service. *Mais non*.'

He lifted his glass and considered its contents, then replaced it on the table. No wonder I always finished my drink before him. I tilted my head back for a good swig. The story had jolted a memory, but I couldn't bring it into sharp focus. I listened, feet drawn up on the chair, hugging my knees to my chest. Rosanno continued, speaking as though this were the kind of thing countries went to war over.

'*C'est scandaleux*,' he fumed. 'Luisa. For three years she has worked as a sales assistant in a shoe store on Lista di Spagna. Her language skills are used to sell Made-in-China sandals to tourists. *Terrible, n'est-ce pas?*'

Pretty disheartening, I had to agree. I reached over to the stove and turned off the gas jets. There was no need to stand up and walk to it – one advantage of my thumbnail-sized kitchen. And that's when I remembered. Of course: Elizabetta, Signor Natalino's daughter. She, too, had excelled at languages but, like Luisa, could not find suitable work in Venice. Paris was now her permanent home, and a high-flying career with Christian Dior had replaced her menial work in a Venetian fashion boutique. How had I forgotten that?

'So many young Venetians feel a sense of hopelessness,' Rossano said.

He reflected on the problems facing Venetian youth while I tossed squid through pasta and placed the bowl on the table. *Alors*. This might not be the time to mention my happy afternoon with an American dad and his location-scout son. I wondered if Evan spoke six languages. Somehow I doubted it.

I pulled the curtains closed, sealing off the outside darkness, then lit candles. The smell of sandalwood spread through the kitchen. Rain continued in a steady drizzle and the central heating purred as we sat in candlelight, ringed by our flickering shadows. The world came to an end a few paces away, at the front door. I twisted pasta onto my fork and stole a sidelong glance at Rossano. He wasn't done yet.

'I worked for years in a good job but retired with little money. That's how it is for most Venetians.' He refilled my wineglass, already empty. The level in his glass stood a centimetre below its starting point.

Oh, don't be such a wet noodle, I wanted to say. *You may not have cash, but you have cachet.* It didn't sound as good, though, in French. *Vouz avez le cachet, si non l'argent.* It lost its ring. And wet noodle stood no chance.

Without a doubt, I had overestimated my language abilities. The subtle complexities of language were grasped only by living in a country and speaking its native tongue. And not even then, sometimes. Rossano had a talent for talking. It had been part of his job, before listening became his job. I wondered, not for the first time, if he missed dialogue beyond the scope of French Language and Conversation.

We finished our meal and I set the *caffettiera* on the gas ring. Rossano sat with his elbows on the table, not smiling but at least no longer frowning. I moved to his side of the table and hugged him.

'Here's an idea,' I said, my smile searching his face. 'Perhaps you could visit Australia?'

Visiter. A simple verb. I know I didn't make a mistake.

A pause developed and lengthened. '*Ah, l'Australie,*' Rossano said. He lifted his cup and set it back down again, as he had done with his wineglass. Adequate hydration could become his biggest issue with this degree of indecision. Seconds of silence thudded by until he turned to me with a disbelieving gaze, like a child being told that Father Christmas is make believe. He spoke a single word.

'*Pourquoi?*'

Why? *Why?* Because I live there. Because the weather is better. Because ... A dozen reasons spluttered to mind, only to stall as they hobbled along my rickety neural pathway on their way to verbalisation.

'But I am happy here,' Rossano said. '*J'adore Venise. Ah, oui. Venise, c'est superbe.*' A stubborn, you-can't-budge-me expression held his features. 'I would never leave, never. To go to the other side of the world?'

As in, to go to the dark side of the moon?

I wondered how Rossano could acknowledge the problems facing his city but still think of it as the best place on earth, the centre of the universe. Venice: the cherished artefact he'd polished for so long that he no longer saw the cracks beneath its high sheen. I felt like flinging my arms out and returning his question. *Pourquoi?* Instead I sat down again, sliding lower in my chair. A visit to Australia, an escape from the Venetian winter. That was all I had suggested.

Rossano's billowing discontent lifted. He sat with his elbows balanced on the table, holding his steepled fingers in front of him; a teacher thing, I guessed, recalling Mary in the same pose. We were invited to a gallery opening tomorrow, Rossano told me, speaking in glowing terms of the artist whose work was being exhibited. I wished he had run into him that afternoon, rather than Luisa.

My mind wandered as I listened. I sipped coffee and picked at the seam of my pullover in an absent-minded way. There was an indefinable otherness about Rossano, something so self-contained, as though he floated through his life – his Venice – in a sealed-off compartment. *I am a true Venetian, living in the best city on earth. As it slowly sinks beneath rising sea levels. As it suffocates from mass tourism. And we can't offer jobs to our young people, but never mind. I am proud to be Venetian.*

Australia. A clear redundancy.

The challenges of a new, Venetian life might run deeper than just language. I remembered Rossano telling me once that non-Venetians were known as *forestieri*. Outsiders. Think square peg in round hole. Three hundred years ago, the Johnny-come-lately Rezzonicos, Albrizzis and Lasbias had got the drift. Their vast fortunes were mobilised to gain acceptance from families – the true and proud Venetians – whose lineage dated back a thousand years. And now here I was, planning to live in Venice, to be a Venetian. Would I need to build a palazzo or two? Host lavish parties? Throw crockery out the window and into a canal? It was something to think about, alright.

But later that evening when I lay in bed, stretched on my back and with my eyes open, my mind was as blank as the ceiling I gazed at.

✹

That was it, then. My day at the fair had come to an end. No more fairy floss and toffee apples, just the plain, nutritious diet of real life. The adventure was over.

I pulled my suitcase through the hotel lobby and out to the unlovely Lista di Spagna. The irony wasn't lost on me. My last night in Venice, and I'd spent it in the neighbourhood I liked the least. But heavy rain was forecast and I'd moved from my flood-challenged apartment to be close to the *ferrovia*. I didn't want to be stranded behind a lake, with a suitcase, at six in the morning.

The hotel door slid closed behind me. Fog seeped along the *calle* and I started the walk to Ferrovia Santa Lucia, my steps as slow as a reluctant school-child bound for the classroom. Platform ten. Milano Centrale. A wavering splotch of darkness hung in my thoughts; sadness ready to move in like a weather system. I slid the suitcase along the train's floor, then pushed it into a space below the luggage racks.

Leaving.

A soundless glide towards the scribble of intersecting tracks, then out of the *ferrovia* and across the lagoon.

Leaving Venice.

Rossano and I went to a concert last night, in Chiesa di San Giovanni Evangelista. I'd never been so cold: it was as though six centuries of perishing cold were trapped within the church's stone walls. My feet turned numb inside my boots and I pushed my hands further into my coat pockets. Snuggled closer to Rossano.

Chunk-a-chunk-a-chunk. Onto the mainland. Venice behind me, somewhere out there in the mist, slipping away like a wave from the shoreline. I rested my elbow near the window and gazed at the greyness. Then I widened my eyes to stop tears from spilling out.

After the concert Rosanno walked with me to the hotel. I stood in the circle of his arms and looked down at our feet, arranged like ballroom dancing instructions on the paving. There were no rules of behaviour governing farewells, no agreed words to run to and take shelter behind. I felt off balance, a top at the end of its spin, about to fall over.

Rossano tilted my face upwards and smiled, as if he'd been practising.

Au revoir.

The Trenitalia inspector moved along the aisle, pausing while I rummaged through my bag. I found my ticket, folded into last night's concert program. The inspector moved on and I looked back to the window. Fog lifted, replaced by the greyness of Mestre concrete.

Phone me when you get home.

Had it been folly, this trip to Venice? A clumsy, impetuous rush towards … what, exactly? Nothing had changed. I looked down at a button on my coat, twisting it. Why had I gone back?

I'd gone to Venice …

I'd gone to Venice with an immense, private hope. I'd wanted any decisions – all decisions – taken out of my hands and settled for me. By Rossano. That wasn't going to happen. Rossano made his way through life in a noncommittal fashion, a responder rather than an initiator. And there was no reason why he should be otherwise.

I'd gone to Venice imagining that, as if by magic and without so much as a hiccough, I could slot into Venetian life. That wasn't going to happen either. Language and culture had shaped me as much as they had Rossano. We each had places where we identified and belonged, our safe places in the world. Different places.

Warm air filtered through the train. I stood and took off my coat, then folded it into the overhead luggage compartment. You can't make things happen with your sheer desire for them.

CHAPTER 17

... AND ENDINGS

I wrote but half of what I saw.

Marco Polo, Venetian-born explorer, at the time of his death

The curtain lifts on a new day. Dawn moves over the city, splintering blackness. Buildings detach from night-time shadow.

Across the canal, a light is switched on. Shutters creak and windows swing open. A woman leans out, looks down to the *fondamente*, then turns her face heavenward, watching the sky whiten. I wave to her, smiling as she waves back. A soft idleness wraps around me and I lift my arms, stretching, yawning.

I'd had in mind an early start today, writing postcards and catching up with emails. An hour ago I came into the kitchen and filled the *caffettiera*, all set to strike a blow. Instead I'm still at this spot by the window. I pause here often, looking out at flawless blue skies or listening to a summer thunderstorm. I watch as morning delivery barges tie up to the *fondamente*, or gondolas set out on their evening circuit.

Four years have passed since I walked along a fog-smudged *calle*, pulling my suitcase to the *ferrovia*, destination Milan.

And in each of those years I've come back to Venice. Sebastiano's apartment is my home for two months, and San Polo and Dorsoduro again become my backyard. I can't imagine summertime without Venice.

But I can imagine Venice without Rossano.

I wait for the coffee to bubble, stretching again. I think back to an earlier Venetian summer, the one that followed my unscripted October return. How keen I was! And how hopeful still, despite the misgivings I'd carried home with me. I packed them away like so many tasteless holiday souvenirs, the ones you regret as soon as they are bought. Minor ills and spills, I'd convinced myself, nothing that couldn't be ironed out with perseverance and a bit of give and take. The language thing, for starters, could be sorted.

Clearly, French Language and Conversation wasn't winning the game. Success lay with a planned attack, and L'Alliance Française shaped up as my best shot on goal. I kicked off with three hours every Thursday night, when my classmates and I tackled verb conjugations and possessive adjectives, simple past tense versus imperfect past tense. Group discussion saw the whole team out to score points.

'What 'ave you done over zee weekend?' our tutor wanted to know. One by one we recounted our Saturday–Sunday adventures, drawing on new vocabulary to ask each other testing, insightful questions. I could now hold up my end in any conversation about lawn mowing, for instance. Bound to be useful in Venice.

Still, those Thursday nights paid off. My language skills notched up a level and from time to time I made that giant leap: I actually *thought* in French, bypassing the French-to-translation-to-English-to-talk process altogether.

But a stronger grasp of language didn't translate to a stronger hold on what I most wanted.

A rebalancing was underway between Rossano and me, subtle but undeniable. It wasn't immediate or instant. There was no single, lightning-bolt moment when I acknowledged the recast nature of our relationship. With each visit, our times together became less frequent. Change just happened; a mutual, unspoken progression made inevitable by our circumstances. No arguments or sulks or tears. No explanations. Our lives played out in cities on opposite sides of the world, in different countries with different customs. In my mind, I likened our romance to seeing just the middle section of a film: I didn't know enough of what went before to understand the plot, and I wouldn't be around for the end.

Coffee bubbles and its warm scent spreads through the room. I reach to turn off the gas, then pour a cup. Craning my neck I can see La Rosa dei Venti across the canal, its green awning rolled up and the shutters closed. In the ashy light of dawn it seems forlorn, unloved.

Rossano and I had dinner there last night. We catch up now as friends, two people who know each other well and can relive shared events. I listen to his observations of Venetian life, its politics and its problems as much as its art and music. I know the time will come, one day, when my summers no longer include Rossano. But not yet.

'The best casual eatery in Dorsoduro,' Rossano had promised when we arranged our date earlier in the day. Anything that carried Rossano's endorsement met with my approval, and I looked forward to the evening.

※

I settled into my seat and opened the menu. Tourism had infiltrated my little corner of Venice: there could be no surer sign of its advance than a menu listing its temptations in multiple languages. *Eh bien.* I worked through the offerings before coming to a snuffling halt. Whoever did these translations?

'*Alors*, Rossano.' I tapped the page, preparing for a good chuckle. 'Sardinians marinated in vinegar and onions? I mean, seriously? How unpleasant for them.'

Rossano looked at my pointing finger, not understanding the Italian to English mistake. '*Oui, oui.* You know sardines are a typical Venetian dish, *n'est-ce pas?*'

I remembered the way his sentences always slanted downwards, even on a question. He smiled at me in a teacher–student way and then, satisfied with his explanation, directed his smile at a corner of the floor.

'Yes, Rossano, I know that. But the translation. It's all wrong. Sardinians are *les Sardaignes*. They are not sardines. It's as if ...' I spoke slowly, giving each syllable its full share of attention as I attempted elucidation. But explaining a joke takes away its humour faster than aspirin dissolving in water. Rossano didn't get it. His eyes rounded. A straightforward case of the Qantas Syndrome. Way over his head.

'Hmph,' he said, fingers drumming a slow beat as he studied the menu like one of his old music manuscripts. *D-rum. D-rum. D-rum.*

I turned to the meat dishes, my eyes tracking down the list and stopping at the chef's recommendation. Affected mixed meats, I read. A perplexing suggestion, and one crying out for clarification. My elbow reached up to nudge Rossano, then fell back by my side in a small, cancelled movement. Why borrow trouble? No point digging myself into a hole when I planned to order black tagliatelle anyway.

Rossano did things to tease me, I knew it. Like now. He ordered the sardinians. Then he smiled at another corner of the floor, pleased with himself, fuller in the face, somehow. His little joke, because he hadn't understood mine. The pinot grigio sat on the table between us and he reached for it, pouring just enough wine to cover the bottom of our glasses.

'A particular favourite, from the area near Trieste,' he said, holding up the glass to admire the colour. The twirling, sniffing thing followed. '*Magnifique, oui?*'

My knowledge of *vino Italiano* didn't extend beyond the six-euro shelf of the local supermarket. Rossano, need it be said, could have written a sommelier's handbook. I was putting together an eloquent response – I had good vocab around the subject – when the waiter arrived, bearing *les Sardaignes*. With a flush of pride he lowered them to the table, like a first-time father presenting his newborn. Rossano beamed at the waiter who beamed at the sardines. I used the moment to upend the *vin magnifique* over my wineglass, then turned my attention to the fare of Dorsoduro's best casual eatery.

Rossano lifted his head and looked at me before his eyes dropped to my plate.

'It is good, *oui?*'

'I think so, but I can't be certain. It keeps melting in my mouth.'

That's what I wanted to say, but of course I couldn't. L'Alliance Française and my lawn-mowing expertise counted for naught at La Rosa dei Venti. Instead I asked about the season's opera: jealous Othello and murdered Desdemona – a love story with an unhappy ending, being performed here in Venice, the city where it was set. I watched Rossano as he spoke of the subject closest to his heart, eyes alight and voice lifting with an enthusiasm that made anything seem possible. I remembered, then, why I came back to Venice that October. If I hadn't, I would have forever asked myself what if.

Personal history would always link me to Rossano, but it no longer registered in that close, inseparable way. Not anymore. Not like the night I sat beside him in Palazzetto Bru Zane and watched those arrows mark out Eduardo's performance. For that night, at least, I had believed in my Venetian future.

The waiter arrived to collect our plates. I listened to the pat and shuffle of feet, the clink of cutlery against china. I wondered when I'd see Rossano again. How many times, in the weeks before I packed my bags and headed off to platform ten, would we sit together, chatting over this and that? And next year? What then? Perhaps it would mark a new first: a trip to Venice that didn't include Rossano. I looked over at him now, finishing off the sardinians. I felt no sadness, no regrets, just a sweet fullness lodging in my chest.

Sometimes a dream is at its best when that's all it is. Just a dream. I'd read that somewhere. And sometimes there really is nothing more to say. Everything is rounded out, a circle completed and the last chapter closed.

❋

But real life continues beyond a book's ending. While Rossano drew me back to Venice, it is the city itself that now holds my heart.

I stay at the window to finish my coffee, catching the scent of jasmine on the morning's cool air. Tomorrow my sister and her husband arrive for a week's visit, but for now I'm alone. It's my time, in my Venice.

On each trip to Venice others join me, for all or part of my stay. They add to my enjoyment of the city and I see it through their eyes, aware again of its pleasures and of its failings. I think back to the year when my bridge partner Domenico stayed with me. A family reunion would take him on to Rome for a week, but while in Venice he would cook, he said, do the shopping and keep house. Pop out for gelati as needed.

With Dom's visit came something special.

*

It was the first day of September. Dom had telephoned Signor Natalino and arranged for us to meet at his shop – we decided around 9 am would suit everyone.

Summer had softened to autumn, and we walked in morning crispness through Cannaregio. In Campo dei Mori, Mr Whippy squatted by the canal, umbrellas furled, tables and chairs stacked away. We turned the corner and saw Signor Natalino outside his shop, farewelling a friend. I introduced him to Dom and they shook hands.

'*Buon giorno.*' Signor Natalino nodded a welcome. He picked up a chair from the pavement and led us inside.

'Please, sit down,' he said, speaking through Dom as he wiped the chair and offered it to me. I sat and looked around. Stock crammed shelves and paperwork stood heaped on the counter, as packed and muddled as I remembered.

'Is your family well?' I asked.

There was a greater sense of ease this time, more than there had been when Pablo acted as translator. Perhaps it was because Dom was closer in age to Signor Natalino, or it may have been that Signor Natalino knew me better. Wife

Lena and son Enzo were both well, he told me, and Enzo and his family remained in Venice. The conversation moved to Elizabetta, the daughter who had left her hometown seeking a career worthy of her talents.

'As you know, she had a senior position with Christian Dior,' Signor Natalino said. 'Now she has been promoted.'

Local girl makes good. I asked Dom for details. He conferred with Signor Natalino and then turned to me with a brief explanation. 'She's the boss,' he said, deploying an Australian colloquialism to describe a Venetian working in Paris.

'And Renato,' I asked, remembering Signor Natalino's English-speaking friend. 'How is Renato?'

I owed a great deal to Renato. I thought back to the day when I first stood on the *fondamenta*. How I'd taken a deep, steadying breath and gathered up courage before walking through an open doorway and into this tiny shop. Renato had been there, ready to translate my halting conversation. *Next door is Tintoretto's house.* That was how I'd begun, and were it not for Renato that would also have been where I finished. Signor Natalino and his Venice would have remained unknown to me.

'Renato has moved overseas. They are no longer in touch.' Another of Dom's brief explanations before he and Signor Natalino resumed their conversation, chatting away like old mates. Was I in the way here? My eyes wandered to the sunlit entrance where a figure stood in silhouette. As my vision adjusted, I saw an elderly woman holding shopping bags in each hand.

'*Ciao, Antoinetta.*' Signor Natalino beckoned her inside. She joined us, placing her shopping bags on the floor to shake hands with Dom and me. Someone local to the area,

I imagined, as she relaxed into easy conversation. I waited in silence while they talked, well out of my conversational depth. Although I could understand a smattering of Italian, a fast-paced dialogue between friends was no place for my novice skills. The only word I could positively ID was Australia. It seemed they were talking about me.

Antoinetta's face lit up. She looked at me, raising both hands to her mouth.

Dom assumed an in-charge expression and took up translator duties. 'Antoinetta asks if you would like to see her home. She lives next door.'

Blood whooshed through my ears. Next door? That could only mean Tintoretto's house. *An apartment on the second floor is owned by an elderly lady. It has views over the canal and the use of a private courtyard. It is for sale at the moment.* Renato's words sounded above the noise-surge happening in my head.

Antoinetta was the owner! Inviting me to come on in! As I live and breathe … Then the apartment's eye-watering price tag slid front-of-mind, and I hoped the preceding conversation had not suggested I might be a prospective buyer. Should I perhaps err on the side of caution and decline? But it *was* Casa Tintoretto. And there stood Antoinetta, smiling as though inviting a stranger into her home were the most natural thing in the world. I lifted one of the shopping bags – heavier than I'd imagined – and followed her from the shop.

A few paces along the *fondamenta*, Antoinetta unlocked the street door and led me into a wide vestibule. She took the shopping bags and placed them on a wooden bench before walking to the far end of a passageway. Three-storey buildings, unchanged over the centuries, enclosed a small garden. Between some overgrown shrubs, tall weeds had taken over – tough plants with stringy stalks, small leaves and tight little flowers. Survivor weeds, designed to outlay energy on nothing but getting their seed pods up towards the sun. Newspaper remnants flattened themselves against one wall.

Antoinetta turned from the garden and walked to the bench where we had left the shopping. Picking up a bag, I followed her to the stairwell. Dusty shafts of light filmed the steps and I focused my attention on a safe arrival at Antoinetta's front door. No handrail offered assistance. I put my hand against the wall for support, rubbing its gritty surface. On the first landing we paused.

'Here?' I nodded hopefully to a door on my left.

'No.' An upwards head tilt and we set off again.

Antoinetta preceded me up another flight of steps, steady and confident, unhindered by the shopping bags in each hand. She unlocked a door on the right of the stairs, the side of the building facing the *fondamenta*. *Thank heavens*, I thought, exhaling through puffed cheeks. Antoinetta held the door open for me, not at all breathless. *Venetians and stairs*, I thought, remembering Sebastiano's two-at-a-time leaps.

'*Non parlo Italiano*,' I said as we walked into the kitchen. '*Français, peut-être?*'

'*Ah oui, oui.*' Antoinetta smiled and her eyes glinted. Green eyes, I noticed, like old gemstones.

With the language barrier removed, Antoinetta sensed a good chat. She sat me down at the kitchen table and put on coffee, moving between cupboards and benchtop as she unpacked her shopping. Out came a bunch of grapes. She carried them to the sink and washed them, all the time talking over her shoulder. The grapes made their return to the table, dried and cut into clusters. Fresh *cornetti* joined them, also plucked from a shopping bag.

'Eat, eat,' she urged, fluttering between table and benchtop, pausing en route for a *cornetto*. At this rate she'd be back down the stairs for a second round of shopping by mid-afternoon.

The kitchen was small, with the table placed at its centre. A window above the sink lit the room with southern light. Antoinetta poured coffee and sat beside me. I listened as she told me of her family connections to Australia.

'My grandfather went to live in Australia as a young man. He was there during the war, and he was placed in, um ... *comment on dit* ... a prison camp? For several years he stayed there.'

A blush found its way to my cheeks. Although Australia was not alone in consigning citizens of foreign birth to internment camps, it was not something to be proud of. Antoinetta shrugged; she carried no grudges, it was all part of history. A branch of the family had remained in Australia and prospered.

'But you wanted to see my home?' She tilted her head with the question, gathering the empty cups and moving them to the sink.

'*Oui, merci.* I'd love to. I could never afford to buy it, though.' Best to get that out there.

Antoinetta laughed, her eyes two merry slits. 'Most people say this.' Her face shone as she relived private memories. 'I have been so happy here. But it is too big for me now. I would like to live in a smaller home, with my daughter.'

She led me from the kitchen into a knot of rooms. No central hallway defined the space, and one room led straight off another. Several bedrooms and two sitting rooms, along with a small bathroom, completed the apartment. I thought of other residences I'd seen in Venice: the apartment I'd shared with Jenny in Cannaregio, my little home under the eaves in Dorsoduro. Rossano's apartment. They too followed this pattern. A great deal of renovation would be needed to transform them into homes acceptable to modern Australian tastes.

And the garden, down those two flights of stairs. What incentive was there for Antoinetta to maintain it? It wasn't a place to relax with a quick cuppa – just getting there would be a mission. How different from my own home, where al fresco was as easy as moving from one room to another.

And yet ...

The snugness, the *togetherness* of Antoinetta's house charmed me. There were no vast spaces to rattle around in, no sparsely furnished rooms with just one statement piece of furniture or artwork. Instead a sense of homey comfort filled the apartment.

And Tintoretto had lived here. I couldn't shake the feeling. The house seemed to speak not just of Antoinetta but of him, too – still living here, perhaps waiting in another room. I stood at the windows, sharing the view with my favourite Venetian painter. The passage of centuries evaporated.

It was my best moment in Venice, my happiest memory.

Antoinetta walked me to the front door. I may not have found it by myself. We said goodbye and I thanked her with my best L'Alliance French.

'*Mon plaisir. Arrivederci.*' Antoinetta farewelled me with a mix of French and Italian, waving goodbye from the doorway. I picked my way down those rail-less stairs, relieved no one was there to see me. Some things I just didn't want to share.

Dom and Signor Natalino looked up when I walked back into the shop.

'We are talking about life in Australia,' Dom said. 'I say it is good.'

Signor Natalino had once considered emigrating to Australia, before he met Lena and decided to make a future in Venice. Looking at him now I could not imagine him anywhere except this little shop on Fondamenta dei Mori. I said goodbye for another year and walked with Dom towards the *campo*. Mr Whippy remained locked and shuttered, as though in silent acknowledgement: *It's official. Summer is over.*

Dom tapped a finger to his lips in contemplation. 'I will make linguini for lunch. Yes. With artichokes I buy from Rialto markets. A little melon first, with prosciutto.'

I smiled; at him, and at the autumn day. *We each have our priorities*, I thought, *the things that bring us happiness*. For me it was the fulfilment of doing something I'd never imagined. I'd been inside Tintoretto's house. And I couldn't say why, but it made my own home in Perth seem all at once *right*. As though another circle was completed. Another chapter closed.

✳

The city yawns, rubs its eyes and wakes.

Early explorers walk the *fondamente*, an advance party for the cavalry that will follow by mid-morning. Chairs grate on paving and umbrellas flap open, signalling the start of breakfast time at Downstairs. Gulls screech their welcome to the day. A sense of ownership rings through their cries: *Our place. Our city.*

For the next two months I'll share their city. Neighbourhoods consigned to memory for the last year will again become familiar and homelike – my backyard, in my Venice. I'll visit the church of the Mendicoli, waiting by the docks to welcome its parishioners, just as it has for longer than a millennium. I'll sit in tucked-away *campi* as dusk falls, watching children at their games. Boys chasing a soccer ball. Young girls practising cartwheels, a spinning chain across the pavement. Simple pleasures. The things that bring me back to Venice.

And Torcello waits. A forgotten island in the far north of the lagoon lies close to my heart. I remember blackberry vines clinging to fruit trees in an overgrown orchard, and I hear the tinny hum of insects in quiet gardens. Torcello is where the city began. It's where Hemingway lived and wrote. It's part of my Venice.

Place and home. Venice and Perth.

For several years I imagined a permanent home here in Venice. A costly apartment in Tintoretto's house, with a costly renovation to match, never figured in my calculations. But, at the other end of the spectrum, a tiny, nest-like home under the eaves was doable; somewhere like my October home, the apartment I'd rented near Calle Lunga San Barnaba. Others had moved countries to establish a new home and their stories, or at least the ones I knew, told of satisfaction at having found the courage to make such a change. *I could never go back,* I was often told.

But I wondered. Would I ever quite belong in a city whose residents called on the history of a millennium? I thought of the steps leading to my apartment, of their indentations. Of lives having worn their mark in hard stone. Caution whispered and doubts wriggled from their hiding spots.

Locked in my thoughts was a remark Rossano once made. Marco Polo, Rossano asserted, should never be considered a Venetian because, although born in Venice, his family were of Dalmatian origin. That the city's most famous son was subject to such a distinction made me question my chances.

Neither had great wealth always facilitated acceptance. Peggy Guggenheim's American–Jewish background meant Venetian grand families held her at arm's length and important invitations failed to appear in the palazzo letterbox. For two decades she remained isolated from *haute volée* Venice, reliant for companionship on sundry lovers, the expat community and a constant stream of international visitors.

The word *forestieri* had currency.

My life in Perth was not one of a visitor waiting outside, hoping to be invited in. Perth was the place of my history, the place that gave order and sense to my life. Other people had shaped it, and were part of it still. Could I disconnect from that secure niche and recreate it on the other side of the world? I didn't think so.

And so, setting aside the occasional euphoric outburst, I came to accept that Venice would only ever be my second home. My summertime place. Back in Perth, whenever I found myself wishing I were here – sitting in a certain *campo*, perhaps, or walking beside this or that canal – I'd turn to the place in my heart where memories are kept. I'd remember the people I met and the fun I had, all that I saw and all that I learned. All that I felt. And I'd think of it this way: I was caught up in the magic of Venice and I wanted more. I wanted to be a part of it.

Toujours. Always.

AUTHOR'S NOTE

The devastation wrought by the 1966 *acqua alta* and the increase in serious flooding events drove government determination to rectify the problem. The MoSE project was adopted as policy by the national government in 1982. MoSE is the acronym for the project's full title, *Modulo Sperimentale Elettromecanico,* but it became immediately and universally known by its diminutive. Moise is the Italian word for Moses, the Old Testament prophet who held back the waters of the Red Sea and saved his people. The same cannot be claimed for the Venetian MoSE.

In essence, the MoSE project consists of seventy-nine steel barriers placed across the three points where the Adriatic Sea enters the Venetian Lagoon (at Porto di Chioggia, Porto di Malamocco and Porto di Lido). These barriers lie on the seabed and are electronically activated to rise to the vertical position when sea levels rise. The two-kilometre barrier, in its upright position, prevents water from entering the lagoon and thus protects the city from flooding. The original plan for MoSE envisaged its design, assembly and maintenance to be undertaken by a private consortium of engineering companies, known as Consorzio Venezia Nuova (CVN).

The original deadline for completion of the project was 1995. Come the deadline (thirteen years after the project was approved by the Italian government), there was nothing to show of this engineering triumph but the forlorn prototype of a barrier segment anchored in the lagoon off the Arsenale. As arguments raged about the future of MoSE, serious and more frequent flooding became commonplace.

Forced into action, the Italian government placed MoSE at the head of its to-do list. In May 2003, the then Italian prime minister, Silvio Berlusconi, launched the construction of the first barrier (now twenty years after the plan for MoSE was adopted as official government policy). Berlusconi was defeated in the general election of 2006. His successor, Romano Prodi, halted work while he conducted a financial audit of every major infrastructure project in the country. Whatever misgivings Prodi had about MoSE, he agreed that the survival of Venice depended on the project's completion. Work recommenced.

Some opponents of MoSE alleged from the start that it would be a giant palm-greasing exercise. In 2014, following a three-year investigation, criminal charges were brought against Giovanni Mazzacurati, the head of CVN, the consortium in charge of construction, and Giorgio Orsoni, the incumbent mayor of Venice. Thirty-three others, including several politicians, were also charged. Of the 5.6 billion euro funnelled into MoSE, as much as 1 billion euro had gone astray – corruption on a grand scale. Three independent commissioners were appointed by the National Anti-Corruption Authority to oversee CVN's operations.

So how does it stand now? MoSE was successfully activated in 2020 and is expected to be fully operational by the end of 2021. But in the forty years since its adoption as official government policy, new problems have emerged to challenge its success. Sea levels are rising and flooding events more common. To be effective in protecting Venice, the barrier will need to be used as a semi-permanent wall. This, in turn, will prevent the lagoon's drainage and interaction with the Adriatic Sea. The Venetian lagoon could become a stagnant pool, further disrupting a fragile ecosystem already compromised during MoSE's construction phase.

A lot of money has been directed towards an ineffective project likely to become obsolete. And a lot of money has found its way into private pockets.

❈

The environmental impacts of Venice's thriving tourism industry are significant. After years of protests, petitions and threats of being put on UNESCO's endangered list, the Italian government has acted: in August 2021, it banned cruise ships exceeding 180 metres in length or weighing more than 25 000 tons from sailing along the Giudecca Canal and through the centre of Venice. These ships are now rerouted through the Venetian lagoon to five temporary berths at the industrial port of Marghera until permanent docking facilities can be constructed outside the lagoon. Maghera, although on the mainland, is still accessed via the lagoon.

REFERENCES

NON-FICTION

Barzini, Luigi, *The Italians*, Penguin Books Ltd., London, 1968

Berendt, John, *The City of Falling Angels*, Hodder and Stoughton, London, 2005

Buckley, Jonathan, *The Rough Guide to Venice and the Veneto*, Rough Guides Ltd., London, 2016

Cipriani, Arrigo, *Harry's Bar: The Life and Times of the Legendary Venice Landmark*, Arcade Publishing, New York, 1996

Comerlati, Doriana (ed.), *Veronese: Gods, Heroes and Allegories*, Skira Editore, Milano, 2004

Da Mosto, Francesco, *Francesco's Venice*, BBC Books, London, 2004

Dearborn, Mary V, *Mistress of Modernism: The Life of Peggy Guggenheim*, Houghton Mifflin, Boston, 2004

Emmerling, Leonhard, *Jackson Pollock 1912–1956: At the Limit of Painting*, Taschen Publishing, Los Angeles, 2016

Fasolo, Andrea, *Palaces of Venice*, Arsenale Editore Srl, Verona, 2014

Ferraro, Joanne, *Venice: History of the Floating City*, Cambridge University Press, Cambridge, 2010

Gill, Anton, *Art Lover: A Biography of Peggy Guggenheim*, HarperCollins, London, 2001

Hale, John, *The Civilisation of Europe in the Renaissance*, HarperCollins, London, 1993

Hooper, John, *The Italians*, Penguin Books, London, 2015

Hussey, Andrew, *Paris: The Secret History*, Viking, London, 2006

Jonglez, Thomas and Zoffoli, Paola, *Secret Venice,* Jonglez Publishing, France, 2014

Littlewood, Ian, *A Literary Companion to Venice*, Penguin Books, London, 1991

Lovric, Michelle (ed.), *Venice: Tales of the City,* Little, Brown, and Company, London, 2003

Mackrell, Judith, *The Unfinished Palazzo: Life, Love and Art in Venice*, Thames and Hudson, London, 2017

Morris, Jan, *A Venetian Bestiary*, Thames and Hudson, Japan, 1982

Norwich, John Julius, *Paradise of Cities: Venice and its Nineteenth-Century Visitors*, Vintage Books, New York, 2004

Plant, Margaret, *Venice: Fragile City*, Yale University Press, New Haven and London, 2002

Prose, Francine, *Peggy Guggenheim: The Shock of the Modern*, Yale University Press, New Haven and London, 2005

Steinbach, Alice, *Without Reservations: The Travels of an Independent Woman*, Bantam Books, New York, 2002

Strathern, Paul, *The Medici: Godfathers of the Renaissance,* Jonathan Cape, London, 2003

Valcanover, Francesco, *Jacopo Tintoretto and the Scuola Grande of San Rocco*, Sorti Edizione, Venice, 2013

Vidal, Gore, *Vidal in Venice,* Simon & Schuster, New York, 1987

Vircondelet, Alain (ed.), *Venice History*, Flammarion, Paris, 2008

Weideger, Paula, *Venetian Dreaming: Finding a Foothold in an Enchanted City*, Simon & Schuster, London, 2004

FICTION

Leon, Donna, *The Girl of His Dreams*, William Heineman, London, 2008

Leon, Donna, *The Golden Egg*, William Heineman, London, 2013

Vickers, Salley, *Miss Garnet's Angel,* Random House, London, 2001

ACKNOWLEDGEMENTS

Many people are involved in transforming an idea into a manuscript and then a book.

I am grateful to Andrew Levett for teaching me the principles of storytelling and for working with me through the earliest drafts. The completed manuscript benefited from the attention of my assessor, John Harman, whose astute feedback shaped the final draft.

Thanks are due to Jenny Shipstone, Jenny Walkden, Dom Musitano and Dennis Gillespie for chapter reviews, suggestions and corrections.

The path to publication began when my manuscript was accepted by Hachette Australia. I thank my publisher, Sophie Hamley, for the trust she placed in my work, and the entire team at Hachette for their unfailing support and encouragement. Special acknowledgement is due to my editor, Stacey Clair, for her diligent and always kindly assistance through each phase of the editorial process.

The staff at Cambridge Library assisted with locating references and providing technical support, as did Tim

Barnden-Brown of Helium Advertising, and friend David Burn.

To booksellers and readers, my special thanks. No book could make its way to bookshelves and out into the world without your support.

And, of course, my sincere gratitude goes to the citizens of Venice, who each year offer hospitality and share their wonderful city with me. *Grazie mille.*

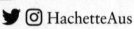
hachette
AUSTRALIA

If you would like to find out more about
Hachette Australia, our authors, upcoming events
and new releases you can visit our website or our
social media channels:

hachette.com.au
HachetteAustralia
HachetteAus